AF560290

HEALTH, GENDER AND DEVELOPMENT

HEALTH, GENDER AND DEVELOPMENT

Editor

DR. L.N. DASH

REGAL PUBLICATIONS

New Delhi

HEALTH, GENDER AND DEVELOPMENT

ISBN 978-81-8484-423-8

Typeset by
RAHUL COMPOSERS
New Highway Apartments, Lakshmi Niwas
760, Pocket-D, Lok Nayak Puram, New Delhi - 110 041

Printed in India at
MAYUR ENTERPRISES
WZ Plot No. 3, Gujjar Market, Tihar Village, New Delhi - 110 018

Published by
REGAL PUBLICATIONS
F-159, Rajouri Garden, New Delhi - 110 027
Phone : 45546396, 25435369
E-mail : regalbookspub@yahoo.com, regaldeepbooks@yahoo.com

Contents

A Prelude

Women's health status is interwoven with a wider set of economic, social and familial circumstances in which women live. The health of women in a country has profound implications not only for women themselves but of children and the economic well-being of households. The adverse effects of pervasive ill-health extend beyond the woman herself. A woman's ill-health and nutritional status influence her newborn's birth weight and chances of survival, her capacity to nurse and nurture her child, etc. In households that depend on the labour of their women, the income of the household falls when poor health prevents the women from working. A mother's death is not just a human tragedy but also an economic and social catastrophe for the family. Her children lose an opportunity of mother's nurture and too often the chance of education, leading the family even further into poverty. Maternal deaths are both caused by poverty and a cause of it.

The emerging focus on women's rights as human right brought about a tectonic shift from the earlier UN-led international conferences in Bucharest (1974) and Mexico (1984) which narrowly focused on limiting population growth and expanding family planning services. The health condition of women in one phase of life not only affects subsequent phases of her life, but it has an impact on future generations. This intergenerational link is unique to women. Therefore, the Global Commission on Women's Health was established in 1993 to promote the adoption and implementation of effective measures at all levels for improving women's health and to carry out international and national advocacy on behalf of women's health concerns. The Cairo Programme of Action addressed broader issues of gender equity and sexual rights as well as reproductive health. At the 1995 UN Fourth World Conference on Women in Beijing, women's sexual and reproductive health and rights were once again contentious issues. Those committed to the Cairo agenda fought hard to ensure that the realities of women's lives were taken into account in policy -making and programming. Pockets of progress were also witnessed. Of late, we have seen examples of genuine integration of sexual and reproductive health. In addition, a growing body of policy frameworks and activism has advanced the concept of sexual rights. The launch of the Millennium Development Goals (MDGs) further intensified efforts to improve the health of women. When the MDGs were first issued in 2000, there was no mention of reproductive health. Women's health appeared only in the form of maternal health. It was also narrowly circumscribed. The MDGs set the target to reduce by three quarters, between 1990 and 2015, the maternal mortality ratio in part by increasing the proportion of births attended by a skilled health professional. Therefore, the MDGs once again marginalised sexual and reproductive health and rights. Only in 2004, reproductive health was added to the MDGs. Both the Bucharest and the Mexico City conferences had in common an emphasis on demographic analysis and on lowering fertility. In contrast, the Cairo Conference represented a conceptual shift from a concern for population growth to a broader concern for sexual and reproductive health.

Global events had an impact at the country level. National policies and programmes were evolved in response to local needs. Soon after the UN International Conference on Population and Development (IPCD) in Cairo, the Government of India initiated the Reproductive and Child Health (RCH) Programme. The National Population Policy adopted in Feb. 2000 further legitimized the paradigm shift. The National Population Policy provided a framework for achieving the twin objectives of population stabilization and promoting reproductive health. In 2001, the Government also adopted a National Policy for the Empowerment of Women. In 2005, the Reproductive and Child Health (RCH) Programme was integrated with the National Rural Health Mission (NRHM). The goal of the NRHM programme is to provide comprehensive health care to the poor, marginalised rural communities, especially to women and children.

The feminization of AIDS epidemic in India has led to growing concern to address women's sexual and reproductive health and rights. In 2008, women constituted 38 percent of the total HIV-infected population, which was only 21 percent in 2001. The increasing number of HIV positive women has opened a new domain of research to address their needs.

The total fertility rate (TFR) in India declined from 6.6 percent in 1951 to 3.5 percent in 1993 and 2.68 percent in 2010. In more than 10 states, the TFR is at or below the replacement level fertility. However, the pace of fertility decline in the north-eastern states has been slower with TFRs ranging between 3 percent and 3.6 percent.

India contributes about 20 percent to the global toll of maternal deaths. Maternal mortality ratio (MMR) in India stagnated for decades; but has shown a positive trend in the recent decades. It declined from 677 per 100,000 live births in 1980 to 254 in 2008. There is growing pressure to achieve MDG-5, i.e. to reduce MMR by 75 percent from 1990 to 2015. Consequently, in April 2005, a nation-wide programme called the *Janani Suraksha Yojana* was launched. This programme aims to reduce maternal and infant mortality by encouraging institutional deliveries and providing care to women during pregnancy and the post-partum period. Cash incentives are provided to women and community-level workers to encourage institutional deliveries. Data show that there has been a dramatic increase in the number of institutional deliveries from 0.8 million in 2005 (when the programme was launched) to about 10 million in 2010. This is the largest conditional cash transfer programme in the world. Currently, health facilities are unprepared to copeup with the sudden and exponential rise in the number of deliveries. Sixty percent of maternal deaths occur within six weeks after delivery and half of these occur on the first day of birth. Two-thirds of neonatal deaths occur in the first week. Therefore, skilled care at birth can save the lives of millions of both mothers and newborns. Millions of girls in India are undernourished. Anaemia during pregnancy is a major contributor to maternal mortality and morbidity as well as low birth weight. Growing recognition about the fact that family planning programmes can reduce the life time risk of maternal deaths by one-third. Nutrition, a neglected issue, has also begun to receive attention in the past years.

An Indian girl child aged 1-5 years is 75 percent more likely to die than an Indian boy, making this the worst gender differential in child mortality for any country in the world. Infant (0-1 year) and child (1-5 years) mortality are declining in India and across the world, though not as fast as it was hoped in India. Simultaneously, most of the world is experiencing a faster fall in female infant and child mortality than in male. However, India along with China bucks this trend. The UN Department of Economic and Social Affairs (UN-

DESA) data for 150 countries show that India and China are the only two countries in the world where female infant mortality is higher than male infant mortality in the 2000s. In China, there are 76 male infant deaths for every 100 female infant deaths compared with 122 male infant deaths for every 100 female infant deaths in the developing world as a whole (Table 1). India has better infant mortality sex ratio than China with 97 male infant deaths for every 100 female, but this is not in tune with the global trend or with its neighbours Sri Lanka (125) or Pakistan (120). The high girl child mortality in India is explained by socio-cultural values. The discrimination against the girl child in areas like food and nutrition, and health care give rise to high girl child mortality in India. Of these, neglect of health care of the girl child is the most direct determinant of mortality. Studies have shown that health-related neglect may involve waiting longer before taking a sick girl to a doctor than a sick boy, and is also reflected in lower rates of immunization for girls than boys. Moreover, since the outrage over India's poor child sex ratio was seen a campaign against female feticide was undertaken. But this is not a complete solution. Pre and post-natal discrimination are complementarily contributing to the gender imbalance.

TABLE I

Ratio of Male to Female Mortality

(per 100 Females)

Country	*Infant (0-1 Year)*	*Child (1-5 Years)*
India	97	56
China	76	97
Pakistan	120	100
Sri Lanka	125	111
Less Developed Regions	122	111
World	122	116

Source : UN data.

In India, girls continue to marry and get pregnant at very young ages. Forty-six percent of women between the ages of 18 and 29 in India were married before the age of 18, according to the National Family Health Survey (NFHS)-3. Worldwide 60 million girls become child brides every year. It is estimated that there are 23 million child brides in the country, around 40 percent of child brides globally. Global human rights NGO 'Breakthrough' found that over 60 percent of women between the ages of 20-24 were married before 18 in the districts of Hazaribagh and Gaya in Bihar and Ranchi in Jharkhand. Underage girls are deprived of early health and reproductive rights. This later has implications on child and maternal mortality. According to the NGO's data the trend is worse in rural areas. In Jharkhand, 71 percent of girls in rural areas were married before 18 years compared to 33 percent in urban areas. In Bihar, 65.2 of girls were married before 18 years compared to 37 percent in urban areas. When these girls become mothers, they are more vulnerable to complications or death during delivery. These mothers often do not have adequate access to health care before, during, and after pregnancy, resulting in untreated complications and higher risk of death.

Gender-related differences in health status have led to an unbalanced sex ratio during the last decade. Gender discrimination at each stage of the female life cycle contributes to the imbalance. Neglect of girl children, reproductive mortality and poor access to health care for girls and women have all been the reasons for this difference. Among children up to 15 years old, there are 1.8 crore fewer girls than boys, giving rise to a sex ratio of 914 girls per 1,000 boys. This is the depressing picture of the fate of girls emerging from Census data 2011. Among infants less than a year old, boys outnumber girls by over 9 lakh. But by 6 years, the difference increases to nearly 60 lakh. In other words, it gives rise to a sex ratio of about 920 girls per 1,000 boys. The story does not end here. There is an appalling drop in the population of girls after that. The difference in the population of boys and girls in the 7-15 age group rises to nearly 1.1 crore. That is a sex ratio of 911 for this age group. (Census 2011). The skewed sex ratio makes life tough for women.

All these make the point clear that health status of women and girls is in a deplorable condition. In order to achieve women's empowerment and gender equality, and fulfill the MDG goals, and augment human resource development, there is an urgent need to enhance the health status of women in India. This book which is a compendium of articles on various aspects of gender and health tries to take a stock of the health status of women and girls in India. The articles incorporated in this book not only deal with various aspects of women's health but also focus on women's health issues in the country in general and in different states in particular.

List of Contributors

Adibabu Kadithi, Research Analyst, Novo Nordisk Education Foundation.

Bidyadhar Dehury, IIPS, Mumbai (Maharashtra).

Binod Bihari Jena, Research Scholar, Jawaharlal Nehru University (JNU), New Delhi.

Biranchi Jena, Project Manager, Programmes & Research, Novo Nordisk, Education Foundation.

Clifford D'Souza, Project Manager, Changing Diabetes Barometer, Novo Nordisk, Education Foundation.

D.S. Sampath Kumar, Assistant Professor, Department of Sociology, Bharathidasan University, Tiruchirappalli (T.N.).

Divya Karikkan, Assistant Professor, Department of Applied Economics, Kannur University, Thalassery campus, Palayad (Kerala).

Divya Singhal, Assistant Professor, Goa Institute of Management, Goa.

Fernanda Andrade, Research Associate, Goa Institute of Management, Goa.

Jitendra Gouda, International Institute for Population Science (IIPS), Mumbai (Maharashtra).

K. Gangadharan, Professor and Head, Department of Applied Economics, Kannur University, Thalassery Campus, Palayad (Kerala).

Kabita Kumari Sahu, Lecturer in Economics, North Orissa University, Baripada (Odisha).

Kalpa Sharma, Research Officer, Institute of Health Management Research, Jaipur (Rajasthan).

M.S.R. Murthy, Retired Professor, Tirupati (A.P.).

M.N.V. Prasad, Research Consultant, Emergency Management and Research Institute, Secunderabad (A.P.).

P. Anbalagan, Associate Professor of Economics, Presidency College, Chennai (T.N.).

R. Maruthakutti, Associate Professor, Department of Sociology, Manonmaniam Sundaranar University, Tirunelveli (T.N.).

Raman Shetty, Trustee, Novo Nordisk Education Foundation.

Ranjan Kumar Prusty, International Institute for Population Science (IIPS), Mumbai (Maharashtra).

Sherly Thomas, Professor of Economics, Avinashilingam Institute of Home Science & Higher Education (Deemed University), Coimbatore (T.N.).

Sudhakar Patra, Head, Department of Economics, Ravenshaw University, Cuttack (Odisha).

Uma Shankar Majhi, Research Scholar, International Institute for Population Sciences (IIPS), Mumbai (Maharashtra).

V.L. Lavanya, Research Scholar, Department of Economics, Avinashilingam Institute for Home Science and Higher Education for Women, Coimbatore (T.N.).

Vinay Ransiwal, Trustee, Novo Nordisk Education Foundation.

1

Gender, Health and Development in India

L.N. Dash

The human right to health has been recognised in numerous international instruments. That health is a basic human right is understood from the Preamble of the Constitution of the World Health Organisation. The right to health has been reaffirmed by the Commission on Human Rights. The Indian Constitution deals with the subject of health in a substantive manner under the Directive Principles of State Policy. There has been judicial recognition about the various aspects of the right to health. India has ratified various international conventions and human rights instruments. The 1990s witnessed various international conferences aimed at improving the health status of women. One such is the International Conference on Population and Development (ICPD) which was held in Cairo in Sept. 1994. The ICPD linked reproductive health to women's status and to overall economic development. One year after the Cairo Conference, the Fourth Conference on Women was held in Beijing in 1995. The Beijing Platform of Action advanced the progress made in Cairo by supporting ICPD Plan of Action. In Sept. 2000 at the Millennium Summit 189 nations agreed on the Millennium Development Goals (MDG) which had four health goals.

Notwithstanding all these, women are still subjugated and face various kinds of discrimination in the society. The most important is women's vulnerable health condition. This paper, therefore, makes an attempt to focus on the health status of women in India. While doing this gender-specific diseases of women will be brought to the fore.

WOMEN, HEALTH AND NUTRITION

Women's nutrition, health and mortality are influenced by the nature of India's social environment. Nutrition influences women's ability to cope with diseases, infections and rigours of everyday life. It has been found that boys and girls receive similar types and amounts of food until 10-12 years. Large differences begin to occur only when women and girls are not given adequate nutrition to support their activity levels. Then they begin to experience the ill effects of malnutrition. The gender difference in the average intake of nutrients is negligible in children aged 7-9 years. They become prominent only after the age of 12. In their teens girls consume fewer cereals, pulses and milk products. After the age of 18, women consume less energy-rich food. Pregnant women's intake is deficient by 1100 calories. Consumption pattern also differs among classes. Low income women's calorie intake is deficient by 500-600 calories. On the contrary, men and boys receive more nutritious food than women and girls. The differences and deficiencies manifest themselves in signs and symptoms, such as low body mass and anaemia.

Almost half of the girls (49.2 percent) are underweight for their age and 20.3 percent are severely underweight. More than half of the girl children are stunted (56.1 percent) and 36.8 percent are severely stunted. About 24.6 percent of girl children are wasted. Negative signs and symptoms of gender differences in nutrition are visible to a greater extent during adolescent and adult years. For example, more women (36.3 percent) than men (28.6 percent) have chronic energy deficiency. On the contrary, more men (62.1 percent) than women (59 percent) have normal Body Mass Index (BMI) grades. This demonstrates how gender differences in nutrition leads to health differences.

Anaemia is a major outcome of malnutrition among women in India. It has been found that large-scale anaemia is found in married women. Pregnant women with hemoglobin levels of less than 10.9 grams/deciliter and non-pregnant women who have hemoglobin

Table 1.1

Nutritional Status of Women and Men in India (State-wise)

States	*Women whose Body Mass Index is below normal (percent)*	*Men whose Body Mass Index is below normal (percent)*
Andhra Pradesh	33.5	30.8
Arunachal Pradesh	16.4	15.2
Assam	36.5	35.6
Bihar	45.1	35.3
Chhattisgarh	43.4	38.5
Goa	27.9	24.6
Gujarat	36.3	36.1
Haryana	31.3	30.9
Himachal Pradesh	29.9	29.7
Jammu & Kashmir	24.6	28.0
Jharkhand	43.0	38.6
Karnataka	33.5	33.9
Kerala	18.0	21.5
Madhya Pradesh	41.7	41.6
Maharashtra	36.2	33.5
Manipur	14.8	16.3
Meghalaya	14.6	14.1
Mizoram	14.4	9.2
Nagaland	17.4	14.2
Odisha	41.4	35.7
Punjab	18.9	20.6
Rajasthan	36.7	40.5
Sikkim	11.2	12.2
Tamil Nadu	28.4	27.1
Tripura	36.9	41.7
Uttar Pradesh	36.0	38.3
Uttarakhand	30.0	28.4
West Bengal	39.1	35.2
Delhi	14.8	15.7
India	35.6	34.2

Source : Government of India (2008), *National Health Profile, 2008*, New Delhi: Government of India, Ministry of Health & Family Welfare.

levels below 11.9 grams/deciliter are considered to be anaemic. The incidence of anaemia is the result of diet deficient in requisite quantities of iron, protein, vitamins, and minerals essential for production of hemoglobin in the human body. Nutritional anaemia is a serious problem that affects 60 to 70 percent of pregnant women. Anaemia increases the risk of low birth weight of a child and premature birth, pre-natal and neo-natal mortality, and increases the risk of maternal morbidity and mortality. Different studies show a correlation between anaemia in pregnancy and poor economic status, illiteracy, poor antenatal care received by the mother. The NFHS-3 data show that 55 percent women and 24 percent of men are anaemic. Although the prevalence of anaemia among women varies widely among the states, it is widespread in every state. The highest prevalence of anaemia in women, i.e. more than 60 percent is found in eight states such as Jharkhand, Bihar, Odisha, etc. (Table 1.2). Similarly, severe anaemia is highest in Assam and Arunachal Pradesh. The lowest levels of anaemia are in five states, such as Punjab, Manipur, Mizoram, Goa and Kerala. Even in these states more than 30 percent women are anaemic. It is revealed that incidence of anaemia among women aged 15-49 years varies from 69.7 percent in Assam to 36.4 percent in Goa. It is also high in Bihar (63.4 percent), Odisha (63 percent) and West Bengal (62.7 percent) (Table 1.2). The number of pregnant women who are anaemic has jumped from about 49 percent to over 54 percent in the period from NFHS-II and NFHS-III. Anaemia is higher among women belonging to ST as well as those belonging to the lower economic sections. Anaemia among married women continues to be a serious problem in India.

TABLE 1.2

Prevalence of Anaemia among Women (in percent)

States	*Mild anaemia*	*Moderate anaemia*	*Severe anaemia*	*Total*
Andhra Pradesh	32.5	14.9	2.4	49.8
Arunachal Pradesh	50.6	11.3	0.6	62.5
Assam	43.2	25.6	0.9	69.7
Bihar	42.9	19.0	1.5	63.4
Delhi	29.6	9.6	1.3	40.5
Goa	27.3	8.1	1.0	36.4
Gujarat	29.5	14.4	2.5	46.3

Haryana	30.9	14.5	1.6	47.0
Himachal Pradesh	31.4	8.4	0.7	40.5
Jammu & Kashmir	39.3	17.6	1.9	58.7
Karnataka	26.7	13.4	2.3	42.4
Kerala	19.5	2.7	0.5	22.7
Madhya Pradesh	37.5	15.6	1.0	54.3
Maharashtra	31.5	14.1	2.9	48.5
Manipur	21.7	5.3	0.8	28.9
Meghalaya	33.4	27.5	2.4	63.3
Mizoram	35.2	12.1	0.7	48.0
Nagaland	27.8	9.6	1.0	38.4
Odisha	45.1	16.4	1.6	63.0
Punjab	28.4	12.3	0.7	41.4
Rajasthan	32.3	14.1	2.1	48.5
Sikkim	37.3	21.4	2.4	61.1
Tamil Nadu	36.7	15.9	3.9	56.5
Uttar Pradesh	33.5	13.7	1.5	48.7
West Bengal	45.3	15.9	1.5	62.7
India	35.0	14.8	1.9	51.8

Notes : 1. Figures are for undivided state. The states of Bihar, Madhya Pradesh and Uttar Pradesh here include the newly-constituted states of Jharkhand, Chhattisgarh and Uttaranchal respectively.
2. Figures give the percentage of ever-married women classified as having iron-deficiency anaemia by degree of anaemia.

Source : Government of India (2004), *Women and Men in India, 2004*, New Delhi: Government of India.

MATERNAL MORTALITY RATE (MMR)

According to World Health Organisation (WHO), a maternal mortality death is defined as a death of a woman while pregnant or within 42 days of termination of pregnancy. It is expressed as a rate per 1000 live births. Maternal mortality in the world is estimated to be 529,000 deaths per year. It comes to a global ratio of 400 maternal deaths per 100,000 live births. Together, the regions of Sub-Saharan Africa and South Asia accounted for 86 percent of the world's maternal deaths in 2005. The world's MMR is declining too slowly to meet the Millennium Development Goal-5 which aims to reduce the number of women who die in pregnancy and childbirth by three-quarters by 2015. While an annual decline of 5.5 percent in MMR between 1990 and 2015 is required to achieve MDG-5, figures show an annual decline of less than 1 percent.

India is among those countries which have a very high maternal mortality rate. Avoidable complications during childbirth are killing 78,000 women in India every year. This means on an average one woman dies from complications related to pregnancy and childbirth every seven minutes. India is followed by Nigeria (59,000), Congo (32,000), and Afghanistan (26,000). India along with 10 other countries accounted for almost 65 percent of global maternal deaths in 2005. The maternal mortality rate (MMR) in India is 407 deaths per 100,000 live births in 2001. In comparison, Congo had an MMR of 740, Nigeria 1,100 and Afghanistan 1,800 per 100,000 births. India's neighbours are far better-off. While Bangladesh reported 21,000 deaths with an MMR of 570, Pakistan recorded 15,000 deaths with MMR of 320, China had 7800 deaths with MMR of 45 and Nepal 65,000 deaths with MMR of 830 in 2005. Sri Lanka recorded 190 deaths with MMR of 58. It has been estimated that an Indian woman is 300 times more likely to die in childbirth from pregnancy-related complications than women in the USA or UK (UNICEF, 2009). The NFHS-III found that women in India lack quality care during pregnancy and childbirth. In India, more than two-thirds of all maternal deaths occur in a handful of states—Uttar Pradesh, Bihar, Jharkhand, Odisha, Madhya Pradesh, Chhattisgarh, Rajasthan and Assam. In Uttar Pradesh, one in every 42 women faces the risk of maternal death, compared to one in 500 women in Kerala. Almost one in four women (23 percent) who gave birth in the last 10 years, received no antenatal care, ranging from one percent or less in Kerala and Tamil Nadu to 66 percent in Bihar. At least 40 percent of pregnant did not get any antenatal care in Jharkhand, Arunachal Pradesh and Nagaland. The quality of antenatal care also needs improvement in India. Only 65 percent of women receiving antenatal care received iron and folic acid supplements for at least 90 days. Only 4 percent of expectant mothers took a deworming drug during pregnancy. Failure to take an iron supplement and deworming drugs increases the risk of anaemia, a major problem for mothers and children in India. Maternal Mortality in India shows a declining trend. It was 20 per 1000 live births in 1938 and declined to 10 per 1000 live births in 1959. According to SRS Reports for the year 1997, maternal mortality for India was 407 per 100,000 live births. In 2003, it declined to 301 per 100,000. During the period from 1997 to 2003, it has declined substantially by 24 percent. Nevertheless, it has come down to 212 in 2007-09. The age distribution of maternal deaths from 2001 to 2003 shows that more than two-thirds of the maternal deaths are in the age group of 20-34 years. The major causes of maternal mortality are hemorrhage (38 percent), sepis (11 percent), hypertension (5 percent), obstructed labour (5 percent), abortion (8 percent) and other conditions (34 percent). With more than half a million maternal deaths annually, more women in India die during pregnancy or childbirth than in any other country in the world. The

TABLE 1.3

Maternal Mortality Ratio, Deliveries Conducted by Skilled Personnel, Antenatal Care Coverage and Life Time Risk of Maternal Deaths in Some Developing and Developed Countries

Country	*Antenatal care coverage (percent) (1996-2004)*	*Deliveries conducted by skilled personnel (percent) (1996-2004)*	*Life time risk maternal death (one in) (2000)*	*Maternal mortality ratio (per 100,000 live births) (2000)*
India	60	43	48	407
Bangladesh	49	13	59	380
Bhutan	—	37	37	420
Indonesia	92	72	150	230
Myanmar	76	57	75	360
Nepal	28	15	24	740
Thailand	99	92	900	44
Sri Lanka	95	96	430	92
Pakistan	43	23	31	500
China	89	96	830	56
Japan	100	100	6000	10
Singapore	100	100	1700	30
UK	—	99	3800	13
USA	99	99	2500	17
World	71	63	74	400

Source : Park, K. (2007), *Park's Textbook of Preventive and Social Medicine*, Jabalpur: Banarasidas Bhanot, p. 454.

probability that a girl will die from a complication-related pregnancy and childbirth during her life time in India is 1 in 48 in 2001. It, however, increased to 70 in 2005. On the other hand, it was 1 in 3800 in UK, 2500 in USA, 1700 in Singapore and so on.

TABLE 1.4

Maternal Mortality Ratio (per 100,000 live births)

Major States	*1997-98*	*1999-01*	*2001-03*
India	398	327	301
Andhra Pradesh	197	220	195
Assam	568	398	490
Bihar	531	400	371
Gujarat	46	202	172
Haryana	136	176	162
Karnataka	245	266	228
Kerala	150	149	110
Madhya Pradesh	441	407	379
Maharashtra	166	169	149
Odisha	346	424	358
Punjab	280	177	178
Rajasthan	508	501	445
Tamil Nadu	131	167	134
Uttar Pradesh	606	539	517
West Bengal	303	218	194

Source : Government of India (2007), *Family Welfare Statistics in India, 2006*, New Delhi: Government of India, p. A-65.

REPRODUCTIVE HEALTH

Fertility rate of women tells upon the health of women. According to the Sample Registration Survey, 53.7 percent of girls aged 15-19 years had children including 60.7 percent of rural and 31.5 percent urban adolescents. Comparison of Age Specific Marital Fertility Rates (ASMFRs) and Maternal Fertility Rates (MFRs) show that women who marry early have high rates of fertility. About one-third of the total disease burden in women from 15 to 44 years in developing countries is linked to reproductive health problems. Government interventions in Reproductive and Child Health (RCH) can contribute directly to reduced infant, child, and maternal mortality. The expected benefits from investing in RCH programmes are likely to be greater than other investment opportunities. There are indirect benefits to a programme that promotes RCH as well. First, a focus on improving information and access to high quality maternal and child health care is likely to yield significant monetary savings in India. It is because nearly 50 percent of aggregate health spending is a primary curative health service. These resources could be used to add to India's base of human capital. Secondly, improved health of mothers and infants contributes to the national output via its effects on the quality and size of the labour force. An effective programme of RCH could do much to reduce the burden of disease among reproductive age women. Right to reproductive health also includes the right to safe termination of pregnancies, information about various health issues and most importantly to make decisions about childbirth and birth spacing. In 1997, 45.4 percent of the couples used contraception. Similarly, Medical Termination of Pregnancies (MTP) is one reproductive choice that allows women to opt out of unwanted or unintended pregnancies. In 1998-99, 0.82 lakh terminations were conducted at national level, while from 1972-99 a total of 11.36 million terminations were affected. At the state level, the number of MTP centres are highest in Maharashtra (1808) followed by Tamil Nadu (645), Uttar Pradesh (576) and Gujarat (557). In Bihar and Madhya Pradesh, there are five such centres for a population of one million people. These states have high rates of maternal mortality as well. MTP remains a contentious issue because it has both negative and positive applications. On the one hand, it provides women with reproductive health and birth spacing option, but on the other it is used for sex selective abortions that lower the number of girl children born. The issue, therefore, presents a challenge to policy-makers committed to upholding women's rights.

Antenatal care includes medical care, diet advice and the provision of iron and folic acid tablets to pregnant women. Currently 77 percent of mothers receive antenatal checkups (Table 1.5), 53.8 percent receive tetanus toxic injections and 50.5 percent receive iron and folic acid supplements. The trend in antenatal care in India shows that the percent of women who receive antenatal care has gone up from 65 percent during NFHS-1 to 77 percent during NFHS-3. However, the rural areas show grim picture as compared to the urban areas (Figure 1.1). The state level analysis presents a diversified picture. In Kerala, 100 percent women receive

TABLE 1.5
Women Who Received any Antenatal Check-up

States	*Percentage*
Kerala	100
Tamil Nadu	99
Andhra Pradesh	95
Maharashtra	93
Karnataka	92
Himachal Pradesh	91
West Bengal	91
Punjab	90
Jammu & Kashmir	88
Haryana	88
Gujarat	88
Chhattisgarh	79
Odisha	76
Madhya Pradesh	74
Rajasthan	68
Uttaranchal	63
Assam	62
Uttar Pradesh	58
Jharkhand	52
Bihar	38
India	77

Source : International Institute of Population Science, *National Family Health Survey- III, 2005-06,* Mumbai: IIPS.

antenatal check up followed by Tamil Nadu (99 percent), Andhra Pradesh (95 percent), Karnataka (92 percent), and Maharashtra (93 percent) etc. (Table 1.5). On the other hand, 38 percent women in Bihar, 52 percent in Jharkhand, 58 percent in Uttar Pradesh, etc. receive antenatal check-up. This shows that the southern and western states are better at providing antenatal care services. With low number of women receiving antenatal care tend to have higher number of maternal deaths.

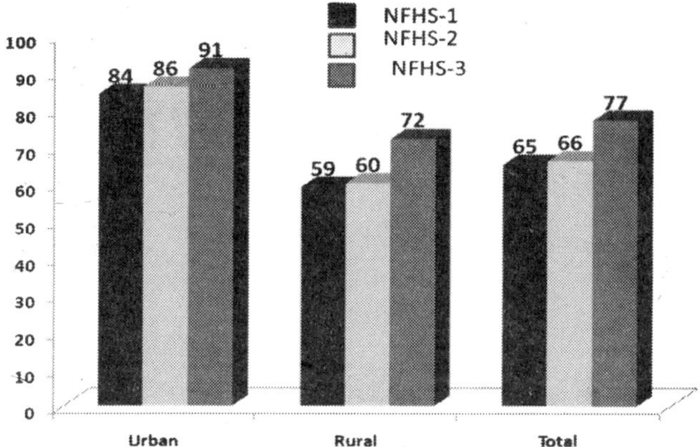

Figure 1.1 : Trend in Antenatal Care
(Percent of Women who had any ANC)

Institutional support during and after birth influences reproductive health. It contributes significantly to the reduction of maternal morbidity and mortality. Forty-one percent of women had institutional delivery, showing an increase of 7 percentage points since DLH Round-1 (Table 1.7). Thirty percent of women had institutional delivery in rural areas as against 70 percent for their

TABLE 1.6

State-wise Percentage of Deliveries Attended by Trained Personnel in India

States	*Births assisted by a doctor/nurse/LHV/ ANM/other health personnel (percent)*	*Institutional births (percent)*
(1)	*(2)*	*(3)*
India	46.6	38.7
Andhra Pradesh	74.9	64.4
Arunachal Pradesh	30.2	28.5
Assam	31.0	22.4
Bihar	29.3	19.9
Chhattisgarh	41.6	14.3

(Contd.)

TABLE 1.6 (*Contd.*)

(1)	*(2)*	*(3)*
Gujarat	63.0	52.7
Haryana	48.9	35.7
Himachal Pradesh	47.8	43..0
Jammu & Kashmir	56.5	50.2
Jharkhand	27.8	18.3
Karnataka	69.7	64.7
Kerala	99.4	99.3
Madhya Pradesh	32.7	26.2
Maharashtra	68.7	64.6
Manipur	59.0	45.9
Meghalaya	31.1	29.0
Mizoram	65.4	59.8
Nagaland	24.7	11.6
Odisha	44.0	35.6
Punjab	68.2	51.3
Rajasthan	41.0	29.6
Sikkim	53.7	47.2
Tamil Nadu	90.6	87.8
Tripura	48.8	46.9
Uttar Pradesh	27.2	20.6
Uttarakhand	38.5	32.6
West Bengal	47.6	42.0

Source : International Institute of Population Science. *National Family Health Survey-III, 2005-06,* Mumbai: IIPS.

urban counterparts. Institutional delivery is lower among illiterate women (21 percent). The proportion of safe delivery below the national average of 48 percent is found in 14 states. It ranges 50-75 percent in 15 states (Table 1.8). The proportion of safe delivery is found to be lowest in Jharkhand (28 percent) followed by Uttar Pradesh (29 percent), Chhattisgarh (29 percent), Bihar (30 percent) and highest in Kerala (98 percent). The delivery assisted by skilled persons is quite low, i.e. more than 60 percent in 185 districts in India. The proportion of deliveries assisted by skilled persons is

TABLE 1.7
Institutional Delivery by Background

Characteristics	*Percentage*
Total	41
Rural	30
Urban	70
Caste	
Scheduled Castes	33
Scheduled Tribes	22
OBC	40
Others	54
Education	
Illiterate	21
0-9 years	51
10 and above	79

TABLE 1.8
Percentage of Safe Delivery

States	*Safe Delivery (In percentage)*
(1)	*(2)*
Kerala	98
Tamil Nadu	89
Jammu & Kashmir	73
Andhra Pradesh	69
Karnataka	67
Punjab	64
Maharashtra	63
Gujarat	62
West Bengal	54
Himachal Pradesh	51
India	48
Rajasthan	44
Odisha	44

(*Contd.*)

TABLE 1.8 (*Contd.*)

(1)	*(2)*
Haryana	43
Madhya Pradesh	36
Assam	33
Uttaranchal	33
Bihar	30
Chhattisgarh	29
Uttar Pradesh	29
Jharkhand	28

Note : Either institutional delivery or home delivery assisted by a doctor/ nurse/ANM is termed as safe delivery.

Source : International Institute of Population Science, *National Family Health Survey- III, 2005- 06*, Mumbai: IIPS.

below 40 percent in 184 districts. Phekh district of Nagaland has the lowest practice of safe delivery and Alappuzha district of Kerala has the highest percentage of safe delivery in India.

MORTALITY

Mortality is affected by different factors depending upon women's age, residence and classes. In younger years, mortality is more due to neglect and social biases that devalue girls while in older years it is caused by the environment in which they work their ability to prevent or obtain treatment for diseases and infections. Apart from maternal deaths and deaths caused by pregnancy and childbirth, communicable diseases also kill large number of women in the reproductive age group. Mortality, therefore, is closely linked with the ability to prevent communicable diseases through access to quality health care facilities. This is evident from the high mortality during young ages and the declining sex ratio.

Girls start out having lower mortality rates than do boys during the first month of life (neonatal period) which accounts for their lower rates of infant mortality. Death rates in the post-neonatal period (age one month to one year) and in the period up to age five (under-five mortality) are higher for girls. Girls have higher childhood mortality despite the fact that boys are reported to have higher prevalence of acute respiratory infections and similar levels of diarrhoea and anaemia. This is explained by the fact that boys are more likely to receive health care. An estimated 66.5 percent of boys with acute respiratory infections are taken to a health provider compared with 60.8 percent of girls. Girls also have marginally higher rates of malnutrition which places them at higher risk of severe illness and death. Therefore, even if a number of girls should be present in India's population, they are not there. This is reflected in a low child sex ratio. The sex ratio for girls aged 0-6 years has declined from 976 in 1961 to 927 in 2001, indicating that fewer girls in this age group survive. Wide national, state and district level variations in this ratio show regional attitudinal differences towards girls. Consequences of discrimination are also visible in child mortality statistics. Data in this regard show that more girls than boys die before the age of 14. Of the total population of women and girls, 30.67 percent die before they turn 15 years.

All these factors give rise to low life expectancy for women. There has certainly been improvement on this front. In 1951, an Indian woman could expect to live no longer than 32 years. The figure has now doubled and it stood at a little over 63 years in 2001and 67 years in 2011. However, it is less than some of the countries like Tajikistan, Vietnam and Mongolia who are poorer than India. Women in these countries can expect to live 70.4 years, 72.5 years and 70.2 years respectively. There are also inter-state variations. In Kerala, a woman's life chances are better (75 years) than other states. The situation is different in Madhya Pradesh where a woman has a life expectancy of only 57 years. Further, there are wide differences in life expectancy of women between urban and rural areas. Women in urban areas live almost three years longer than women in rural areas.

There are a number of other factors like access to quality health facilities and mental health that influence mortality. The major causes of death in women aged 15-44 are venomous animal contact, infections and parasitic diseases and pregnancy, child birth and puerperium. At the national level, burns (6.4 percent), cancer (5.5 percent) and heart attacks (5.3 percent) account for a major number of deaths. Although anaemia causes health problems for a number of women, it has directly caused the death of less than 5 percent of women. At the state level major causes of death vary. In Andhra Pradesh, Gujarat, Haryana, Odisha, Tamil Nadu and Uttar Pradesh many women take their own lives, while in Bihar, Madhya Pradesh, Rajasthan and Karnataka tuberculosis kills a large number of women. In Kerala, most women die from cancer while in Maharashtra and

Punjab most die from burns and heart attacks. India's maternal mortality ratio is remarkably high in comparison to countries like China and Sri Lanka. The major causes of maternal deaths in the country are due to haemorrhage (29.7 percent), anaemia (10 percent), sepsis (16.1 percent), obstructed labour (9.5 percent), abortion (8.9 percent), toxaemia (8.3 percent) and so on. The causes confirm to the fact that deaths are not only due to the low status of women in general, but due to the lack of adequate health facilities during pregnancy and child birth. Cancer is another illness that affects Indian women. Currently, India has 25 percent of world's cervical cancer cases. About 50,000 women die of cervical cancer each year in the country. Among urban women, 80,000 new cases of breast cancer are diagnosed and 35,000 women die every year. Therefore, issues around cancer also highlight the importance of health care facilities to women's health. Another crucial health issue is mental health. Women and girls have equal right with men to grow in mentally and physically healthy environments where their full potentialities are recognized. Despite this, women experience psychological abuse and low self esteem. They live in environments that restrict or discourage them from developing their potentialities. Mental health problems among women have social and cultural roots such as dowry harassment, sexual violence, poverty, spousal alcohol abuse and a lack of personal choice. Given this many women commit suicide. Incidents are high, especially among older women.

In most of the countries where the HIV/AIDS virus is spreading rapidly women have become far more vulnerable to it than ever. Women account for about 43 percent of the world's 33 million people living with AIDS. The facts on infection among women are startling though most countries have not yet formulated strategies to deal with this factor. In France, AIDS cases among women have doubled in the last couple of years. In Africa the risk for girls is two to one in relation to boys. In sub-Saharan Africa, infected women outnumber men. In India the ratio is 4:1, but the rate of infections in women is increasing since the mid-1990. Women are biologically at greater risk and in addition face a number of social factors which contribute to making them more vulnerable to HIV. Across the social spectrum, they face limited access to health care. Most Indian women suffer from anaemia as a result of which they require more blood transfusion than men. This increases their risk of being infected. Myths and superstition heighten the risk of women. Even younger female partners are in the belief that they are less likely to contract any disease. In parts of India, the myths still persists that sex with a virgin actually cures men of various STDs. With increasing violence against women, rape has become a high risk factor for transmission. Therefore, with the AIDS virus poised to go into overdrive in India, a number of strategies have to be developed to reduce women's vulnerability. Access to information, education and skill regarding HIV/AIDS is to be improved. Women must be provided services and technologies which will lessen their chances of risk and prevention programmes that effectively address gender-related factor in HIV/AIDS.

SEX RATIO

The average number of females per 1000 males is 990 in the world. It is 1064 females per thousand males in Western Europe and 1015 in Africa. The ratio in Asia is 953. India shows a dismal picture in this regard as the sex ratio stands at 933 in 2001. This has of course registered marginal increase in 2011 as the overall sex ratio has increased to 940. The top five states/UTs with high sex ratios are Kerala (1084), Puducherry (1038), Tamil Nadu (995), Andhra Pradesh (992), and Chhattisgarh (991). On the other hand, the states/UTs with low sex ratios are Chandigarh (818), Delhi (866), Andaman and Nicobar Islands (878) and so on. In India, sex ratio is skewed in favour of males and has continued to rise in various forms. Indicating a continuous preference for boys in society, the Child Sex Ratio (CSR) in India has dropped to 914 against 1,000 males—the lowest since Independence. Despite a slew of measures to prevent female foeticide and schemes to encourage families to have girl child, the ratio has declined from 927 females against 1000 males in 2001 to 914 in 2011. Though an increasing trend in Child sex ratio (0-6 years) has been seen in Punjab, Haryana, Himachal Pradesh, Gujarat, Tamil Nadu, Mizoram and Andaman and Nicobar Islands, in all the

TABLE 1.9

Sex Ratio and Child Sex Ratio (0-6 years) in India

Year	*Sex Ratio*	*Child Sex Ratio*
1991	927	945
2001	933	927
2011	940	914

Source : *The Economic Times*, 31st March 2011.

remaining states the child sex ratio shows decline over the Census 2001. Haryana's Jhajjar (774 females) and Mahendragarh (778 females) districts have the lowest sex ratio while Lahul and Spiti district of Himachal Pradesh has the highest sex ratio of 1013 females.

CONCLUSION

Health is considered as fundamental to human right. Good health is both the means and the end of development. Yet, the *Alma Ata* Goal of 'health for all' is a distant dream for a large percentage of women in India. No doubt, India has created a large network of health care facilities during the last six decades, but women are yet to receive significant benefits. There have been improvements in antenatal care, institutional deliveries and assistance at delivery by health professional, but the changes over time have been slow. The sex ratio remains pitted against women. India continues to share the lowest rung in comparison to the world average sex ratio. Even countries like Nigeria, Tajikistan, Vietnam, Brazil and Indonesia fare better. In order to bring about an overall change in the health condition of women, the NGOs and village panchayats can be involved. The public-private partnership model can also be adopted to bring about improvement in the health condition of women in the country.

References

Anand, Anita and Salvi Gouri (1998), *Beijing! UN Fourth World Conference on Women*, New Delhi: Women's Feature Service.

Cahill, Kevin M. (1976), *Health and Development*, New York: Orbis Books.

Government of India (1997), *Women in India: A Statistical Profile*, New Delhi: Department of Women and Child Development.

Government of India (2004), *Health Information of India, 2002*, New Delhi: Government of India, Ministry of Health and Family Welfare.

Government of India (2005), *Report of the National Commission on Macroeconomics and Health*, New Delhi: Government of India, Ministry of Health and Family Welfare.

Government of India (2007), *Bulletin on Rural Health Statistics in India, 2007*, New Delhi: Government of India, Ministry of Health and Family Welfare.

Government of India (2007), *Statistical Abstract of India 2007*, New Delhi: Government of India.

Government of India (2008), *National Health Profile 2008*, New Delhi: Government of India.

Government of India (2007), *Family Welfare Statistics in India, 2006*, New Delhi: Government of India.

International Institute of Population Science (2005), *National Family Health Survey- III, 2005-06,* Mumbai: IIPS.

Kumar, Ashok and M.E. Khan (2010) "Health Status of Women in India: Evidences from National Family Health Survey-3 (2005-06) and Future Outlook", *Research and Practice in Social Sciences,* 6(2), Aug., pp. 1-21.

Mahabub ul Haq Human Development Centre, (2005) *Human Development in South Asia 2004: The Health Challenge,* Oxford: Oxford University Press.

UNICEF (2009), *State of the World's Children, 2009.*

2

Socio-economic Differential and Determinants of Overweight and Obesity Status among Men and Women in Urban India

RANJAN KUMAR PRUSTY AND JITENDRA GOUDA

INTRODUCTION

According to the World Health Organization (WHO), there will be about 2.3 billion overweight people aged 15 years and above, and over 700 million obese people worldwide in 2015. Overweight and obesity are the fifth leading risk for global deaths. At least 2.8 million adults die each year as a result of being overweight or obese. In addition, 44 percent of the diabetes burden, 23 percent of the ischemic heart disease and between 7 percent and 41 percent of certain cancer burdens are attributable to overweight and obesity. (WHO, 2012) Once considered as a high-income country problem, overweight and obesity are now on the rise in low and middle-income countries, particularly in urban settings.

India has already witnessed a rise in overweight or obesity in recent time. The last quarter of the Twentieth Century witnessed faster growth of overweight or obesity population in the country.

India has more than 30 million overweight and obese population. (IIPS, 1999) It has grappled children, adult and also old people in the country. (Chhatwal *et al.*, 2004) The National Family Health Survey (NFHS) evidently reports that obesity among women has increased from 11 percent in 1998-99 to 15 percent in 2005-06. (Chhatwal *et al.*, 2004; IIPS, 2006) Furthermore, the rate of increase is much faster in urban than in rural India. In urban areas of the country, prevalence of overweight and obesity is three times more than in rural India. (IIPS, 2006) The reasons of overweight or obese are many. However, lack of physical work, intake of energy-dense food and sedentary lifestyles are the main factors leading to overweight or obese. (Prentice, 2006; Sinha and Kapoor, 2010) Like any other disease, overweight or obesity also has an adverse impact on health, many times chronic in nature and causes premature deaths. Cardiovascular diseases, hypertension and type-2 diabetes mellitus are the most common chronic health problems that can occur due to overweight or obese condition. (Misra *et al.*, 2009; Chhan and Woo, 2010) It certainly reduces productivity and economic gain at the individual level. At country level, the problem obviously puts additional pressure on the economic and health system. Now, it has to tackle overweight or obesity on the one hand and hunger or malnutrition on the other hand which are yet to be resolved completely. (Mithu, Mukhopadhyay and Bose, 2005)

Despite the severity of the problem, there are very few studies which document the prevalence of overweight or obesity among sub-groups of the population in India. Furthermore, the associated covariates of being overweight and obesity for different socio-economic groups are least explored in India. Nevertheless, a study which intends to explore the covariates of overweight or obesity among women in north India stated that women's risk to get the problem increases with their age and parity. Other social factors like education and media exposure are also associated positively which increase the risk for women in India. (Agarwal and Mishra, 2004) However, the magnitude of the problem and associated covariates of overweight and obesity for men remains unexplored in India. Moreover, a comparative assessment of women and men incorporating the degree of prevalence with associated covariates of overweight or obesity is yet to be understood fully. Therefore, any comprehensive analysis to determine the sex differential in the prevalence of the problem and the associated covariates will be helpful for better policy implications to curb the situation in the country.

With these viewpoints, the study attempts to shed light on the prevalence of overweight or obesity by sex groups in urban India. Based on this perspective, the specific objectives of the study are to:

1) Document the prevalence of overweight and obesity among men and women in urban areas of India; and
2) To analyze the prevalence differentials and determinants for socioeconomic and demographic characteristics of men and women in urban India.

DATA AND METHODS

The study uses the National Family Health Survey (NFHS-3) third round data for the assessment of overweight and obesity among women and men in urban India. The survey is an Indian version of Demographic Health Survey (DHS) which is conducted in more than 80 countries all the world over. The NFHS-3 collects information from a nationally representative sample of 109,041 households, 124,385 women in the reproductive age of 15-49 years and 74,369 men aged 15-54 years. The sample is a multistage cluster sample with an overall response rate of 98 percent. Details of the sample design, including sampling frame and sample implementations, are provided in the basic survey report. (IIPS, 2006) For the present study, we consider urban women and men in the age group of 15-49 years.

OUTCOME VARIABLES

Overweight and Obesity: In NFHS-3, each woman and man aged 15-49 years were weighed using a solar-powered scale with an accuracy of $\pm$100 GM. Their height was measured using an adjustable wooden measuring board, specifically designed to provide accurate measurements (to the nearest 0.1 cm) in a developing-country field situation. The weight and height data were used to calculate the body mass index (BMI). Women who were pregnant at the time of the survey or women who had given birth during the two months preceding the survey were excluded. (IIPS, 2006) The BMI can be used to estimate the prevalence of underweight, as well as the prevalence of overweight and obesity. A BMI of less than 18.5 kg/m^2 is defined as underweight, indicating chronic energy deficiency. A BMI in the range of 18.5 and 24.9 kg/m^2 is defined as normal, 25.0 and 29.9 kg/m^2 as overweight, and more than 30.0 kg/m^2 as obese.

(WHO, 2003) Based on these cut-offs, the present study uses a three-category variable of nutritional status of women and men, merging underweight and normal, indicating as 'not obese' while keeping all others same as 'overweight' and 'obese'.

PREDICTOR VARIABLES

Age of Respondent: The survey collected information on each single age in the reproductive span of women and men from 15 to 49 years. Three category of age of respondent variables were used in this study, by merging 15 to 24 years as 'one', 25 to 35 years as 'two' and 35+ years as 'three'.

Religion: The NFHS-3 collected information from eleven different religions, i.e. Hindu, Muslim, Christian, Sikh, Buddhist/Neo-Buddhist, Jain, Jewish, Parsi/Zorastrian, No religion, Donyi Polo and others in India. This study uses a four-category religion variable wherein, Sikh, Buddhist/Neo-Buddhist, Jain, Jewish, Parsi/Zoroastrian, No religion, Donyi Polo and others are merged into one as 'Others' while keeping all others same.

Caste of the Household Head: The caste system in India is a social institution where social stratification of communities is defined by several endogamous inherited groups called *Jatis*. The castes in modern India can be classified into four classes: Scheduled Castes (SCs), Scheduled Tribes (STs), Other Backward Castes (OBCs) and other castes. There are a number of studies which provide evidence of caste-based inequalities and fosters that SCs/STs are socio-economically backward compared to other castes. (Srinivas, 1957)

Educational Attainment: Information on four educational variables i.e. no education, primary, secondary and higher level were collected in the NFHS-3 survey. However, this study uses three category variable wherein secondary and higher level are merged together for 'Up to higher level' while keeping all other same.

Marital Status: NFHS-3 collected information on marital status of respondents (women and men) and used in this study for the analysis of overweight and obesity variations.

Work Status: The income generation activity information for women and men were collected in the NFHS-3 Survey. The study used a two-category variable indicating whether the woman or man is working or not working for any income generation for the analysis of overweight and obesity variation.

Wealth Index: In the NFHS third round survey, the economic status information for women and men were collected and used in this study for the analysis of overweight and obesity variations.

Exposure to Mass Media: This study used media exposure variable with two categories, exposed to media and not exposed to media, to analyze the overweight and obesity variation in India. Mass media exposure includes reading newspaper or listening to radio or watching television at least once in a week.

STATISTICAL ANALYSIS

Descriptive statistics are used to know the level of overweight and obesity among urban women and men and by different socioeconomic demographic characteristics in India. The results are presented in percentages. Ordinal logistic regression is used to estimate the adjusted effects of selected demographic and socioeconomic variables on the prevalence of overweight and obesity among urban women and men in India. The ordinal logistic regression is used due to the nature of the outcome variable. The outcome variable has three categories namely, not obese, overweight and obesity (coded as 0, 1 and 2 respectively) are in order of BMI. The results are presented in the form of Odd Ratios (OR) with 95 percent confidence interval. In all our analysis, weights are used to restore the representativeness of the sample. The analysis is conducted using software IBM SPSS 20.0 and STATA 10.

RESULTS

Sex Differentials in the Prevalence of Overweight and Obesity in India

The prevalence of overweight and obesity among adult men and women in India is presented in Figure 2.1. Seventeen percent of women and 14 percent of men are overweight in addition to 6 and 3 percent of obese women and men in urban India. In rural India, 6 and 3 percent of women are overweight and obese respectively. Furthermore, 5 percent and only one percent of men are overweight and obese, respectively. Comparing between sexes, women are more overweight or obese across the country. However, the prevalence is higher in urban areas for both sexes than their counterpart group in rural area.

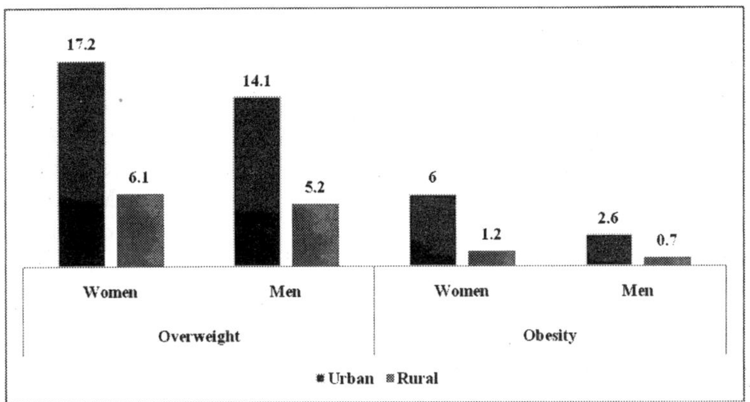

Figure 2.1 : Sex Differentials in the Prevalence of Overweight and Obesity in India, 2005-06 (in percent)

Overweight among States and Selected Cities in Urban India

The state-wise variation in overweight and obesity among women and men is presented in Table 2.1. Different states of India report different prevalence rate among women and men in India. Kerala records the highest of 27 percent prevalence of overweight for women whereas for men it is 21 percent in Punjab. The state of Punjab with 24 percent holds the second highest overweight women whereas Kerala's men are the second highest overweight in the country. Arunachal Pradesh (9.4 percent) and Bihar (7.3 percent) have the lowest overweight women and men respectively in India. For most obese population, Punjab holds majority both for women and men in the country. However, the prevalence is higher for women (12 percent) than men (6 percent). Meghalaya (0.8 percent) records the lowest obese women whereas other north-eastern states, such as Tripura and Arunachal Pradesh have no record of obese men. However, except Sikkim and Mizoram where men are more overweight than women, in all other states including the capital city of Delhi women are more overweight or obese than men in India. In states like Sikkim and Mizoram obesity is more prevalent among women than men.

The prevalence of overweight and obesity by the metropolitan cities is also analyzed in India. Among all the cities, Chennai records higher prevalence of overweight and obesity among both men and women in India while Nagpur has the lowest. However, the prevalence is higher for women than men in all selected cities in the country (Figure 2.2).

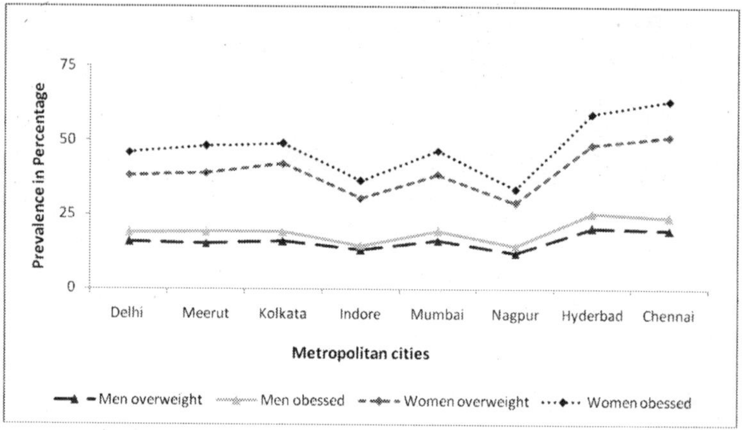

Figure 2.2 : Prevalence of Overweight and Obesity among Women and Men in Selected Cities in India, 2005-06

TABLE 2.1
Sex Differential in the Prevalence of Overweight and Obesity in India, 2005-06

States	*Overweight*		*Obesity*	
	Women	*Men*	*Women*	*Men*
Jammu & Kashmir	22.7	13.0	7.4	1.8
Himachal Pradesh	22.4	15.9	6.7	2.4
Punjab	24.2	21.3	11.9	5.6
Uttaranchal	18.8	12.7	4.9	1.6
Haryana	20.2	17.1	8.0	4.0
Delhi	19.0	15.8	7.9	3.2
Rajasthan	13.3	12.2	3.7	2.5
Uttar Pradesh	14.8	13.2	4.4	2.6
Bihar	9.8	7.3	2.7	1.5
Sikkim	15.7	16.2	4.4	1.3
Arunachal Pradesh	9.4	7.9	1.9	**
Nagaland	11.0	9.9	1.6	1.2
Manipur	16.4	13.3	3.2	1.6

Mizoram	12.7	14.9	2.1	.9
Tripura	14.0	12.4	3.1	**
Meghalaya	7.4	4.8	.8	.4
Assam	16.2	10.7	3.0	.5
West Bengal	19.2	11.7	5.4	1.2
Jharkhand	11.9	9.9	3.1	1.0
Odisha	14.4	10.9	3.2	3.6
Chhattisgarh	12.1	12.0	4.3	2.5
Madhya Pradesh	13.7	9.6	4.2	.5
Gujarat	18.4	14.6	7.4	3.4
Maharashtra	16.1	15.2	6.1	2.6
Andhra Pradesh	18.2	17.8	7.7	3.6
Karnataka	18.3	15.9	7.5	3.1
Goa	17.7	16.4	6.2	2.7
Kerala	26.9	19.5	6.0	2.8
Tamil Nadu	21.2	16.0	8.3	2.9
India	17.2	14.1	6.0	2.6

Source : NFHS-3 Survey.

Socio-economic and Demographic Differentials among Men and Women

The prevalence of overweight and obesity among women and men by different background characteristics is presented in Table 2.2. Comparing people of different age groups, it is evident from the Table that both men and women at later ages are more overweight or obese than their counterparts from younger ages. The prevalence of overweight and obesity increases with each passing year for both the sexes. However, the magnitude of increase in the prevalence rate is much higher for women than men. Women and men from the higher caste are more overweight and obese than their counterpart from lower caste groups. Furthermore, women from higher caste groups are more overweight and obese than men from this caste background. Nearly one-fifth and 8 percent of women from higher caste characteristics are overweight and obese respectively. In contrast to this, only 13 and 2 percent of men from the corresponding caste groups are overweight and obese in India. Comparing women and men from different religions, it is seen that except 'other' religions where men are more overweight than women, in all other religions

TABLE 2.2
Overweight and Obesity among Urban Men and Women for Selected Background Characteristics in India, 2005-06

Characteristics	Overweight		Obesity		Sample Size	
	Women	Men	Women	Men	Women	Men
(1)	(2)	(3)	(4)	(5)	(6)	(7)
Age						
15-24	6.7	4.9	1.3	0.7	19362	12277
25-34	19	14.7	5.4	2.5	16626	9656
35+	27.3	21.8	11.9	4.3	17204	10653
Caste						
SC[1]	13.3	5.8	3.4	0.7	8351	11866
ST[2]	10.6	3.1	1.9	0.3	4541	8600
OBC[3]	16.4	7.7	5.6	1.1	16043	25092
Others	20.3	12.5	7.6	2.4	22055	21373
Religion						
Hindu	17.2	14	5.8	2.5	37484	24933
Muslims	16.3	11.8	6.5	2.1	8437	5472
Christian	19.4	17.2	6.7	3.5	4709	2673
Others	21	24	8.5	4.7	2501	1569

Education						
No Education	13.3	6.9	4	0.7	10196	3016
Up to Primary	16.1	8.9	5	2	6203	4144
Secondary or above	18.8	15.8	6.9	2.9	36785	27478
Wealth Index						
Poorest	3.6	3.7	0.8	0.2	867	497
Poorer	5.6	3.0	1.3	0.5	2363	1511
Middle	9.4	6.3	1.9	0.6	6334	4554
Richer	14	10.0	3.7	1.1	15369	10938
Richest	23.1	20.6	9.2	4.4	28259	17153
Work status						
No	17.7	6.2	6.5	1.1	38008	6374
Yes	16	15.7	4.7	2.9	15089	28265
Media Exposure						
No Exposure	8.1	3.4	2.5	1.3	2756	511
Have Exposure	17.9	14.3	6.3	2.6	50428	34134

* Includes underweight and normal Men/Women, 1=Schedule Caste, 2=Schedule Tribe and 3=Other Backward Classes.

category women are more overweight and obese than men. Further, more women from 'other' religions are obese than men.

The prevalence of overweight or obesity increases with higher education for both the sexes. It is found that the scale of increase is much faster for women than men. Nearly 7 percent of women and 3 percent of men who had education up to secondary level are obese. In addition, more women are overweight than men with this reference level of education in India. A similar pattern is also observed in the economic standard of both the sexes. With rising economic standard the proportion of the problem increases. More than one-fifth of women (23 percent) and slightly lower than this level of men (21 percent) from affluent families are overweight. Similarly, more working women are either overweight or obese than men with any income generating activities. This apart, exposure to the media is also found to have influenced women more to be overweight or obese than men in India.

MULTIVARIATE ANALYSIS

To understand factors associated with overweight and obesity among men and women different covariates were modeled using ordered logistic regression. The adjusted effect of selected covariates of overweight and obesity both for women and men are presented in Table 2.3. It is observed that both men and women are at greater risk of being overweight or obese with increase in age. While men who are more than 35 years old are about 4 times (OR=3.53, CI=3.09-4.05) more likely to be obese than younger men of less than 25 years. Similarly, women of more than 35 years of age are six times

TABLE 2.3

Ordered Logistic Regression Showing Different Covariates Associated with Overweight and Obesity among Urban Women and Men in India, 2005-06

Characteristics	*Women*		*Men*	
	Odds Ratio	*95 percent CI*	*Odds Ratio*	*95 percent CI*
Age				
15-24®				
25-34	2.71***	2.50-2.93	2.28***	2.02-2.59
35+	5.94***	5.48-6.44	3.53***	3.09-4.05

Caste				
[1]SC®				
[2]ST	0.55***	0.48-0.63	0.78**	0.61-0.98
[3]OBC	1.16***	1.08-1.25	1.07	0.96-1.18
Others	1.19***	1.11-1.28	1.17**	1.06-1.30
Religion				
Hindu®				
Muslims	1.35***	1.26-1.44	1.07	0.96-1.18
Christian	1.02	0.92-1.14	1.37***	1.13-1.65
Others	1.31***	1.18-1.45	1.72***	1.49-1.96
Education				
No Education®				
Up to Primary	1.13*	1.04-1.24	1.29*	1.08-1.55
Secondary or above	1.48***	1.38-1.58	1.74***	1.48-2.04
Wealth Index				
Poorest®				
Poorer	1.48**	1.05-2.07	0.96	0.60-1.54
Middle	2.22***	1.62-3.03	1.78**	1.17-2.71
Richer	3.56***	2.62-4.85	2.77***	1.84-4.16
Richest	7.18***	5.28-9.76	6.86***	4.56-10.31
Marital Status				
Unmarried®				
Married	2.04***	1.87-2.22	1.82***	1.63-2.04
Work status				
No®				
Yes	0.85***	0.81-0.90	1.25***	1.09-1.42
Media Exposure				
No Exposure®				
Have Exposure	1.41***	1.24-1.62	1.96**	1.28-3.00
Cut1	**5.16**	**4.83-5.48**	**5.79**	**5.21-6.37**
Cut2	**6.92**	**6.60-7.25**	**8.17**	**7.38-8.55**

®=Reference category,1=Schedule Caste, 2=Schedule Tribe and 3=Other Backward Classes. *p<0.1 **p<0.05, and ***p<0.01. The variables like region is controlled in the model. Other religions means people belonging to Non-Hindu, Non-Christian and Non-Muslim religion.

(OR=5.94, CI=5.48-6.44) more likely to be obese than younger women of the same age. Women from higher caste are 19 percent more likely of being overweight or obese than women from scheduled caste (SC) category. Muslim women are at (OR: 1.35; CI: 1.26-1.44) more risk of being overweight or obese than Hindu women. Men from higher caste group are (OR: 1.17) also more overweight or obese than SC category men. Comparing men of different religions, men of other religions and the Christian religion are 1.72 and 1.37 times more likely of being overweight or obese respectively than Hindu men.

Education and economic status of both men and women show significant and positive association with overweight and obesity. Women from higher education category (OR: 1.48; CI: 1.38-1.58) and belonging to the richest wealth quintile (OR: 7.18; CI: 5.28-9.76) have a very odds of being overweight/obese than illiterate and poorest women respectively. In case of man, the odds are lower than man. For example, men with education of up to secondary level are 1.74 times more likely to be overweight or obese than illiterate men. The marital status and media exposure of both men and women show a statistically significant and positive association with overweight and obesity status whereas work status shows a negative association for women. For example, working women are 15 percent less likely to be obese than those not working.

DISCUSSION

The present study tries to examine the sex differentials in the prevalence of overweight and obesity in India. Like many other studies on similar issue, this study also found that overweight or obesity is more of an urban problem and both the sexes have been affected more than their counterpart groups from rural India. However, the problem is more noticeable among women than men. It substantiates the available literature which documents that women are affected more than men. (Janghorbani *et al.*, 2007; Case and Menendez, 2009) In addition, women in metropolitan cities are markedly more overweight or obese than men corroborating the result further. The finding could well be compared with other studies carried out in western and other developing countries wherein women in urban or mega cities are more overweight or obese. (Janghorbani *et al.*, 2007; Case and Menendez, 2009) The reasons for high prevalence among women could be many. There are studies from western and other developing countries documenting childhood nutrition deprivation, depression and high socioeconomic status as the potential reasons for the high prevalence of overweight or obesity among women. (Case and Menendez, 2009; World Bank, 2011; Gruebner, 2011) Contrary to this, there are also studies which argue that women from low economic background are more overweight or obese than women from affluent families. (Gordon-Larsen *et al.*, 2003; Anuradha *et al.*, 2011) Furthermore, many studies have documented that women's risk of being overweight or obesity increases with each of her additional age and parity. (Wardle *et al.*, 2002) Nevertheless, it is also evident in the present study that the risk of being overweight or obese increases phenomenally with each additional age for both sexes, but the rate of increase is much faster for women than men. A similar pattern is also noticed between the risk of being overweight or obese and economic standard. Women and men from affluent families are more overweight or obese than their counterpart group of poor households. The result of ordinary logistic regression substantiates these arguments further. Richest women are more than 8 times at risk to get the problem. However, men have 5.64 times more risk from this economic background. Beside, women and men aging 35 and above years are 6.62 and 4.17 times more likely to be overweight or obese respectively in India. Other social factors like marital status and media exposure are associated positively and increase the risk for being overweight or obese for both men and women. Nevertheless, the magnitude of the prevalence is much higher among women than men for these selected covariates.

The adverse health outcomes of being overweight or obese are out of the purview of this study. Nevertheless, there are studies which document that women are always at greater health risk due to their overweight or obese condition. Women's reproductive and pregnancy related complications are the most worrisome thing in recent times. There are studies which state that overweight or obese women are more likely to have still birth or terminated pregnancy than normal women. (Agarwal and Mishra, 2004) In addition to this, as research from developing countries suggests cancer (breast cancer), type-2 diabetes mellitus and hypertension are on a continuous rise in Asian countries including India and, in most cases overweight or obese conditions are attributed as the primary determinant for these health consequences. (Routley, 2011; Yoon *et al.*, 2006) Therefore, considering the high prevalence of overweight or obesity among women in the country it would be justifiable to assume that the chronic diseases which are on the rise among women probably are due to overweight or obese condition. This definitely needs further exploration with longitudinal or other suitable researches in medical settings.

CONCLUSION

Considering rapid urbanization and increasing participation of women in economic and other social sectors in India, it can well be presumed that the prevalence of the disease will rise further probably at a higher rate than before. However, the current health programmes or policy in the country are not in place to consider this growing epidemic. The existing health policy or programmes have overlooked this new epidemic focusing priorities to other traditional issues like hunger and malnutrition. Thus, the growing demand which might appear in the near future is to have appropriate policy or programme measures to address the issue stringently for the restoration of good health more noticeably of women in India.

LIMITATIONS

The study used anthropometric technique i.e. BMI as the only measurement to estimate the prevalence of overweight or obesity in India. However, there are many studies which argue that BMI is not an ideal measure for the estimation of obesity especially in Asian countries due to various physiological reasons. (WHO Expert Consultation, 2004; Pan and Wen-Ting, 2008) The studies consider waist circumference (WC), waist to hip ratio (WHR) and percentage of fat in the body as better measures of overweight or obese and are able to recognize the associated health risks at an early stage. Beside this, the paper deliberately excludes some of the demographic covariates which might have more significance like, parity of women, to determine the degree of prevalence among women. This is done to maintain uniformity in the selection of covariates to make the analysis comparable among women and men.

References

Agarwal, P., V. Mishra (2004), "Covariates of Overweight and Obesity among Women in North India," Population and Health Series, Honolulu, East-West Centre Working Papers 2004.

Anuradha, R., G. Ravivarman and Timsi Jain (2011), "The Prevalence of Overweight and Obesity among Women in an Urban Slum of Chennai," *Journal of Clinical and Diagnostic Research,* 5 (5), 957-60.

Bhadra, Mithu, A. Mukhopadhyay and K. Bose (2005), "Overweight and Obesity among Adult Bengalee Hindu Women of Kolkata, India," *Human Ecology Special Issue*, 13, 77-83.

Case, Anne and Alicia Menendez (2009), "Sex Differences in Obesity Rates in Poor Countries: Evidence from South Africa," *Economics and Human Biology*, 7, 271-82.

Chan, R.S.M., J. Woo (2010), "Prevention of Overweight and Obesity: How Effective is the Current Public Health Approach," *Int. J. Environ. Res. Public Health*, 7(3), 765-83.

Chhatwal, Jugesh, Manorama Verma and Sandeep Kaur Riar (2004), "Obesity among Pre-Adolescent and Adolescents of a Developing Country (India)," *Asia Pacific Clinical Nutrition*, 13 (3), 231-35.

Gordon-Larsen, Penny., Linda S. Adair and Barry M. Popkin (2003), "The Relationship of Ethnicity, Socio-economic Factors, and Overweight in U.S. Adolescents", *Obesity Research*, 11 (1), 121-129.

Gruebner, O., R. Staffeld, M.M.H. Khan, K. Burkart, A. Krämer, P. Hostert (2011), "Urban Health In Megacities Extending The Framework For Developing Countries," *IHDP Update Human Health and Global Environmental Change*, Vol. 1, 42-49.

International Institute for Population Sciences (IIPS) and Macro International (2007), *National Family Health Survey (NFHS-3), 2005–06: India*, Volume I. Mumbai: IIPS.

International Institute for Population Sciences (IIPS)(1999), and Macro International (2000) *National Family Health Survey (NFHS-2) Report 1998-99: India*, Volume I, Mumbai: IIPS.

Janghorbani, Mohsen *et al.* (2007), "First Nationwide Survey of Prevalence of Overweight, Underweight, and Abdominal Obesity in Iranian Adults," *Obesity*, 15, 2797-2808.

Misra, A. *et al.* (2009), "Consensus Statement for Diagnosis of Obesity, Abdominal Obesity and the Metabolic Syndrome for Asian Indians and Recommendations for Physical Activity, Medical and Surgical Management," *Journal of the Association of Physicians of India*, 57, 163-70.

Misra, Anoop and Gulati Seema, "Obesity: The Indian Perspective," Presented at Head, Nutrition Research Group, National Diabetes, Obesity and Cholesterol Foundation (N-DOC) & Center for Nutrition & Metabolic Research (C-NET).

Pan, W.H., Y. Wen-Ting (2008), "How to Define Obesity? Evidence-Based Multiple Action Points for Public Awareness, Screening, and Treatment Extension of Asian-Pacific Recommendations," *Asia Pacific Journal of Clinical Nutrition*, 17, 370-74.

Prentice, A.M. (2006), "The Emerging Epidemic of Obesity in Developing Countries," *The International Journal of Epidemiology*, 35, 93-99.

Report of a joint WHO/FAO expert consultation. Technical Report Series No. 916.

Routley, Vanessa M. (2011), "The Emergence Epidemic of Type-2 Diabetes—An Asian Pacific Perspective," *On the Risk*, 27 (3).

Sinha, R., A.K. Kapoor (2010), "Cultural Practices and Nutritional Status among Premenopausal Women of Urban Set-up in India," *The Open Anthropology Journal*, 3, 168-71.

Srinivasan, M.N. (1957), "Caste in Modern India," *Journal of South Asian Studies*, 16 (4), 529-48.

The World Bank (2011), *The Growing Danger of Non-Communicable Diseases Acting Now to Reverse Course,* Washington, D.C.: The World Bank.

Wardle, Jane, Jo Miller and Martin J. Jarvis (2002), "Sex Differences in the Association of Socio-economic Status with Obesity," *American Journal of Public Health*, 92 (8).

WHO Expert Consultation (2004), "Appropriate Body-Mass Index for Asian Populations and Its Implications for Policy and Intervention Strategies," *Lancet*, 363, 157-63.

World Health Organization (2003), *Diet, Nutrition and the Prevention of Chronic Diseases.*

World Health Organization (2012), *Obesity and Overweight Factsheet*, Washington, D.C., WHO Media Centre, Accessed at: http://www.who.int/mediacentre/factsheets/fs311/en

Yoon *et al.* (2006), "Epidemic Obesity and Type-2 Diabetes in Asia," *Lancet*, 368: 1681-88.

3

Maternal Health Status of Empowered Action Group (EAG) States

Findings from Annual Health Survey

KALPA SHARMA

INTRODUCTION

Improving maternal health and reducing maternal mortality is one of the Millennium Development Goals (MDG). (UN, 2013) The WHO's International Statistical Classification of Diseases and Related Health Problems, 1992 defines maternal death as the death of a woman while pregnant or within 42 days of pregnancy, irrespective of the duration and site of the pregnancy from any cause related to or aggravated by the pregnancy or its management but not from accidental or incidental causes. (WHO, 2013) Maternal Mortality Ratio (MMR) is a key indicator for monitoring progress towards the achievement of MDG-5. Reducing MMR by three-quarter between 1990 and 2015 is the goal MDG-5. (Government of India, 2013) The MMR reflects a country's level of socio-economic development and quality of life and it is an indicator for monitoring and evaluating population, health programmes and policies. According to the

Sample Registration System (SRS), MMR was 398 per 1,00,000 live births in 1997-99 which declined to 212 per 1,00,000 live births in 2007-09. (SRS, 201)

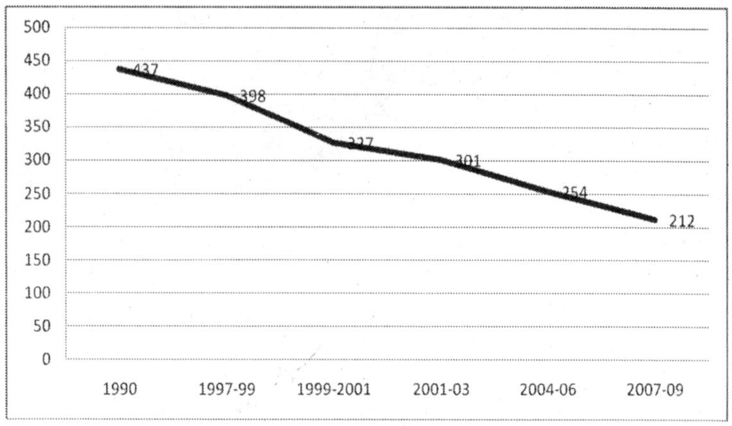

Source : Sample Registration System, Registrar General of India

Figure 3.1 : Trend in Maternal Mortality Ratio in India

Antenatal Care: Care provided during the time of pregnancy is critical to ensure the health of the mother and child. Antenatal care is one of the important factors that affect maternal death. Mothers who didn't undergo for ANC are more prone to maternal death as compared to mothers who received ANC. Antenatal care is a type of preventive care with the goal of providing regular check-ups and allows health care providers to treat and prevent potential health problems during the course of pregnancy while providing healthy lifestyles that benefit both mother and child. (Wikipedia, 2013)

Care at Delivery: Care during delivery is critical to ensure not only the immediate survival of mother and child but also to improve the long -term health and nutrition of mother and child. Delivery conducted by untrained health workers is the leading cause of maternal death.

Postnatal Care: Care provided to a mother after the birth of a baby is very important. The postnatal period is defined as the first six weeks after birth and it is critical to the health and survival of a mother and her newborn. (Wikipedia, 2013) The most vulnerable time for both is during the hours and days after birth. Lack of care during this time period may result in death or disability as well as missed opportunities to promote healthy behaviour affecting women and newborns. Half of all postnatal maternal deaths occur during the first week after the baby is born and the majority of these occur during the first 24 hours after childbirth.

TABLE 3.1
Maternal Health Indicators of India

Health Indicators	*Percentage of Women*
Antenatal Care	
Do not receive any ANC	22.8
Received 3 or more ANC	52.0
Took IFA for 90 days or more	23.1
Received two or more TT injections	76.3
Care at Delivery	
Delivery at health facility	38.7
Deliveries at home	61.0
Deliveries conducted by skilled providers	Maternal 46.6
Postnatal Care	
Do not received any PNC	57.6

Source : *National Family Health Survey–3 (NFHS-3).*

According to the National Family Health Survey-3 (NFHS-3), (IIPS, 2006) more than 20 percent women do not receive any ANC and only 53 percent receive 3 or more ANC. Data depict that 23 percent women take IFA for 90 days or more and nearly 75 percent women receive 2 or more TT injections. As far as delivery is concerned, survey findings show that more than 60 percent of the deliveries occur at home and 39 percent at health facilities. Only 47 percent deliveries are conducted by skilled providers. It is also observed that 58 percent of women do not receive any PNC.

In India, the socio-economically eight backward states such as Bihar, Chhattisgarh, Jharkhand, Madhya Pradesh, Odisha, Rajasthan, Uttaranchal and Uttar Pradesh, referred to as the Empowered Action Group (EAG) states, have weak socio-demographic and health indicators. According to the *Annual Health Survey*, about two-third maternal deaths occur in the EAG states. Uttar Pradesh has the highest MMR (345) among the EAG states followed by Rajasthan, Madhya Pradesh and Bihar. The average MMR of the EAG states is 289 which is higher than the nation's average MMR of 212. (Table 3.2)

TABLE 3.2
Maternal Mortality Ratio in EAG States

EAG States	*Maternal Mortality Ratio*
Bihar	305
Chhattisgarh	275
Jharkhand	278
Madhya Pradesh	310
Odisha	277
Rajasthan	331
Uttar Pradesh	345
Uttarakhand	188
Average EAG States	289
India	212

Source : Annual Health Survey, 2010-11.

TABLE 3.3
Antenatal Care in EAG States

EAG States	*Mothers who received any ANC*	*Mothers who received 3 or more ANC*	*Mothers who received at least one TT injection*	*Mothers who consumed IFA for 100 days or more*
Bihar	84.5	34.0	84.4	10.0
Chhattisgarh	90.1	57.1	90.1	23.8
Jharkhand	86.1	56.3	85.7	15.1
Madhya Pradesh	88.6	68.1	94.8	17.5
Odisha	95.6	76.0	95.1	21.6
Rajasthan	84.8	47.5	84.3	12.3
Uttar Pradesh	82.1	29.6	80.9	6.5
Uttarakhand	84.4	52.3	83.6	14.9
Average EAG States	87.0	52.6	87.4	15.2

Source : Annual Health Survey 2010-11.

Data from the EAG states depict that 87 percent of the pregnant women received any ANC but only 53 percent received 3 or more ANC. Findings show that 87 percent of the women received at least one TT and 15 percent consumed IFA for 100 days or more. (Table 3.4) Among the EAG states, the situation of Uttar Pradesh was found to be grave as only 82 percent women received any ANC and less than 30 percent received 3 or more ANC. However, ANC indicator of Odisha, Chhattisgarh and Madhya Pradesh is better than the EAG states average.

TABLE 3.4
Delivery Care in EAG States

EAG States	*Institutional Delivery (percent)*	*Delivery at home (percent)*	*Delivery at home conducted by skilled health personnel (percent)*	*Safe delivery (percent)*
Bihar	47.7	52.0	18.4	53.5
Chhattisgarh	34.9	65.0	39.6	49.5
Jharkhand	37.6	62.0	24.7	47.1
Madhya Pradesh	76.1	23.5	26.0	82.2
Odisha	71.3	28.1	20.5	75.2
Rajasthan	70.2	29.5	32.3	76.2
Uttar Pradesh	45.6	53.8	21.8	51.3
Uttarakhand	50.5	49.0	32.0	56.9
Average EAG States	54.2	45.3	26.9	61.5

Source : Annual Health Survey, 2010-11.

Only 54 percent deliveries are conducted at institutions in the EAG states. (Table 3.4) Data indicate that 70 percent deliveries which happen at home are conducted by unskilled personnel. Sixty-one percent deliveries were safe deliveries in the EAG states. Data also show huge variation among the EAG states. In Madhya Pradesh, Odisha and Rajasthan more than 70 percent of the deliveries are conducted at health institutions and more than 75 percent of the deliveries were found to be safe. (Table 3.4) However, in Chhattisgarh and Jharkhand more than 60 percent of the deliveries are conducted at home and more than half of the deliveries are unsafe.

On an average, more than 50 percent of the women stay for less than 24 hours at institution after delivery. Data depict that more than

TABLE 3.5
Postnatal Care in EAG States

EAG states	*Less than 24 hrs. stay in institution after delivery (percent)*	*Mothers who received postnatal check-up within 48 hrs. of delivery (percent)*	*Mothers who received postnatal check-up within 1 week of delivery (percent)*	*Mothers who did not receive any post natal check-up (percent)*
Bihar	66.6	60.8	54.1	30.4
Chhattisgarh	36.8	64.8	70.1	23.2
Jharkhand	42.5	59.1	64.0	34.4
Madhya Pradesh	27.2	74.2	76.6	22.1
Odisha	53.5	74.5	78.5	19.6
Rajasthan	38.0	73.3	76.1	23.0
Uttar Pradesh	64.7	68.4	71.6	28.1
Uttarakhand	40.5	59.1	61.4	35.8
Average EAG States	46.2	66.8	69.0	27.0

Source : *Annual Health Survey, 2010-11.*

25 percent of women did not receive any postnatal care. However, 67 percent women received postnatal care within 48 hours after birth. (Table 3.5) In Bihar, Uttar Pradesh and Odisha more than 50-70 percent of the women stay for less than 24 hours after birth. As far as postnatal care is concerned, data show that 30-40 percent of the women did not receive any postnatal care in Uttarakhand, Jharkhand and Bihar.

Use of contraception is an important and effective primary prevention strategy to reduce maternal mortality in developing countries. Satisfying the unmet need of family planning is one of the essential interventions to reduce the number of maternal deaths. According to the recent studies, contraceptive use in developing countries has brought down the number of maternal deaths by 44 percent (about 270,000 deaths averted in 2008) but could prevent 73 percent of the full demand for birth control were met. (Cleland *et al.*, 2012; Ahmed *et al.*, 2012) According to WHO, women with unmet need are those who are fecund and sexually active but are not using any method of contraception, and report not wanting any more children or wanting to delay the birth of their next child. (WHO, 2013)

TABLE 3.6

Family Planning Method Usage in EAG States

EAG States	*Percentage of currently married women*	
	Using any method of contraception	*Unmet need of contraception*
Bihar	37.6	39.2
Chhattisgarh	53.9	26.4
Jharkhand	47.8	30.5
Madhya Pradesh	61.2	22.4
Odisha	56.2	23.2
Rajasthan	64.5	19.6
Uttar Pradesh	49.9	29.7
Uttarakhand	62.7	23.2
Average EAG States	54.2	26.8

Source : Annual Health Survey, 2010-11.

Findings show that the use of contraception is nearly 55 percent and unmet need of family planning method is nearly 27 percent in the EAG states. (Table 3.6) In Rajasthan, usage of family planning methods is found to be satisfactory as 65 percent of the currently married women aged 15-49 years are using any method of contraception and the unmet need of family planning is less than 20 percent. However, the situation of Bihar is found to be grim among all EAG states where unmet need of family planning method is nearly 40 percent.

CONCLUSION

According to the *World Health Report, 2005*, the major causes of maternal deaths worldwide are severe bleeding/haemorrhage (25 percent), infections (13 percent), unsafe abortions (13 percent), eclampsia (12 percent), obstructed labour (8 percent), other direct causes (8 percent) and indirect causes (20 percent). For all obstetric complications, basic and emergency medical care is essential to prevent death and life threatening complications of pregnancy. The three-tier healthcare delivery system has been developed by the Government of India to reach out to remote areas to provide primary care at the village level, secondary care at the sub-district and district levels, and tertiary care at the regional level. To improve the availability of and access to quality health care, especially for those residing in rural areas, the poor, women, and children, the Government had launched the National Rural Health Mission (NRHM) in 2005 to carry out necessary architectural correction in the basic health care delivery system in India. One of the important goals of the NRHM is to provide access to improved health care at the household level through female Accredited Social Health Activists (ASHA), who act as interface between the community and the public health system. The ASHA acts as a bridge between the Auxiliary Nurse Midwife (ANM) and the village, and she is accountable to the Panchayat. She helps promote referrals for universal immunization, escort services for RCH, construction of household toilets, and other health care delivery programmes. The ASHA scheme has improved community mobilization efforts significantly. ASHA has given the responsibility to identify pregnant women to make sure that they receive adequate antenatal care, natal care, and postnatal care. The Janani Suraksha Yojana (JSY) which was then converted into Janani Shishu Suraksha Yojana (JSSY) was launched to promote institutional deliveries. Under this scheme there is provision for cash transfer for institutional deliveries in government and selected private health institutions. Despite these government efforts, India is unlikely to achieve the MDG-5. To improve the pace of improvement in MMR, special attention should be given to EAG states.

References

Accredited Social Health Activist. Ministry of Health and Family Welfare, National Rural Health Mission. http://www.nrhm.gov.in/communitisation/asha/about-asha.html. (Last accessed on 2013, January 15)

Ahmed, S.Q. Li, L. Liu, A. Tsui (2012) "Maternal Deaths Averted By Contraception Use: An Analysis of 172 Countries," *The Lancet*, 380 (9837), 111-25.

Annual Health Survey. http://censusindia.gov.in/vital_statistics/AHSBulletins/ahs.html. (Last accessed on 2013, January 15)

Cleland, J., A. Conde-Agudelo, H. Peterson, J. Ross, A. Tsui (2012), "Contraception and Health", *The Lancet*, 380 (9837), 149-56.

Government of India (2006), *National Family Health Survey-3*, Mumbai: IIPS.

Government of India (2011) *Millennium Development Goals, India Country Report,* New Delhi: Central Statistical Organization. Ministry of Statistics and Programme Implementation, Government of India.

International Classification of Diseases, 10th Revision, Geneva, World Health Organization. http://www.who.int/classifications/icd/en/index.html. (Last accessed on 2013, January 15).

Janani Shishu Suraksha Karyakram, Ministry of Health and Family Welfare, National Rural Health Mission. http://www.nrhm.gov.in/nrhm-components/rmnch-a/maternal-health/janani-shishu-suraksha-karyakram/background.html. (Last accessed on 2013, January 15).

Janani Suraksha Yojana, Ministry of Health and Family Welfare, National Rural Health Mission. http://www.nrhm.gov.in/nrhm-components/rmnch-a/maternal-health/janani-suraksha-yojana/background.html. (Last accessed on 2013, January 15).

National Rural Health Mission (NRHM), http://www.mohfw.nic.in/NRHM/RCH/Index.htm. (Last accessed on 2013, January 15).

National Rural Health Mission (NRHM). Mission Document. http://www.mohfw.nic.in/NRHM/Documents/Mission_Document.pdf. (Last accessed on 2013, January 15).

Post-natal care. Wikipedia. http://en.wikipedia.org/wiki/Postnatal. (Last accessed on 2013, January 15).

Pre-natal care. Wikipedia. http://en.wikipedia.org/wiki/Prenatal_care. (Last accessed on 2013, January 15).

Sample Registration System (SRS) (2011). Registrar General of India. Vital Statistics Division, New Delhi.

The World Health Report (2005), *Make Every Mother and Child Count*. http://www.who.int/whr/2005/whr2005_en.pdf. (Last accessed on 2013, January 15).

United Nations Development Funds, Millennium Development Goals. Available from http://en.wikipedia.org/wiki/Millennium_Development_Goals (Last accessed on 2013, January 15).

World Health Organization, Unmet need of family planning. http://www.who.int/reproductivehealth/topics/family_planning/unmet_need_fp/en/index.html (Last accessed on 2013, January 15).

4

Determinants of Reproductive Spans among Muslims

Evidence from NFHS Data

M.S.R. Murthy

INTRODUCTION

Reproductive spans, i.e. difference between age at effective marriage and age of sterilisation have been compressing over the years in many countries. It is due to early acceptance of family planning. Certain religious groups may have higher fertility. However, social factors influence the religious groups to adopt family limitations. Muslims constitute the second largest religious group in India and the largest religious minority. According to the 2001 Census there were about 138 million Muslims in India. The Muslim population of India comes next to Indonesia and exceeds the Muslim population of Pakistan and Bangladesh. Most of them live in West Bengal, Bihar, Maharashtra and Uttar Pradesh and they are relatively younger population too. The total fertility rate of Muslims according to 2001 Census was 3.06 (Rural: 3.52 and Urban: 2.29) whereas TFR of Hindus stood at 2.47 (Rural: 2.77 and Urban: 1.72).

Low levels of contraceptive use among Muslims have been associated with low socioeconomic and differential influence of religious leaders (Weigl, 2010). Mishra (2004) opines that religious differentials in contraceptive use are transitional phenomena and fertility is falling among Muslims too. Lack of autonomy and social and economic handicaps of women might have promoted low contraceptive use among Muslims (Weigl, 2010). The largest ever survey of Indian Muslim women (in 2004) demonstrates that neither cultural restrictions nor religion influences the status of women. Community specific disadvantages arise out of poverty. The status of Muslim women is determined by social and economic class, urban and rural residence and regional location (TPMS, 2008). In Kerala too Muslims have lower uptake of family planning methods than Hindus (Rob Stephenson, 2006).

OBJECTIVES

1. To know the reproductive span of Muslim women in different states of India.
2. To know the decline in the reproductive span of Muslims over the years, and
3. To understand if Muslims are influenced by local cultures in their reproductive behaviour.

METHODOLOGY

The sample considered for the study has been ever married Muslim women at the all India level. National Family Health Survey data (NFHS-1, NFHS-2, and NFHS-3) have been utilized for analysis. These data sets pertain to individual data. Age at sterilization and reproductive spans of women (difference between effective age at marriage and age at sterilization) has formed the variables for the study. Several socio-economic and demographic variables have been considered as independent variables. Using life table, median reproductive spans have been computed for rural and urban residents and marriage cohorts and states of India. Cox proportional hazard analysis has been used to see the determinants of reproductive spans.

RESULTS AND DISCUSSION

Variables considered were education status of wife and husband, type of residence, work status of the respondent, current age of the respondent, marriage cohort, and ever terminated pregnancy. (Table 4.1) Women's education has shown that illiterate Muslims have progressively accepted sterilization over the decades. Women with primary level education have also accepted sterilization in

TABLE 4.1

Socio-economic and Demographic Characteristics of Total and Sterilised Respondents

Variable	*NFHS 1*		*NFHS 2*		*NFHS 3*	
	Total	*Sterilised (Total/male)*	*Total*	*Sterilised (Total/male)*	*Total*	*Sterilised (Total/male)*
(1)	*(2)*	*(3)*	*(4)*	*(5)*	*(6)*	*(7)*
Respondents education						
No education	63.1 (5956)	13.94 (830/93)	57.3 (6170)	17.88 (1103/75)	41.0 (6870)	18.78 (1290/50)
Primary	19.7 (1857)	22.13 (411/33)	18.5 (1994)	24.87 (496/16)	14.7 (2467)	23.67 (584/15)
Secondary	15.8 (1496)	15.78 (236/15)	19.7 (2123)	23.27 (494/16)	39.2 (6560)	14.28 (937/16)
Higher	1.3 (126)	10.32 (13)	4.5 (483)	14.91 (72/3)	5.0 (845)	7.57 (64/2)
Total	9435	15.79 (1490/141)	10770	20.1 (2165/110)	16742	1717 (2875/83)
Partner's education						
No education	39.8 (3740)	12.38 (463/51)	34.9 (3746)	16.42 (615/37)	32.8 (3961)	20.78 (823/32)
Primary	30.5 (2870)	20.52 (589/59)	20.2 (2167)	24.13 (523/26)	17.6 (2132)	27.53 (587/15)
Secondary	24.9 (2340)	15.6 (365/25)	33.8 (3626)	21.84 (792/31)	42.1 (5092)	24.69 (1257/32))
Higher	4.8 (451)	15.3 (69/6)	11.1 (1196)	18.9 (226/16)	7.5 (904)	20.02 (181/3)
Total	9401	15.81 (1486/141)	10735	20.08 (2156/110)	12089	23.56 (2848/82)
Type of place of residence						
Urban	37.5 (3555)	19.21 (683/40)	38.5 (4143)	25.63 (1062/47)	55.3 (9262)	19.94 (1847/44)
Rural	62.5 (5930)	13.68 (811/102)	61.5 (6632)	16.63 (1103/63)	44.7 (7480)	13.74 (1028/39)
Total	9485	15.75 (1494/142)	10775	26.68 (2165/110)	16742	17.17 (2875/83)

Current age of the respondent						
Below 30	52.6 (4989)	8.44 (421/12)	49.1 (5291)	9.66 (512/9)	59.6 (9971)	5.93 (591/4)
Above 30	47.4 (4496)	23.87 (1073/130)	50.9 (5484)	30.14 (1653/101)	40.4 (6771)	33.73 (2284/79)
Total	9485	15.75 (1494/142)	10775	26.68 (2165/110)	16742	17.17 (2875/83)
Marriage cohort						
1950-59	2.4 (232)	14.22 (33/8)				
1960-69	17.1 (1624)	24.82 (403/71)	5.6 (602)	25.75 (155/15)		
1970-79	28.8 (2732)	25.04 (684/55)	23.0 (2478)	32.36 (802/67)	11.3 (1380)	38.7 (534/38)
1980-89 (94)	51.6 (4897)	7.64 (374/8)	33.1 (3570)	26.55 (948/22)	28.2 (3456)	36.78 (1271/35)
1990-99 (00)			38.3 (4125)	6.3 (260/6)	35.8 (4379)	22.47 (984/9)
2000-05					24.7 (3019)	2.85 (86/1)
Total	9485	15.75 (1494/142)	10772	20.1 (2165/110)	12234	23.5 (2875/83)
Ever terminated pregnancy						
No	79.4 (7532)	15.14 (1140/113)	78.0 (8397)	19.69 (1653/82)	85.9 (14376)	16.73 (2405/68)
Yes	20.6 (1952)	18.14 (354/29)	22.0 (2375)	21.56 (512/28)	14.1 (2364)	19.88 (470/15)
Total	9484	15.75 (1494/142)	10772	20.1 (2165/110)	16740	17.17 (2875/83)
Work status of the respondent						
No	81.4 (7718)	14.54 (1122/100)	77.4 (8338)	18.61 (1552/78)	74.7 (12480)	16.51 (2061/49)
Yes	18.6 (1761)	21.07 (371/42)	22.6 (2431)	25.22 (613/32)	25.3 (4219)	19.15 (808/34)
Total	9479	15.75 (1493/142)	10769	20.1 (2165/110)	16669	17.21 (2869/83)

similar way. At secondary and higher levels of education, higher acceptance of sterilization have been decreasing from 141 in 1990 to 110 in 1999 and 83 in 2005.

A higher proportion of Muslims in recent years (2005) has been living in urban areas than rural areas. Around two-fifth of the respondents lived in urban areas in 1990 (37.5 percent) and during 1999 it was 38.5 percent compared to more than half (55.3 percent) in 2005. Though more Muslims were found in rural areas during 1990 and 1999, sterilization practices were more in urban areas than rural areas. During 2005 also more sterilization were found in urban areas than in rural areas.

The current age of the respondent shows that one-third women above 30 years have accepted sterilization while it was around one-tenth for women below 30 years. Further, middle marriage cohorts have high acceptance of sterilization. Women who terminated their pregnancy for some reason or other too have higher acceptance of sterilization.

The present work status of women revealed that more proportion of working have high levels of acceptance of sterilization than non-working people (Table 4.1). In general, Muslims are presumed to practice polygamy. As per NFHS-3, a few men (254) had more than one wife where as 34, 4 and 17 men had two, three and four wives, respectively. The state-wise data indicate that 39 men in West Bengal, 38 men in Assam, 29 men in Andhra Pradesh, 20 men each in Uttar Pradesh and Kerala had more than one wife.

TOTAL FERTILITY RATES

The Muslim TFR has been 4.4, 3.6 and 3.4 for the three Survey periods. Fertility rate of Hindu women has declined from 3.3 to 2.6 whereas Muslim fertility rate came down from 4.4 to 3.4 (NFHS- I, II and III). Kerala interestingly had TFR of more than two children during the three Surveys. A personal account of a Kerala resident has revealed that the Kerala couples prefer odd number of children: three children instead of two.

MEDIAN AGE OF FIRST MARRIAGE, FIRST BIRTH AND STERILIZATION (BASED ON LIFE TABLE ANALYSIS)

In general, differences were minimal during the three periods in median age at marriage, first birth and sterilization. It is found that all the southern states and Goa which are at the threshold of transition

TABLE 4.2

Mean Age at First Birth, Age at First Marriage and Age at Sterilisation among Indian Muslim Women, by Region and State, NFHS I, 2 and 3 (Life Table Analysis)

Region and State	*Median age at first birth (20-49)*			*Median age at first marriage (20-49)*			*Median age at sterilisation (20-49)*					
	NFHS 1	*NFHS 2*	*NFHS 3*	*NFHS 1*	*NFHS 2*	*NFHS 3*	*F*	*M*	*F*	*M*	*F*	*M*
(1)	*(2)*	*(3)*	*(4)*	*(5)*	*(6)*	*(7)*	*(8)*	*(9)*	*(10)*	*(11)*	*(12)*	*(13)*
India	18.6	18.6	19.1	17.3	17.2	17.7	27.6	26.0	27.4	26.1	26.8	26.2
North												
Delhi	19.1	18.5	17.9	17.9	17.2	18.02	29.8	25	28.3	22.5	28.0	—
Haryana	19.4	18.6	20.4	17.8	17.1	17.5	35	35	28.8	35	22.5	—
Himachal Pradesh	18.8	18.2	20.4	17.8	17.5	19.02	25	30	25	25.8	25.6	22.5
Jammu	18.9	18.9	20.20	17.2	17.5	18.64	30.3	26.7	28.2	27.3	28.8	27.5
Punjab	20.2	19.6	20.43	19.1	18.4	18.34	28.75	—	27.5	—	24.6	—
Rajasthan	18.8	18.2	19.1	17.4	16.9	17.11	27.5	27.5	29.3	27.5	27.8	28.8
Central												
Madhya Pradesh	18.5	17.8	19.00	17.5	16.7	17.45	28.1	27.5	28	27.5	27.5	25
Chhattisgarh	—	—	19.22	—	—	17.85	—	—	—	—	27.3	—
Uttar Pradesh	19.08	17.98	19.00	17.7	16.9	17.90	33	28.3	31.5	32.5	30	32.5
Uttaranchal	—	—	19.24	—	—	17.54	—	—	—	—	28.1	22.5

(*Contd.*)

TABLE 4.2 (*Contd.*)

(1)	(2)	(3)	(4)	(5)	(6)	(7)	(8)	(9)	(10)	(11)	(12)	(13)
East												
Bihar	18.7	18.1	18.20	17.2	16.8	17.01	31	30	30	23.8	28.6	37.5
Odisha	18.2	17.9	19.07	16.5	17.9	18.25	30.6	22.5	28.8	—	32.5	—
West Bengal	17.8	17.7	18.22	16.0	16.4	17.07	26.9	—	25.8	23.8	26.2	21.25
North East												
Arunachal Pradesh	—	—	17.16	—	—	16.10	—	—	—	—	27.5	—
Assam	17.6	17.9	18.4	15.8	16.7	16.9	28.0	26.3	27.4	25	25.8	22.5
Manipur	19.14	15	18.88	18.5	15	17.56	32.5	17.5	32.5	32.5	33.8	32.5
Meghalaya	19.11	22.5	20.13	18.1	17.5	18.28	—	27.5	27.5	—	35	—
Mizoram	22.50	20	27.5	22.5	20	22.50	26.3	—	30	—	32.5	—
Nagaland	20.62	—	19.6	17.5	—	17.42	22.5	—	—	—	31.3	—
Tripura	—	—	18.17	—	—	16.40	—	—	—	—	25	—
West												
Goa	19.6	20	20.6	18.1	17.7	18.90	27.2	23.8	30	—	26.7	—
Gujarat	20.3	18.8	19.92	19	17.9	18.10	29	26.3	27.7	22.5	27.1	32.5
Maharashtra	18.2	18.4	19.44	17.1	17.12	18.15	27.1	26.3	27	27.5	26.2	25
South												
Andhra Pradesh	18.1	17.8	19.01	16.9	16.5	17.60	25.6	29.2	25.2	25	25.4	25
Karnataka	18.3	17.6	19.12	17.2	16.4	17.8	26.3	23.8	25.7	26.3	24.9	—
Kerala	18.6	18.8	19.35	17.6	17.72	17.87	27.1	25.5	27.2	22.1	26.7	24.2
Tamil Nadu	19.5	19.5	20.52	18.2	18.1	18.41	26.1	27.5	26.6	—	25.1	37.5

had age at marriage and age at first birth below 20 years except in Tamil Nadu whose age at first birth during NFHS-3 (2005-06) period has been 20.52 years. Most of the Muslim women in India have married at less than 20 years except in Mizoram.

Muslims in Andhra Pradesh have accepted sterilization at around 25 years of age which supports the finding that compression of reproductive spans is taking place in Andhra Pradesh Pradesh (Padmadas, Hutter and Willekens, 2004). The remaining states have more than 25 years as age at sterilization. Punjab, Meghalaya and Mizoram did not have any case of male sterilization during the three Survey periods while Goa and Odisha did not have any case of male sterilization during NFHS-1 and NFHS-2 periods only (Table 4.2).

MEDIAN AGE AT STERILIZATION ACCORDING TO CURRENT AGE OF MUSLIM WOMEN

Less than one-fifth of couples have accepted sterilization as a method of family planning around the age of 25 and below during the three Survey periods. For instance, it was 17.6 percent during NFHS-1, 24.78 percent during NFHS-2 and 16.26 percent during NFHS-3. Similarly, about one-third were found in the age group of 25-29 (27.21 percent during NFHS-1, 38.32 percent during NFHS-2 and 37.02 percent during NFHS-3.) It came down to about one-fifth during the age of 30-34: 19.07 percent in 1990, 22.28 percent in 1999 and 22.41 percent in 2005. (Table 4.3)

STATE-WISE DISTRIBUTION OF STERILISATION

Most of the southern states and developed states of India have better practices of sterilisation than northern states. It was around one-third among the former states and the remaining states have less than ten percent practice. The north-eastern states seem to have less Muslim population hence lower practice of sterilisation. A few states have one-third participation of family planning: Andhra Pradesh (35.77, 36.33 and 34.17 percent), Tamil Nadu (25.3, 34.55 and 39.59 percent), Karnataka (26.43, 36.66 and 34.13 percent), Kerala (25.02, 34.5 and 31.29 percent), and Goa (32.5, 32.73 and 23.27 percent) for the three Survey periods. Himachal Pradesh was one of the states with two-third acceptance for the NFHS-1 and 2 while it has decreased to one-fifth (21.43 percent) during NFHS-3. Tamil Nadu was the only state, among the Indian states, with two-fifth (39.59 percent) acceptance of sterilisation by Muslims during NFHS-3.

TABLE 4.3

Age at Sterilisation among Muslims According to NFHS I, 2 and 3

Age at Sterilisation	*NFHS-1 (1990-91)*		*NFHS-2 (1998-99)*		*NFHS-1 (2005-06)*	
	Total	*Sterilised*	*Total*	*Sterilised*	*Total*	*Sterilised*
(1)	*(2)*	*(3)*	*(4)*	*(5)*	*(6)*	*(7)*
Below 25	3126	17.59 (550)	3120	24.78 (773)	7194	16.26 (1170)
25-29	1863	27.21 (507)	2171	38.32 (832)	27777	37.02 (1028)
30-34	1531	19.07 (292)	1854	22.28 (413)	2222	22.41 (498)
35-39	1261	9.67 (122)	1585	7.7 (122)	1978	8.14 (161)
40-44	985	2.13 (21)	1202	1.66 (20)	15.20	1.05 (16)
45-49	719	0.28 (2)	843	0.59 (5)	1051	0.1 (1)
Total	9485	15.75 (14.94)	10775	20.09 (21.65)	16742	17.17 (2875)

Source : IIPS, NFHS 1, 2 and 3.

TABLE 4.4
Broad Categorisation of States According to Percentage Acceptance of Sterilisation by Muslims

Participation in Sterilisation	*NFHS-1*	*NFHS-2*	*NFHS-3*
(1)	*(2)*	*(3)*	*(4)*
India	15.75	20.09	17.17
One-third and above	Andhra Pradesh (35.77), Himachal Pradesh (33.3), Goa (32.5)	Karnataka (36.6), Andhra Pradesh (36.33), Himachal Pradesh(34.58), Tamil Nadu (34.55), Kerala (34.5), Gujarat (33.33), Goa (32.73)	Tamil Nadu (39.59), Andhra Pradesh (34.17), Karnataka (34.13), Kerala (31.29)
One-fifth and above	Karnataka (26.43), Madhya Pradesh and Tamil Nadu (25.3), Maharashtra (24.32), Gujarat (21.93), Jammu (20.71)	Maharashtra (26.2), Jammu (29.2), Madhya Pradesh (27.61)	Maharashtra (26.2), Madhya Pradesh (24.49), Goa (23.27), Gujarat (24.18), Chhattisgarh (21.53), Himachal Pradesh (21.43),
One-tenth	West Bengal (15.06), Odisha (10.98)	West Bengal (19.93), Haryana (13.68), Delhi (12.56)	Jammu (17.51), West Bengal (16.49)
Below one-tenth	Delhi (8.36), Assam (6.93), Haryana (5.94), Bihar (4.84), Uttar Pradesh (3.92)	Odisha (7.61), Bihar (5.75), Assam (4.82), Uttar Pradesh (4.44)	Jharkhand (8.81), Delhi (6.85), Odisha (6.25), Bihar (5.75), Uttar Pradesh (5.42), Haryana (3.85), Assam (3.74)

Source : IIPS, NFHS 1, 2 and 3.

Maharashtra and Madhya Pradesh have two-fifth acceptance of sterilisation by Muslims during all the three Surveys. West Bengal has slightly less than one-fifth acceptance in all the surveys. Bihar and Uttar Pradesh were the other states which fall under one-tenth acceptance of sterilisation. Thus, there seems to be a marked divide among northern and southern states.

According to different data set (NFHS-3) it shows that southern states have better acceptance of sterilisation than other states followed closely by Chhattisgarh, Maharashtra, Gujarat and Madhya Pradesh (Table 4.4).

OTHER METHODS OF FAMILY PLANNING

Other methods of family planning practice have increased over the years. They include use of condoms, pills, periodic abstinence, withdrawal, and intra-uterine devices. Injections have been other temporary methods of family planning followed in the NFHS-3 Survey. In general, higher acceptance of temporary methods of

TABLE 4.5
Use of Other Methods of Family Planning among Muslims

Other methods	*NFHS-I*	*NFHS-II*	*NFHS-III*
Pill	6.17 (167)	9.89 (389)	11.15 (671)
IUD	6.35 (172)	5.4 (208)	3.84 (220)
Injections	0.22 (6)	0	0.7 (40)
Diaphragm	0	0	0.02 (1)
Condoms	10.53 (285)	11.27 (434)	16.17 (925)
Periodic abstinence	14.04 (380)	8.85 (341)	9.35 (535)
Withdrawal	6.43 (174)	7.17 (276)	7.92 (4.53)
Others	1.07 (29)	1.22 (47)	0
Foam or Jelly	0	0	0.03 (2)
Folkloric method	0	0	0
Female sterilisation	49.94 (1352)	53.35 (2055)	48.79 (2792)
Male sterilisation	5.25 (142)	2.86 (110)	1.45 (83)
Acceptors	2707	3852	5722
Not using	71.46 (6778)	64.25 (6923)	65.76 (10990)
Total	9485	10775	16712

Source : IIPS, NFHS 1, 2 and 3.

family planning was noticed during NFHS-3 Survey, perhaps due to better awareness of temporary methods of family planning. Periodic abstinence has been followed more than any other method during 1990. Later on condoms and pills were used in 1999 and 2006 followed by withdrawal during all the three Surveys. (Table 4.5)

MEDIAN (SURVIVAL) TIME OF REPRODUCTIVE SPAN

Median survival time of reproductive span has been computed using life table technique for all the states. The results show that urban residents have lesser reproductive spans than rural residents. Cohort wise latest cohorts have spans than earlier cohorts. The states that have values less than ten were during NFHS-3 were Goa, Karnataka, Kerala, Punjab, and Tamil Nadu. This list went up during NFHS-2 and they include states like Andhra Pradesh, Gujarat, Himachal Pradesh, Karnataka, Kerala, Maharashtra, Punjab and Tamil Nadu. Some states have come into existence during NFHS-3; Goa (reappeared), Haryana, Chhattisgarh and West Bengal. It shows that transition has been taking place in majority of the states. (Table 4.6)

TABLE 4.6

Duration of Reproductive Span among Muslims

Median duration of reproductive span	*NFHS-1*	*NFHS-2*	*NFHS-3*
India	11.1866	9.6357	9.2472
Below 10	Goa, Karnataka, Kerala, Punjab, Tamil Nadu	Andhra Pradesh, Gujarat, Himachal Pradesh, Karnataka, Kerala, Maharashtra, Punjab, and Tamil Nadu	Andhra Pradesh, Goa, Gujarat, Punjab, Haryana, Himachal Pradesh, Karnataka, Kerala, Chhattisgarh, Maharashtra, Tamil Nadu, and West Bengal

MEDIAN REPRODUCTIVE DURATION IN RELATION TO TYPE OF RESIDENCE, MARRIAGE COHORT AND STATE

From the Table 4.7 it is revealed that reduction in reproductive span has been occurring in both the urban and rural areas. However, rural areas have higher values than urban areas. Marriage cohort has shown decline within and among the National Family Health Surveys.

TABLE 4.7
Median Reproductive Spans in Relation to Type of Residence and States of India

Survival	*NFHS-1*	*NFHS-2*	*NFHS-3*
Type of Residence			
Urban	10.9031	9.2055	8.9425
Rural	11.4286	10.1422	9.9182
Total	11.1866	9.6357	9.2472
Marital Duration			
1950-59	19.4231		
1960-69	15.4318	16.0648	
1970-79	11.3883	12.1452	13.1771
1980-89	7.4802	8.7035	10.1877
1990-99		5.9335	7.6322
2000-07			3.3333

COX REGRESSION

Cox proportional hazard analysis has been done in two ways, such as Enter and Forward conditional methods. The variable such as education status of the respondents and the spouse, type of residence, number of children ever born and the sons and daughters died and marriage cohort and current work status of the respondents have been considered for analysis in the three Surveys. Children ever born and sons and daughters denote the fertility experience of the women whereas marriage cohort shows current age of the respondents and age at marriage. Hence, current age of the respondents and age at marriage have been excluded from the analysis to avoid co-linearity. Current work status shows the participation of women in economic activity. The NFHS-1 does not have standard of living and wealth indices hence current work status has been taken to show the economic empowerment of women.

TYPE OF RESIDENCE

It is found that rural and urban differences in duration of reproductive span have been distinct. The urban areas have lesser duration of reproductive span. The differences are significant between these areas. However, rural-urban differences were not significant during the NFHS-I period. Women's education seems to influence reproductive duration significantly except during NFHS-I. Hence, education is a major determinant, particularly women's education. Rural-urban residence was not significant during the NFHS-I period. Subsequently, this difference became prominent. Rural residents had higher reproductive span than rural women during the NFHS-II and III. Both the Cox hazard regression has shown that rural-urban differences were prominent during NFHS-I and II. Rural areas have higher reproductive spans than urban areas. Partner's education was not significant during NFHS-I. However, primary and higher levels of education, secondary and higher levels were significant during NFHS-II and III. Higher educational levels give rise to lesser reproductive spans than illiterate women. Stepwise regression shows that partner's education is not a variable influencing reproductive span. Those who have resorted to termination of pregnancy have higher reproductive spans in all the three Surveys. Stepwise regression is not significant during NFHS-I only. The variable is not prominent at stepwise regression during NFHS 2 and 3. Marriage cohort has shown inter-survey effects. Younger age cohorts have lesser duration of reproductive spans in all the Surveys. It shows that younger women are more seized of the family size than older cohorts of women.

CONCLUSION

Different opinions and different propositions have been advanced for and against the issue of Muslim fertility and family planning. However, Muslims have been adopting family planning and limiting family size for one reason or the other. Scholars have observed that a number of Indians have converted to Islam several centuries or decades ago. However, they have retained their indigenous cultures and are influenced by their language and social milieu. This is evident from the food habits and different functions followed by Muslims. Murthy (2004) has found that Muslims were performing puberty rituals just like other caste groups in Andhra Pradesh. Differences are noticed in the places such as Uttar Pradesh,

Table 4.8
Cox Proportional Hazard Model (Model: Enter and Forward Stepwise Conditional LR)

	NFHS-1		*NFHS-2*		*NFHS-3*	
	Enter	*Forward step-wise conditional LR (4th step)*	*Enter*	*Forward step-wise conditional LR (5th step)*	*Enter*	*Forward step-wise conditional LR (5th step)*
(1)	*(2)*	*(3)*	*(4)*	*(5)*	*(6)*	*(7)*
Type of residence (Reference: Urban)						
Rural	1.049		.879*	.874*	.843*	.855*
Educational level of the respondents (Reference: No education)						
Primary	.750	.714	1.149*	.937	1.356*	.728*
Secondary	.967	.974	1.283*	1.10	1.308*	.984
Higher	1.014	1.010	.957	1.248*	1.501*	.927
Partner's education						
Primary	.872		.825*		1.133	
Secondary	1.045		.912		1.178*	
Higher	1.054		.870*		1.131	
Ever terminated pregnancy (Reference: No)						
Yes	.796*	.797*	.855*	.855*	.781*	.785*

Sons and daughters who died (Reference: No death)						
One + daughters died	1.466*	1.498*	1.660*	1.671*	1.685*	1.688*
One + sons died	1.062	1.073	1.231	1.247*	1.140	1.150
One + sons and daughters died	1.257*	1.295*	1.366*	1.378*	1.266*	1.277*
Marriage cohort (Reference)						
1950-59						
1960-69	1.583*	1.568*				
1970-79	3.936*	3.867*	1.749*	1.748*		
1980-89	13.535*	13.358*	3.763*	3.743*	1.605*	1.613*
1990-99			14.270*	14.110*	3.418*	3.434*
2000-07					19.319*	19.030*
Respondent currently working (Reference: Not working)						
Working	1.050		1.016		1.131	
-2 Log	18818.20	29078.010	39934.940			

*Significant P < .05.

Bihar, and West Bengal where they are in majority and they follow the Muslim cultures. In the southern part of Kerala Muslims have high fertility rate as 99.4 percent of the STs are Muslims in that part of Kerala. (TPMS, 2008)

The above discussion point out that education of husbands has not been found to be a deciding factor in reproductive span. Men's participation may improve acceptance of family planning and the compression of reproductive spans. Rural Muslims also need attention in several areas. Further, research need to be undertaken to understand the concerns of the Muslim community. The other measures suggested are enhancing age at marriage, reducing child mortality, promotion of better reproductive health services among Muslims, better utilisation of temporary methods of family planning methods and so on.

References

Mohan, P.V. and Mohanchandran Nair (2008-09), "Correlates of Low Reproductive Span in Kerala: Evidence from NFHS-3," *Jan Samkhya*, 26 and 27, pp. 79-91.

Murthy, M.S.R. (2004), "Reproductive Health Practices of Adolescent Mothers: Need for Better Services," in N. Audinarayana, S. Krishnamoorthy, P.M. Kulkarni and C.P. Prakasam (eds.), Perspectives on Population, Gender Empowerment and Health in South Asia, Mumbai: Research Book Centre, pp. 219-27.

Padmadas, Sabu S., Inge Hutter and Frans Willekens (2004), "Compression of Women's Reproductive Spans in Andhra Pradesh," *India International Family Planning Perspectives*, 30(1), pp. 12-19.

International Institute of Population Sciences (IIPS) NFHS-1, NFHS-2, and NFHS-3, Mumbai: IIPS.

Rob, Stephenson (2006), "District Level Religious Composition and Adoption of Sterilisation in India," *Journal of Health, Population and Nutrition*, 24(1).

Weigl, Constanze (2010), Reproductive Health Behaviour and Decision-making of Muslim Women: An Ethnographic Study in a Low-income Community in Urban North India.

5

Maternal Health in Rajasthan

ALPANA KATEJA

INTRODUCTION

Social discrimination against women results in systematic neglect of women's health from womb to tomb. Female feticide, female infanticide, a higher death rate among women, lower literacy levels, higher morbidity, lower work participation rate and an adverse sex ratio are a few manifestations of this discrimination. One of the most serious consequences of this neglect is women's ill-health associated with childbearing. The concept of maternal health recognizes that women have special health needs before, during and just after the childbearing. Maternal health has an impact on the health of women themselves and on the health of next generation and that both are of crucial importance for socio-economic development. India is one of the few countries in the world where women and men have nearly the same life expectancy at birth. The fact that typical female advantage in life expectancy is not seen in India suggests there are systematic problems with women's health.

Poor maternal health finds serious manifestation in the form of maternal mortality. Maternal death is a problem of serious proportions in India as an estimated 136,000 women die each year due to causes related to pregnancy, childbirth and abortion. A huge gap of up to a hundred-fold exists in the risk of pregnancy between women in poor and rich countries, the highest differential of any public health indicator monitored by World Health Organization (WHO). The lifetime risk of dying in pregnancy or childbirth of an Indian woman is one in 37. In developed regions, the comparable risk is one in four thousand (Holysmoke, 2006). Indian women have high mortality rates during childhood, reproductive years and particularly in pregnancy (Velkoff and Adlakha, 1998). The present study tries to probe into the status of maternal health in Rajasthan.

MATERNAL HEALTH IN RAJASTHAN

Development, in the ultimate analysis, must have a positive impact on the quality of life of the masses, especially the poor and deprived sections of society. No doubt, Rajasthan too has made real progress over the past sixty years in achieving more equitable distribution between women and men of the benefits of development. Gender gaps in education and health have narrowed rapidly. Yet much remains to be done. A very simple indication of the level of welfare enjoyed by women in Rajasthan is that their levels of education are amongst the lowest in the world and the levels of maternal mortality are amongst the highest in the world. Whether in socio-economic indicators such as education, health and work participation or in more subtle processes of power, decision-making and self-esteem the inferior position of women has been consistently documented. Status of women, as delineated by various socio-economic indicators, is low in the state across all the districts (Table 5.1) which in turn has culminated in unawareness about nutrition, hygiene, limited access and control over health care, low utilization of health care facilities, low coverage of safe deliveries. NFHS-III data indicate that majority of women have reproductive health and pregnancy-related problems, but only 16.6 percent of all mothers received ante-natal care, 32 percent of all deliveries took place in institutions, and only 29 percent received post-natal care, and there are wide variations between urban/rural, SC/ST and mainstream population, as well as among economic groups. Low coverage of safe deliveries, which includes institutional deliveries and home deliveries assisted by doctor/nurse/ANM, is a cause for concern. The situation is more deplorable in rural areas with only 5.8 percent institutional deliveries, which is the lowest in the country (SRS, 2003).

Among the fifteen major states, Rajasthan ranks 13th with respect to Reproductive Health Index (RHI) (Population Foundation of India, 1998) reflecting poor condition of women in the state. Even Maternal Mortality Rate (MMR) estimates, recognized as the tip of the iceberg of the problems caused by reproduction and sexuality (Sai and Nassim, 1989), places Rajasthan in danger zone. The average maternal mortality rate for the year 1997 was estimated to be 677 (SRS, 1999), which is the highest in India and it is only next to Uttar Pradesh. All the states, including states lagging behind in development like Madhya Pradesh (498), Bihar (451) and Odisha (361) have recorded lower MMR than Rajasthan. The latest SRS figures show decline in MMR to 445. The estimates of MMR, whether according to SRS or NFHS are based on the national level or on a regional level are cross-section data and do not reflect the trends specially at a regional level which has immense practical value in health care and policy matters. Because of deficiencies in vital registration, it may be expected that these estimates are too modest. Nevertheless, it manifests actual critical condition of maternal health prevailing in the state.

The Population Policy of Rajasthan reflects state's strong commitment to improve health status of its population, particularly the poor and vulnerable groups including women, children, and those belonging to scheduled tribes, castes and nomadic groups. The goals set by Rajasthan are similar to the internationally committed Millennium Development Goals (MDGs). While these goals are very relevant, they are also challenging, especially in case of the poor. Poverty and health are intimately related, and poverty is both a cause and consequence of ill-health (World Bank, 2004).

A consistent observation across almost all indicators is that the poor have worse health status compared to the rich and are less likely to use health services. These results are not unexpected or peculiar to Rajasthan; however, the extent of disparities in the state is glaring. There exists a greater inequality in different income groups. There are clear inequalities in health outcomes, which are closely related to incomes. Income is a strong predictor of human development. Practically all indicators of social development—both outcomes and utilization—vary consistently by income quintile, with lower income groups typically having lower values of the indicator. Table 5.2 reveals that the poorer women suffer from double deprivation. All this poses special challenges to providing accessible health care of good quality.

TABLE 5.1

Socio-Economic-Demographic Profile of Rajasthan

Sl. No.	District	Total Population		Decennial Growth Rate	Female Literacy		Female Work Partici-pation Rate	Per capita income of 2000-01 at constant prices of 1993-94	Adjusted per capita income	Life Expec-tancy	Gender Related Develop-ment Index (1999)
		Female %	Backward %	1991-2001	Total	Rural			Female	Female	
(1)	(2)	(3)	(4)	(5)	(6)	(7)	(8)	(9)	(10)	(11)	(12)
1.	Ajmer	48.2	20.1	26.10	49.10	32.72	27.89	9,832	2,817	62.30	0.532
2.	Alwar	47.0	26.0	30.23	43.95	39.16	43.91	9,229	3,228	63.80	0.548
3.	Banswara	49.3	76.6	29.84	27.86	23.78	44.12	7,842	2,597	59.20	0.439
4.	Baran	47.6	38.9	26.19	42.18	38.21	35.80	9,828	2,832	63.30	0.525
5.	Barmer	47.2	21.7	36.83	43.91	42.43	41.76	6,128	1,799	61.60	0.402
6.	Bharatpur	46.1	23.9	27.05	44.12	39.62	32.99	7,772	1,842	60.80	0.484
7.	Bhilwara	49.0	24.7	26.14	33.47	26.09	38.54	9,133	2,884	59.80	0.471
8.	Bikaner	47.1	20.3	33.18	42.55	28.83	27.48	8,509	1,910	68.60	0.525
9.	Bundi	47.6	38.3	24.80	37.76	32.41	40.60	8,536	2,825	61.60	0.504
10.	Chittourgarh	49.1	35.4	21.46	36.45	29.98	46.32	8,590	3,883	56.20	0.497
11.	Churu	48.6	21.7	24.60	53.87	51.45	38.51	6,334	1,865	65.30	0.476

12.	Dausa	47.4	48.0	32.42	43.15	40.83	36.24	7,236	1,864	66.00	0.467
13.	Dholpur	45.3	24.9	31.13	42.36	39.37	34.08	5,946	533	55.90	0.269
14.	Dungarpur	50.5	69.3	26.58	31.22	28.19	45.02	5,090	1,835	58.80	0.420
15.	Ganganagar	46.6	34.5	27.53	52.69	37.74	24.84	11,414	2,918	69.50	0.596
16.	Hanumangarh	47.2	26.8	24.34	52.71	50.01	29.80	10,199	2,918	69.50	0.590
17.	Jaipur	47.3	22.7	35.10	56.18	44.42	22.11	9,157	2,180	66.00	0.547
18.	Jaisalmer	45.1	20.1	47.45	32.25	27.45	29.30	9,027	1,485	60.40	0.430
19.	Jalore	49.1	26.8	26.78	27.53	25.88	46.24	5,856	2,263	59.90	0.430
20.	Jhalawar	48.1	27.6	23.34	40.39	35.51	39.62	6,898	2,374	61.50	0.470
21.	Jhunjhunun	48.6	18.1	20.90	60.10	59.80	32.62	7,611	1,854	68.30	0.529
22.	Jodhpur	47.6	18.6	33.77	39.18	25.10	27.06	8,042	1,945	64.40	0.500
23.	Karauli	46.1	45.6	29.96	45.44	43.84	34.08	6,612	2,335	60.70	0.503
24.	Kota	47.3	28.9	28.52	61.25	50.60	19.14	9,891	2,811	63.30	0.570
25.	Nagaur	48.6	19.9	29.33	40.45	37.58	32.78	6,534	2,478	63.40	0.483
26.	Pali	49.5	23.6	22.39	36.70	31.76	30.70	8,390	2,492	57.80	0.471
27.	Rajsamand	50.1	25.5	19.88	37.89	33.22	29.96	9,598	3,048	60.60	0.486
28.	Sawai Madhopur	47.1	41.6	27.44	35.44	29.69	35.55	8,120	2,335	60.70	0.503
29.	Sikar	48.7	17.6	24.11	56.70	55.70	31.62	7,054	1,408	67.20	0.478
30.	Sirohi	48.5	44.0	30.08	37.37	31.47	30.74	9,137	2,330	59.30	0.460
31.	Tonk	48.3	31.2	24.24	32.30	25.62	38.30	7,600	2,817	59.70	0.475
32.	Udaipur	49.3	27.6	27.37	43.71	35.46	31.82	8,195	2,386	60.80	0.465

Note : All figures refer to the year 2001 mentioned otherwise.
Source : Column 1 – 6: Census (2001), Column 8: Directorate of Economics and Statistics, Rajasthan, Column 8-10: HDR (2002).

TABLE 5.2

Health Outcomes: Inequalities in Rajasthan

Sl. No.	*Indicators*	*Poorest 20%*	*Richest 20%*
1.	Infant Mortality Rate	107.3	55.2
2.	Under 5 Mortality Rate	161.6	69.1
3.	Total Fertility Rate	5.1	3.3
4.	Stunting Children <3 Years	59.2	35.5
5.	Underweight Children <3 Years	60.5	33.2
6.	Body Mass Weight < 18.5 Kg.	38.1	23.0
7.	Expectant women who received NC from a medically trained person (percent)	29.3	85.3
8.	Women delivered by medically trained person (percent)	15.8	79.3
9.	Women delivered at a health facility (percent)	8.2	59.7
10.	Women delivered at a public health facility (percent)	3.0	34.8
11.	Children (12-23) months fully immunized (percent)	4.2	43.4
12.	Children with ARI seen medically (percent)	44.5	86.7
13.	Children with ARI seen medically at a public health facility (percent)	23.9	34.9
14.	Married females using modern contraception (percent)	25.3	55.2
15.	Received ANC from a doctor (percent)	10.5	68.0
16.	Received 3 or more ANC visits (percent)	10.5	63.2
17.	Delivered by a doctor (percent)	7.4	53.6
18.	Women aware of sexual transmission of HIV/AIDS (percent)	27.1	45.1
19.	Adolescent girls (15-19 yrs.) receiving iron folate supplements (percent)	27.5	66.1
20.	Women (20-24 yrs.) married by age 18 (percent)	88.6	54.9
21.	Women (20-24 yrs.) who had a child by age 18 (percent)	53.8	27.5
22.	Adolescent girls (15-19 yrs.) women aware of sexual transmission of HIV/AIDS (percent)	0.7	32.6

Source : IIPS (2002).

DATA AND METHOD

The study aims to investigate the socio-economic and cultural correlates of poor maternal health in Rajasthan for which primary data regarding maternal health and correlates were collected through a field survey in three districts of western Rajasthan namely, Barmer, Jaisalmer and Jodhpur. The total married female population in the reproductive age group in these districts is 8,63,399 of which 76 percent, i.e. 6,57,986 reside in rural areas (Census, 2001). In order to assess the status of maternal health a field survey was undertaken in which 1,500 women who had delivery in two years preceding the survey and/or pregnant were included in the survey. The survey was undertaken in randomly selected eight tehsils of the three districts namely, Gudamalani, Pachpadra and Barmer tehsils of Barmer district, Jaisalmer tehsil of Jaisalmer district and Luni, Osiyan and Jodhpur tehsils of Jodhpur district. Since the rural sample size was comparatively bigger, the survey was conducted in 24 villages of eight tehsils, while for the urban areas only the district headquarters were surveyed. Though the sample size of Jaisalmer rural area was very small, the number of villages covered in the district was maximum, i.e. ten because of very low-density villages. The number of villages surveyed in the other two districts was seven each. Women were asked to provide details about various determinants of ANC seeking behaviour.

To fulfil the specific objective multivariate statistical method used in the study is logistic regression. The equation of logistic regression can be represented by:

$$\text{Logit } P = b_0 + b_1X_1 + b_2X_2 + \dots\dots\dots + b_kX_k$$

Where:

$$\log(odds) = \log it(P) = In\left(\frac{P}{1-P}\right)$$

Maternal health cannot be quantified as such. Hence, availing ANC has been taken as the dependent variable, assuming that pregnant women who avail ANC enjoy better health. Explanatory variables used in the analysis are female education, son preference, cultural practices, place of delivery, nutrition level, media awareness, quality of care, etc.

CAUSES OF POOR MATERNAL HEALTH

The issue of maternal health has received much less attention than it deserves. Not only the magnitude but also the causes of poor maternal health have been long neglected. Rather than simply a medical problem, poor maternal health is ultimately a reflection of the series of social, cultural, economic and environmental factors which are inextricably linked. Examining different causes in India and Rajasthan suggest deplorable condition of the state (Table 5.3).

The present study develops models to relate Antenatal Care (ANC), taken as a proxy variable of maternal health, with some independent variables that affect the ANC seeking behaviour of women which mainly include literacy, place of residence, skilled attendance, intake of nutrition, etc. Antenatal care provides women familiarity with the health system, offers other health services as well as information on birth preparedness. Some women who are at greater risk can be identified with good antenatal care and can be cared for if the women and their families appreciate the seriousness of the complications and if the referral health systems are functional and responsive.

TABLE 5.3
Proximate Factors Affecting Maternal Health

Sl. No.	*Item*	*Year*	*India*	*Rajasthan*
1.	Infant Mortality Rate [a]	2005-06	57	65
2.	Neonatal Mortality Rate [a]	2005-06	39	43.9
3.	Post-Neonatal Mortality Rate [a]	2005-06	18	21.4
Medical Factors				
4.	Percent of Women who receive ANC (any) [a]	2005-06	65.3	62.0
5.	Percent of women who receive full ANC [a]	2005-06	31.8	16.6
6.	Percent of institutional deliveries [a]	2005-06	40.7	32.2
7.	Percent of safe deliveries [a]	2005-06	48.3	43.2
8.	Percent of children who are underweight [a]	2005-06	45.9	44.0
9.	Percent of children suffering from anemia [a]	2005-06	79.2	79.6

10.	Percent of children who received full vaccination [a]	2005-06	43.5	26.5
11.	Mothers who received postnatal care	2005-06	36.4	2.9
Demographic Factors				
12.	Sex ratio [b]	2001	933	922
13.	Total fertility rate [a]	2005-06	2.68	3.21
14.	Percentage of girls married below 18 years [a]	2005-06	28	49.4
15.	Percent of births of order 3 and above [a]	2005-06	42.	47.4
16.	Mean age at marriage of the girls [a]	2005-06	19.5	17.3
Socio-economic Factors				
17.	Population Age 6 + that is literate [a]	2005-06	67.6	57.4
18.	Female literacy [b]	2001	54.2	44.34
19.	Female work participation rate [b]	2001	25.68	33.48
20.	Poverty ratio [c]	2004-05	27.8	21
21.	Health infrastructure [c]	2005-06	31.8	33.2
22.	Per capita state Govt. health expenditure [c]	2001-02	—	110.08
Environmental Factors				
	Percentage of households			
23.	With electricity [b]	2005-06	67.9	66.1
24.	With drinking water (piped or hand pump) [b]	2005-06	42.0	45.4
25.	With a toilet or latrine facility [b]	2005-06	44.5	30.8
26.	Living in a *pucca* house [b]	2005-06	41.4	45.0
27.	Mean House-hold Size [b]	2005-06	4.8	5.2

Source : IIPS, *NFHS-III; Census of India*; Government of India. *The Eleventh Five-Year Plan.*

There is great diversity in number of women availing Antenatal Care (ANC), according to different characteristics. This diversity prevails according to caste, religion, place of delivery, women with mass media awareness, nutrition awareness and work status. Uneducated women, women belonging to backward castes, women opting home/unsafe delivery, women unaware about nutrition and mass media and non-working women are less likely to receive at least one ANC visit. An analysis of differentials in the use of ANC reflects the interrelationship between different variables examined viz. place

TABLE 5.4
Correlation Matrix

	ANC	*PLACE*	*CASTE*	*SELFEDU*	*MEDIA*	*HUSEDU*	*IFA*	*TT*	*SAFEDEL*	*INSTDEL*
(1)	*(2)*	*(3)*	*(4)*	*(5)*	*(6)*	*(7)*	*(8)*	*(9)*	*(10)*	*(11)*
ANC	1.000	.188**	.179**	.230**	.111**	.239**	.226**	.178**	.274**	.410**
PLACE		1.000	.345**	.290**	.182**	.215**	.203**	-.040	.215**	.388**
CASTE			1.000	.290**	.127**	.223**	.045	.034	.127**	.082**
SELFEDU				1.000	.372**	.529**	.297**	.180**	.345**	.187**
MEDIA					1.000	.195**	.135**	-.045	.204**	.126**
HUSEDU						1.000	.311**	.207**	.301**	.177**
IFA							1.000	.271**	.394**	.230**
TT								1.000	.212**	.062*
SAFEDEL									1.000	.201**
INSTDEL										1.000

* Significant at the 0.05 level (2-tailed).
** Significant at the 0.01 level (2-tailed).

of delivery (place), caste, self education (selfedu), media awareness (media), education of husband (husedu), consumption of IFA tablets (IFA), TT injections (TT), safe deliveries (safedel) and institutional deliveries (instdel). Clearly all variables interact; correlation matrix (Table 5.4) exhibits statistically significant correlation coefficients, which are in the expected directions as well.

As it is not possible to assess individual contribution of each element to overall use of ANC, for better understanding of the impact of each variable logistic regression uses ANC (Yes or No) as the response variable, female education as the primary predictor variable and ten demographic and socio-economic variables as controls. Four different alternative logistic regression models are estimated using different combination of variables. Demographic variables, which include age of mothers, religion, caste and birth order, affect the likelihood of ANC but are not easily amenable to change and they are included as controls in all models. To see the impact of mother's education, it has been considered separately. Other socio-economic variables include work status, mass media awareness and nutrition awareness. Supply factors include availability of medical facility within close vicinity of residence and the quality of care available. The results of the multivariate analysis are presented in the form of odds ratios. Table 5.5 presents adjusted effects of mother's education on the likelihood of access to ANC for Rajasthan based on four different models.

TABLE 5.5

Adjusted Effects (Odds Ratios) of Selected Predictor Variables—On Availing ANC

Characteristics	*Model 1*	*Model 2*	*Model 3*	*Model 4*
(1)	*(2)*	*(3)*	*(4)*	*(5)*
	Background factors			
Age				
15-19	1.00	1.00	1.00	1.00
20-24	0.41*	0.70*	0.85**	0.68*
25-29	0.55**	0.47*	0.63*	0.85**
30-44	0.92	1.05	0.88	0.89

(Contd.)

TABLE (*Contd.*)

(1)	*(2)*	*(3)*	*(4)*	*(5)*
Birth Order				
1	1.00	1.00	1.00	1.00
2	0.77**	0.62**	0.73**	0.85**
3	0.91**	0.68**	0.75**	0.97**
4+	0.93**	1.04**	1.20**	1.11**
Religion				
Hindu	2.72**	2.21**	1.87**	1.75*
Muslim	1.00	1.00	1.00	1.00
Caste				
General	1.51*	2.25**	1.81*	1.56*
Backward	1.00	1.00	1.00	1.00
Socio-economic Factors				
Woman's education				
Educated (8+)		8.58**	5.57**	3.06**
Uneducated		1.00	1.00	1.00
Work status				
Working			0.53*	0.26*
Not working			1.00	1.00
Media Awareness				
Aware			2.57	3.36
Not aware			1.00	1.00
Nutrition Awareness				
Aware			1.77	1.24*
Not aware			1.00	1.00
Supply Factors				
Availability of Medical Facility				
Yes				0.97*
No				1.00
Quality of Care				
Good				3.86**
Bad				1.00

**Significant at the 0.01 level (2-tailed); *Significant at the 0.05 level (2-tailed).

Results show that educated mothers are more likely to avail ANC than uneducated mothers, even after controlling for a number of potentially confounding variables. In model-2, with age, birth order, religion and caste controlled by holding them at their mean values in the underlying logistic regression, the odds of access to ANC is 8.6 times higher for educated mothers than uneducated mothers. This effect is reduced to 5.6 when socio-economic variables are additionally controlled in model-3 and further to 3.1 when supply factors are additionally controlled in model-4.

CONCLUSION

In the last decades, the life expectancy of the population has shown remarkable improvement. Yet pregnancy related mortality and morbidity continue to take a huge toll on the lives of women and newborns, and there is little evidence that maternity has become safer. It will, therefore, be difficult to achieve MDG-5 in stipulated time. Certainly, it will be impossible for a state like Rajasthan to attain the goal. The following arguments, some of which have already been stated, are recapitulated in support of this conclusion.

1. The health situation in Rajasthan is far from satisfying. The situation can be judged from the fact that out of the 90 problem districts identified in India where the birth rate and the infant mortality rate are significantly high, 27 districts belong to Rajasthan. The CDR (8) is higher than the national average. The MMR and the infant and child mortality rates are also higher than most of the major states and the national average (SIHFW, 2005).
2. An average of 25,846 rural populations are covered by one PHC reflecting the poor health infrastructure in Rajasthan. As the villages are widely scattered and covered with desert, climatic conditions play a major role in non-availability of appropriate maternal health facilities in Rajasthan. Although more than 12,500 government health care facilities exist in Rajasthan, yet the percentage of institutional deliveries is negligible.
3. Per capita income is also low at Rs. 8,175 in 2000-01 at constant prices of 1993-94. Almost one-third of the total population is underprivileged, belonging to scheduled castes and tribes.
4. Considering the major factor of poor maternal health, i.e.

illiteracy, Rajasthan shows a worse condition of women having only 44 percent female literacy in which rural females have only 37 percent literacy. (*Statistical Abstract of Rajasthan*, 2003)

5. Cultural factors are greatly responsible for poor maternal health in societies like Rajasthan and more so in rural areas. Majority of women do not receive medical care even during pregnancy and delivery as they think it to be unnecessary. Cultural practices prevent them to have a say in any kind of decision-making regarding use of contraceptive or the size of family, etc.

All these factors point to the inescapable conclusion that even hundred percent ANC by the year 2015 will be a herculean task. It is premature to talk on the possibility of attaining MDG when full ANC and institutional deliveries may well prove to be beyond the most determined efforts in the remaining period. As long as high levels of maternal mortality and morbidity persist, a reflection of the poor maternal health of the society, the fruits of development will always remain questionable. Maternal mortality in India is 40 to 50 times more as compared to the developed countries. And Rajasthan is in the high MMR belt. High MMR is simply an evidence of the deplorable maternal health situation prevailing in the state. Rather than simply a medical problem, poor maternal health is ultimately a reflection of the series of social, cultural and economic factors which are definitely not responsive to short term strategies and go beyond the health sector. The most basic long-term solutions are poverty and gender-related — here changes in female status and the expansion of educational and economic opportunities for women, improvement in nutrition and prevention of adolescent marriage are of particular importance.

Short-term benefits to maternal health can be accrued through well-implemented interventions, which address directly medical causes. Such interventions exist but in practice the focus has been on sterilisation only. And maternal and child health care, health and nutrition care, birth spacing have been relatively neglected. At the same time, programmes suffer from poor outreach, quality of services and care and message to the cultural milieu of their beneficiaries. Since medical causes are only immediate causes, any government policy or programme, which targets only reduction in immediate causes in isolation, cannot be a success. Besides improving the maternal healthcare services, it is necessary to improve the social status of women, including the education standard, to reduce the current level of MMR. Medical causes would be automatically addressed in the long run if socio-economic and cultural development were complimented with the improvement of health infrastructure. The socio-economic status including educational status of women greatly influences the maternal mortality and morbidity.

References

Bhat, P.N.M. (2002), "Maternal Mortality in India: An Update," *Studies in Family Planning*, 33(3).

Census. (2001), *Census of India, 2001—Provisional Population Totals,* Series 9 - Rajathan, Jaipur: Directorate of Census Operations.

Holysmoke, (2006), "Maternal Death Rates around the World", Available at www.holysmoke.org/fem/fem0230.htmhttp://www.safemotherhood.org/facts_and_figures/health_around_the_world.htm

Sai, Fred T. and Janet Nassim. (1989), "The Need for a Reproductive Health Approach", *International Journal of Gynecology and Obstetrics*, Supplement 3.

SIHFW (2005), *Health Vision-2025*, Available at: http://rajswasthya.nic.in/HealthVision2025.doc

Statistical Abstract.(2003), *Statistical Abstract, 2003*, Jaipur: Directorate of Economics and Statistics.

World Bank (2004), "Growth, Human Development and Poverty Reduction in Rajasthan: Past Performance and Future Prospects", Available at: http://www.wds.worldbank.org/servlet/WDSContentServer/WDSP/IB/2004/02/24/000160016_20040224122704/Rendered/PDF/268230IN.pdf.

SRS: Various Bulletins, Sample Registration System, Office of Registrar General of India.

Velkoff, Victoria A. and Arjun Adlakha (1998), "Women's Health in India", in *Women of the World*, U.S. Department of Commerce, Economics and Statistics Administration, Bureau of the Census.

6

Inter-district Variation in Utilization of Reproductive and Child Health Services in Uttar Pradesh

MAMTA RAJBHAR AND SANJAY K. MOHANTY

INTRODUCTION

The National Rural Health Mission programme (NHRM) was launched in 2005 to provide effective health care to the rural population in the country with special focus on states having poor health outcomes and inadequate public health infrastructure. The primary focus of the NRHM was to improve access of rural people, especially women and children, to equitable and affordable primary health care. The mission includes basic health care services especially family planning services, pre-natal care, safe delivery, post-natal care, prevention and treatment of other reproductive health conditions. These services are provided free of cost in public health centres.The basic aim of the programme is to reduce infant mortality and maternal mortality by promoting new born care, immunization, antenatal care, institutional delivery and post-partum-care (NHRM 2005-12). The Government of India has taken a slew of measures to augment supply of essential equipment, drugs and consumables, construction of building and staff quarters, filling up vacant post of medical and paramedical staff and in-service training of staff in order to improve the quality of health care services.

Despite free provision of these services and government efforts to improve the quality of health care, utilization of these services varies largely among the states in India. For instance, while 99 percent women in the state of Kerala delivered at health centres, it was less than 28 percent in Bihar and 25 percent in Uttar Pradesh (IIPS and Macro International, 2007). Often studies document that low socio-economic status among women as the barrier in low utilization of services in these states (Becker *et al.*, 1993; Singh and Singh, 2007).

Reduction of inequality in utilization of reproductive and child health services across space and sub-groups has been accorded top priority in global and national developmental agenda. Despite the efforts to improve the quality of health care, utilization of these services varies largely among states and among districts within states of India.

LITERATURE REVIEW

A number of studies have been carried out on utilization in reproductive and child health services in developing countries. Among other things, these studies outline the increasing inequality in the utilization of basic health services among various socio-economic groups (Backer *et al.,* 1993; Gwatkin, 2000; Leon *et al.*, 2001; Wagstaff, 2002; Joe *et al.*, 2008, Anand, 2004; Sen, 1985).

An important proximate determinant of declining mortality is access to and use of quality health services (McCarthy and Maine, 1992). Access to reproductive health services is crucial for improved child survival and increased contraceptive use and consequently fertility decline in the developing countries (Ramachandran, 1989). Although evidence suggests that health services influence fertility behaviour, maternal and child health services often exist in conjunction with family planning services. Maternal and child health services have been promoted as an important influence on couples' fertility-related behaviour as they decrease mortality (Caldwell, 1986; Foster, 1984; Pebley, 1984). However, the spread of these services often accompanies numerous other important social, economic, and institutional changes that affect fertility behaviour (Axinn and Yabiku, 2001; Caldwell, 1986; Hernandez, 1981; Mason, 1997). A study by Brouner *et al.* reveals maternal and child health services as key determinant for increasing fertility limitation in Nepal. Their study found significant and independent relationship between the availability of maternal and child health services, family planning services, and the rate of fertility limitation, even though the provision of these services were positively correlated. Studies found positive impact of utilising antenatal services on improving maternal health in rural Uttar Pradesh (Ram and Singh, 2006).

During the decade, studies have reported growing rich-poor and urban-rural gap in utilisation of basic reproductive and child health (RCH) services (Chattopadhyay and Roy, 2005; Singh and Singh, 2007; Mohanty and Pathak, 2008, Kumar and Mohanty, 2011). In 2005, Chattopadhyay and Roy found wide rich-poor gap with respect to fertility and mortality indicators in India. In the medium size urban centres people are at disadvantage in terms of access to health services, use of family planning and less infant and child mortality. Using NFHS data Kumar and Mohanty (2011) found large gap in utilization of antenatal and natal services and narrowing gap in contraceptive use in urban India. A study by Mohanty and Pathak (2009) observed highest economic inequality in medical assistance at delivery and lowest inequality in contraceptive use in Uttar Pradesh and Maharashtra.

OBJECTIVES

The objective of this paper is to examine the inter-district variation in utilization of reproductive and child health services in Uttar Pradesh

DATA AND METHODS

Data from the third round of District Level Household and Facility Survey (DLHS-3) conducted in 2007-08 are used for the purpose. The DLHS-3 covered a total of 90,415 households from 71 districts in Uttar Pradesh. It covered a total of 87,564 ever-married women aged 15-49 years and 23,110 unmarried women aged 15-24 years. The DLHS-3 collected information on wide range of topics: fertility, family-planning, maternal and child health, living condition of households, health infrastructure and other variables like effectiveness of ASHA and JSY in promoting RCH care. Along with household survey, the facility survey was also conducted to assess the availability of trained staff, equipment and supplies and their utilization at district hospitals, Community Health Centres (CHCs), Primary Health Centres (PHCs) and Sub-centres (SCs) levels. We have used the unit data to understand the inter-district variation in reproductive and child health services in the state.

The analysis was confined to six indicators of reproductive and child health services, namely, ANC visits (at least 3 visits), postnatal care (check-up within 2 weeks of delivery), safe delivery (institutional delivery or home delivery assisted by skilled persons), full immunization (BCG+ 3 injection of DPT+ 3 doses of polio + measles), contraceptive use (current use of any modern method) and unmet need for contraception. A composite index of these indicators has been computed for inter-district comparison. First, each of the indicators has been converted to a dimensional index using the following formula. The composite index is calculated by taking average of all indices. Descriptive analysis has been used to understand the determinants of reproductive and child health services in Uttar Pradesh.

Dimensional index:

For positive indicator : $\frac{Actual\ value - Minimum\ value}{Maximum\ value - Minimum\ value}$

For negative indicator : $\frac{Maximum\ value - Actual\ value}{Maximum\ value - Minimum\ value}$

Results

Table 6.1 presents the data source, mean and standard deviation of the selected demographic, socio-economic and health indicators in the districts of Uttar Pradesh. The mean population size of the districts of Uttar Pradesh was 2.8 million in 2011, while mean population growth rate was 20.15 per decade. The mean total fertility rate was 3.5 while the mean death rate was 8.8 during 2010-11. Though the crude death rate was lower, the mean under-five morality and infant mortality rates were high, 94 and 69 respectively. The schedule caste and Muslim population constitute about 21.5 percent and 17.5 percent of the total population in the state. The percentage of population living below poverty line is 38.6 percent while the mean female literacy and urbanization are relatively low in the state. About 23.1 percent women had gone for three or more ANC visits, 35.8 percent used post-natal care, 32.3 percent women had safe delivery, 28.1 percent women were using modern contraceptive method and about 32 percent women had unmet need for family planning (either spacing or limiting). About 32 percent children in the age group of 12-23 months were fully immunized against all preventable disease.

TABLE 6.1

Data Sources and Descriptive Statistics of Demographic, Socio-Economic and Health Indicators in the Districts of Uttar Pradesh

Sl. No.	*Item*	*Data source*	*Mean*	*SD*
1.	Population Size (million)	Census, 2011	2.82	1.1
2.	Decadal Growth Rate	Census, 2011	20.15	6.12
3.	Crude Birth Rate	Indirect estimates using RSM Census, 2011	25.35	3.03
4.	Crude Death Rate	AHS, 2010-11	8.77	1.39
5.	Total Fertility Rate	Derived from CBR	3.45	0.42
6.	Infant Mortality Rate	AHS, 2010-11	69	14
7.	Under Five Mortality Rate	AHS, 2010-11	94	19
8.	Sex Ratio	Census, 2011	905	44
9.	Child Sex Ratio	Census, 2011	900	29
10.	Percentage population below poverty line	NSS, 2009-10	38.55	15.30
11.	Percentage Schedule Caste population	Census, 2001	21.45	5.58
12.	Percentage Schedule Tribe population	Census, 2001	0.07	0.20
13.	Percentage Muslim Population	Census, 2001	17.47	10.66
14.	Female Literacy Rate	Census, 2011	58.48	8.69
15.	Male Literacy Rate	Census, 2011	79.27	7.00
16.	Percent urban population	Census, 2011	20.54	15.09
17.	Percentage of 3 or more ANC visits	DLHS, 2007-08	23.1	8.86
18.	Percentage of post natal care	DLHS, 2007-08	35.84	21.46
19.	Percentage of safe delivery	DLHS, 2007-08	32.27	11.52
20.	Percentage of contraceptive use	DLHS, 2007-08	28.12	10.66
21.	Percentage full immunization	DLHS, 2007-08	31.46	10.93
22.	Percentage unmet need	DLHS, 2007-08	31.91	8.20

To get the relative position of the districts in reproductive and child health care, a composite index is developed (Table 6.2). The value of each of the dimensional index and the composite index is presented. The Index value ranges from a minimum of 8.9 percent in Budaun and Bahraich to 73 percent in Lucknow (Table 6.2). Based on the index value we have classified districts into three broad categories of utilization namely Low, Moderate and High performing districts. The highest utilization of RCH services are in the districts of Lucknow (73 percent) followed by Deoria (71 percent), Varanasi (70.7 percent), Jhansi (67.3 percent), Kanpur Nagar and Ghaziabad (66.9), Baghpat and Meerut (64.8). The low performing districts in composite index of RCH services are Budaun and Bahraich (8.9 percent) followed by Balrampur (9.5 percent), Shrawasti (10.4 percent), Shahjahanpur (16.7 percent) Farrukhabad (18.1 percent) and Gonda (18.6 percent). The mean value of the poor performing districts is 27.1, among moderately covered districts 49.4 and it is 66.1 among the high performing districts. There are 29 districts classified as low performing districts, 29 districts as moderate and the remaining 12 districts as high performing districts in RCH services (Fig. 6.1). Moreover, the poor performing districts follow a spatial pattern; Budaun, Bahraich, Balrampur, Shrawasti, Shahjahanpur, Farrukhabad, Gonda, Sitapur, Kheri, Hardoi, Fatehpur, Etah, Siddharthnagar, Mainpuri, Kannauj, Pilibhit, Kaushambi, Firozabad, Unnao, Auraiya, Banda, Sant Ravidas Nagar, Chitrakoot, Barabanki, Etawah, Moradabad, Sant Kabir Nagar, Bareilly, and Rae Bareli. Similarly, the high performing districts are Hamirpur, Muzaffarnagar, Gorakhpur, Bijnor, Meerut, Baghpat, Ghaziabad, Kanpur Nagar, Jhansi, Varanasi, Deoria and Lucknow.

Table 6.3 presents differentials in utilization of maternal and child health care indicators by socio-economic characteristics among 3 grouped districts of Uttar Pradesh during 2007-08. It is found that ANC visit is very low in the state and in all groups of districts. Huge differences are also found in post-natal care and safe delivery across the low, moderate and high performing districts. With increase in age, the gap between low and high performing districts decreases for safe delivery. The differential in utilization of ANC visits is more pronounced in urban areas as compared to rural areas. Across caste groups the gap between low and high performing districts is more prominent among other caste women as compared to women belonging to schedule caste and schedule tribes, while for religious

TABLE 6.2

Ranking of Districts in Composite Index of Reproductive and Child Health Services in Uttar Pradesh, 2007-08

State/District	*Index of 3+ANC*[a]	*Index of Post Natal Care*[b]	*Index of Safe delivery*[c]	*Index of Full immunization*[d]	*Index of Contraceptive Use*	*Index of Unmet Need*	*Composite Index of RCH services*	*Percent Indices*
(1)	*(2)*	*(3)*	*(4)*	*(5)*	*(6)*	*(7)*	*(8)*	*(9)*
Budaun	0.006	0.165	0.071	0.041	0.123	0.127	0.089	8.9
Bahraich	0.192	0.000	0.014	0.108	0.046	0.173	0.089	8.9
Balrampur	0.402	0.002	0.000	0.166	0.000	0.000	0.095	9.5
Shrawasti	0.278	0.004	0.080	0.071	0.044	0.147	0.104	10.4
Shahjahanpur	0.087	0.080	0.018	0.223	0.259	0.335	0.167	16.7
Farrukhabad	0.056	0.210	0.113	0.108	0.186	0.411	0.181	18.1
Gonda	0.254	0.064	0.304	0.187	0.125	0.183	0.186	18.6
Sitapur	0.194	0.104	0.297	0.151	0.242	0.274	0.210	21.0
Kheri	0.182	0.083	0.166	0.093	0.334	0.431	0.215	21.5
Hardoi	0.040	0.402	0.101	0.328	0.182	0.340	0.232	23.2
Fatehpur	0.195	0.256	0.221	0.219	0.226	0.320	0.240	24.0
Etah	0.000	0.691	0.343	0.000	0.211	0.244	0.248	24.8
Siddharthnagar	0.319	0.007	0.064	0.603	0.106	0.411	0.252	25.2
Mainpuri	0.018	0.284	0.277	0.363	0.207	0.520	0.278	27.8

Kannauj	0.086	0.515	0.182	0.386	0.213	0.457	0.307	30.7
Pilibhit	0.288	0.096	0.231	0.253	0.438	0.551	0.309	30.9
Kaushambi	0.310	0.324	0.230	0.173	0.326	0.538	0.317	31.7
Firozabad	0.353	0.508	0.417	0.350	0.263	0.162	0.342	34.2
Unnao	0.213	0.132	0.299	0.542	0.328	0.543	0.343	34.3
Auraiya	0.146	0.420	0.186	0.511	0.407	0.416	0.348	34.8
Banda	0.331	0.164	0.310	0.149	0.397	0.739	0.348	34.8
Sant Ravidas Nagar	0.249	0.158	0.522	0.226	0.486	0.525	0.361	36.1
Chitrakoot	0.428	0.153	0.292	0.169	0.526	0.612	0.363	36.3
Barabanki	0.413	0.142	0.380	0.426	0.271	0.551	0.364	36.4
Etawah	0.270	0.344	0.401	0.448	0.380	0.340	0.364	36.4
Moradabad	0.318	0.396	0.352	0.330	0.382	0.434	0.369	36.9
Sant Kabir Nagar	0.427	0.049	0.377	0.761	0.228	0.393	0.373	37.3
Bareilly	0.209	0.580	0.210	0.451	0.345	0.470	0.378	37.8
Rae Bareli	0.503	0.179	0.471	0.439	0.307	0.437	0.389	38.9
JyotibaPhule Nagar	0.286	0.223	0.444	0.411	0.514	0.551	0.405	40.5
Agra	0.324	0.414	0.669	0.291	0.420	0.322	0.407	40.7
Hathras	0.237	0.483	0.528	0.291	0.344	0.594	0.413	41.3
Ghazipur	0.557	0.114	0.569	0.544	0.361	0.426	0.428	42.8
Chandauli	0.254	0.220	0.636	0.287	0.572	0.609	0.430	43.0
Kanpur Dehat	0.330	0.143	0.314	0.687	0.436	0.688	0.433	43.3

(Contd.)

TABLE 6.2 (Contd.)

(1)	(2)	(3)	(4)	(5)	(6)	(7)	(8)	(9)
Mathura	0.340	0.530	0.782	0.193	0.457	0.429	0.455	45.5
Maharajganj	0.557	0.414	0.190	0.532	0.497	0.569	0.460	46.0
Faizabad	0.512	0.257	0.534	0.614	0.303	0.538	0.460	46.0
Rampur	0.222	0.713	0.349	0.480	0.451	0.586	0.467	46.7
Basti	0.521	0.106	0.563	0.886	0.238	0.492	0.468	46.8
Ambedaker Nagar	0.437	0.235	0.536	0.779	0.265	0.579	0.472	47.2
Aligarh	0.322	0.650	0.594	0.389	0.445	0.434	0.472	47.2
Sultanpur	0.520	0.114	0.808	0.702	0.299	0.442	0.481	48.1
Mirzapur	0.277	0.282	0.636	0.254	0.687	0.789	0.487	48.7
Azamgarh	0.710	0.209	0.898	0.527	0.271	0.368	0.497	49.7
Lalitpur	0.312	0.220	0.537	0.322	0.714	0.904	0.501	50.1
Jaunpur	0.483	0.104	0.745	0.726	0.488	0.525	0.512	51.2
Pratapgarh	0.546	0.185	0.703	0.857	0.345	0.437	0.512	51.2
Allahabad	0.553	0.379	0.589	0.293	0.601	0.662	0.513	51.3
Sonbhadra	0.208	0.245	0.447	0.685	0.645	0.858	0.515	51.5
Kushinagar	0.683	0.579	0.431	0.474	0.493	0.523	0.531	53.1
Mau	0.711	0.247	0.811	0.659	0.313	0.485	0.538	53.8
Jalaun	0.290	0.212	0.625	0.427	0.800	0.891	0.541	54.1

Mahoba	0.212	0.409	0.816	0.467	0.762	0.794	0.577	57.7
Bulandshahar	0.446	0.922	0.667	0.352	0.503	0.604	0.582	58.2
Saharanpur	0.412	0.598	0.503	0.584	0.695	0.728	0.587	58.7
Gautam Buddha Nagar	0.422	0.551	0.648	0.440	0.658	0.838	0.593	59.3
Ballia	0.867	0.212	0.702	0.817	0.386	0.607	0.598	59.8
Hamirpur	0.646	0.163	0.613	0.716	0.710	0.782	0.605	60.5
Muzaffarnagar	0.705	0.934	0.540	0.418	0.562	0.500	0.610	61.0
Gorakhpur	0.909	0.345	0.628	0.780	0.551	0.556	0.628	62.8
Bijnor	0.493	1.000	0.646	0.577	0.503	0.596	0.636	63.6
Meerut	0.521	0.664	0.735	0.529	0.610	0.830	0.648	64.8
Baghpat	0.676	0.911	0.550	0.463	0.631	0.657	0.648	64.8
Ghaziabad	0.772	0.579	0.754	0.440	0.674	0.794	0.669	66.9
Kanpur Nagar	0.645	0.394	0.713	0.762	0.676	0.825	0.669	66.9
Jhansi	0.457	0.347	0.787	0.449	1.000	1.000	0.673	67.3
Varanasi	0.335	0.393	1.000	0.866	0.781	0.865	0.707	70.7
Deoria	1.000	0.648	0.777	1.000	0.384	0.452	0.710	71.0
Lucknow	0.884	0.448	0.871	0.903	0.616	0.655	0.730	73.0
Uttar Pradesh	0.359	0.314	0.423	0.411	0.397	0.510	0.402	40.2

a At least three visits for antenatal check-up.
b Check-up within two weeks after delivery.
c Either institutional delivery or home delivery assisted by skilled person.
d BCG, three injections of DPT, three doses of Polio (excluding Polio "0") and measles.

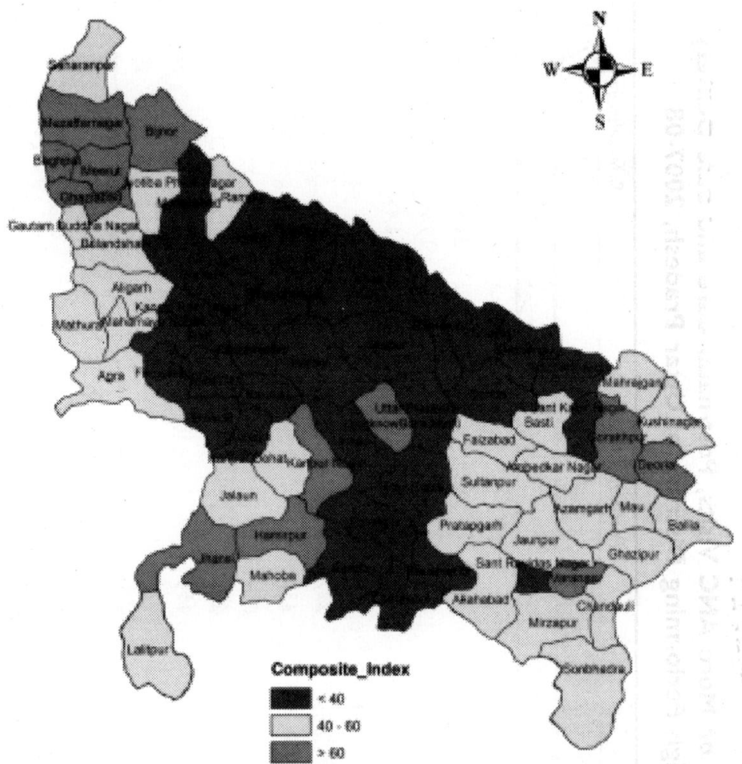

Figure 6.1: Composite Index of Utilization of RCH Services in Districts of Uttar Pradesh, 2007-08

groups the gap is more glaring among Hindu women as compared to other religion women and Muslims women. The differences by educational status are relatively high. As the educational status improve the gap between low and high performing districts increases. The pattern is similar in case of wealth quintiles.

Table 6.4 presents differentials in utilization of full immunization, contraceptive use and unmet need indicators by socio-economic characteristics across low, moderate and high performing districts of Uttar Pradesh during 2007-08. It is found that large differentials in full immunization and contraceptive use across these districts. Differentials in immunization of children are large belonging to younger, urban areas, schedule castes, other religious

TABLE 6.3

Differentials in Utilization of Three or More ANC Visits, Post-natal Care and Safe Delivery Across Low, Moderate and High Performing Districts of Uttar Pradesh, 2007-08

Background variable	*3 or more ANC*[a]			*Post-natal Care*			*Safe delivery*[c]		
	Low	*Moderate*	*High*	*Low*	*Moderate*	*High*	*Low*	*Moderate*	*High*
(1)	*(2)*	*(3)*	*(4)*	*(5)*	*(6)*	*(7)*	*(8)*	*(9)*	*(10)*
Age group									
<25	18.7	27.5	36.3	28.2	37.9	61.1	24.8	42.7	47.5
25-35	16.2	24.7	34.9	25.0	35.4	58.7	19.9	36.4	41.9
>35	12.8	17.0	24.9	19.2	29.8	59.1	14.4	28.5	34.8
Place of residence									
Rural	15.2	23.5	32.3	22.9	33.2	58.0	18.4	35.3	38.5
Urban	27.3	34.8	39.4	43.4	52.3	63.6	39.3	56.0	54.7
Castes									
SC	14.4	19.3	28.0	20.5	29.6	46.4	15.5	28.5	30.8
ST	10.4	13.5	17.8	15.7	20.9	37.8	13.5	20.9	23.9
OBC	15.2	24.4	33.2	24.4	33.9	60.5	18.6	36.2	42.1
Others	23.7	34.6	43.8	33.9	49.7	70.4	34.2	56.4	58.9

(*Contd.*)

Table 6.3 (*Contd.*)

(1)	(2)	(3)	(4)	(5)	(6)	(7)	(8)	(9)	(10)
Religion									
Hindu	16.5	25.2	36.9	25.9	34.8	54.8	20.8	38.0	46.4
Muslim	17.1	23.4	28.5	22.6	40.5	70.5	20.6	38.1	36.0
Others	30.0	33.8	48.1	53.2	66.2	84.6	61.2	50.0	69.2
Education									
Illiterate	12.6	17.7	23.7	19.5	30.4	54.7	14.3	27.3	29.3
<5 years	16.9	21.4	35.0	26.8	37.3	64.3	20.4	40.0	33.3
5-9 years	21.2	28.2	38.7	34.4	38.4	55.9	29.8	44.8	47.1
>=10 years	40.7	50.8	57.3	54.2	53.5	77.3	57.4	71.1	78.2
Wealth index									
Poorest	10.7	15.0	20.3	17.5	26.6	46.2	11.9	23.5	23.0
Poorer	13.2	18.5	26.6	22.5	29.8	52.5	15.9	28.4	31.6
Middle	14.8	21.9	29.4	23.9	31.6	52.8	18.8	34.1	35.3
Richer	19.9	26.9	33.1	29.3	38.0	58.2	24.5	40.5	42.7
Richest	31.3	38.2	46.3	41.3	48.5	71.9	43.7	57.3	60.1
Total	16.6	24.6	33.7	25.5	35.7	59.1	21.0	37.7	41.9

a At least three visits for antenatal check-up.
b Check- up within two weeks after delivery.
c Either institutional delivery or home delivery assisted by skilled person.

TABLE 6.4

Differentials in Utilization of Full Immunization, Contraceptive Use and Unmet Need for Contraception Across Low, Moderate and High Performing Districts of Uttar Pradesh, 2007-08

Background variable	*Child Immunization*[d]			*Contraceptive use*[e]			*Unmet Need*[f]		
	Low	*Moderate*	*High*	*Low*	*Moderate*	*High*	*Low*	*Moderate*	*High*
(1)	*(2)*	*(3)*	*(4)*	*(5)*	*(6)*	*(7)*	*(8)*	*(9)*	*(10)*
Age group									
<25	25.3	36.9	42.3	7.3	12.3	15.6	39.0	34.6	32.8
25-35	23.7	34.4	39.1	24.1	37.4	45.3	39.5	29.9	24.5
>35	19.3	27.3	33.0	26.3	39.7	49.6	34.3	24.2	20.1
Place of residence									
Rural	23.1	34.4	38.5	18.4	30.3	38.1	38.4	29.9	26.8
Urban	29.2	39.0	43.9	29.5	37.5	43.1	32.5	25.0	21.1
Castes									
SC	24.6	31.0	41.9	16.5	28.5	38.1	38.6	29.6	25.8
ST	18.1	22.0	11.8	26.8	27.1	40.2	33.6	25.6	23.4
OBC	21.6	34.1	38.4	17.6	29.7	37.3	39.0	30.2	26.3
Others	30.2	43.7	44.0	28.9	38.6	46.4	33.3	26.4	21.0

(Contd.)

TABLE 6.4 (Contd.)

(1)	(2)	(3)	(4)	(5)	(6)	(7)	(8)	(9)	(10)
Religion									
Hindu	25.2	36.6	48.0	21.2	33.1	44.3	36.6	27.9	22.0
Muslim	18.0	25.2	22.7	13.0	18.4	23.2	43.4	38.4	35.3
Others	22.6	60.0	50.0	46.1	56.3	55.2	20.4	15.1	19.0
Education									
Illiterate	18.4	25.7	26.0	16.4	29.7	35.1	40.3	30.5	28.9
<5 years	24.3	28.2	40.5	19.7	34.0	40.5	35.7	27.9	24.5
5-9 years	32.3	42.7	48.4	24.9	32.5	42.2	33.4	28.3	22.0
> = 10 years	48.5	61.6	64.8	34.2	35.9	47.6	28.9	25.6	19.2
Wealth index									
Poorest	17.1	22.4	28.2	12.8	25.0	27.3	44.5	34.7	35.6
Poorer	18.6	26.6	30.2	15.4	27.2	33.4	40.5	32.3	27.9
Middle	23.4	31.4	32.2	18.6	28.3	36.4	38.2	30.6	26.2
Richer	27.1	37.5	41.7	23.3	32.5	38.4	34.2	27.5	26.3
Richest	40.2	51.3	51.5	31.7	38.3	47.1	29.4	24.9	20.0
Total	24.1	34.6	39.8	19.9	31.0	39.3	37.6	29.3	25.5

d BCG, three injections of DPT, three doses of Polio (excluding Polio "0") and measles.
e Current use of modern contraceptive methods.
f Unmet need for limiting or unmet need for spacing.

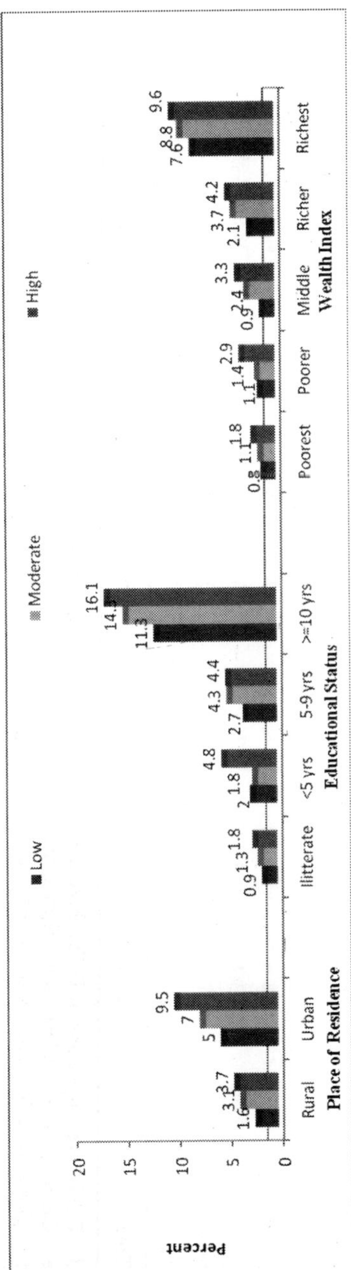

Figure 6.2: Differences in 3 and More ANC Visits Across Low, Moderate and High Performing Districts Women by their Place of Residence, Educational Status and Wealth Quintile in Uttar Pradesh, 2007-08

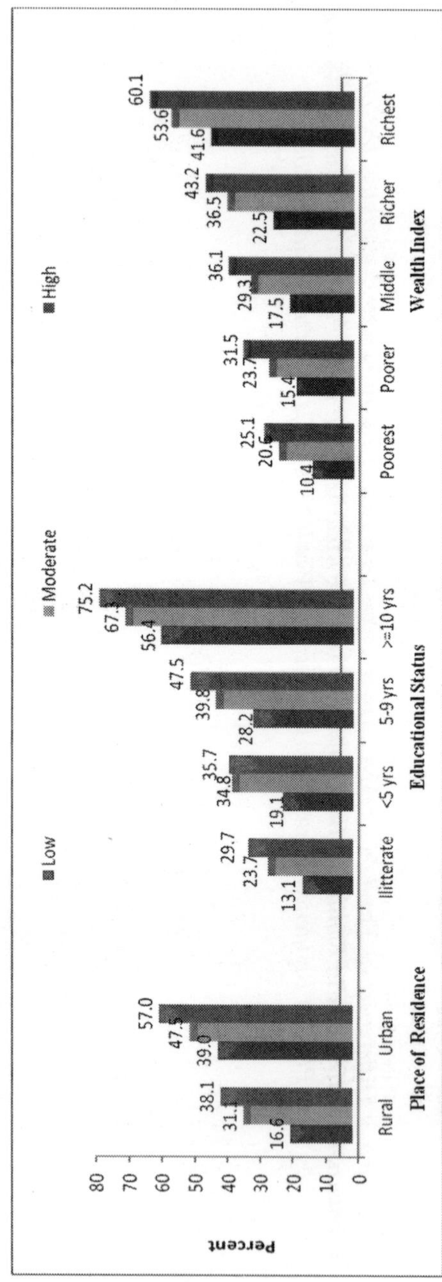

Figure 6.3 Differences in Safe Delivery Across Low, Moderate and High Performing Districts Women by their Place of Residence, Educational Status and Wealth Quintile in Uttar Pradesh, 2007-08

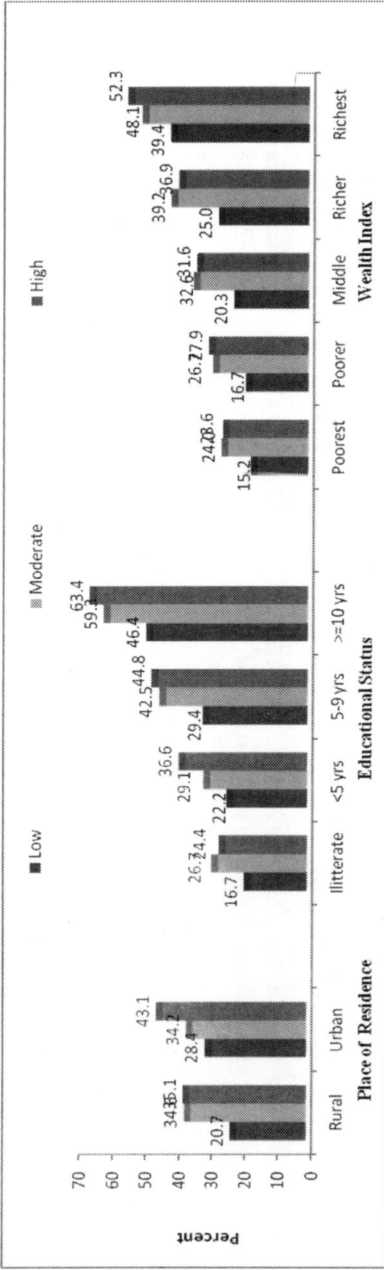

Figure 6.4 : Differences in Child Immunization Across Low, Moderate and High Performing Districts Women by their Place of Residence, Educational Status and Wealth Quintile in Uttar Pradesh, 2007-08

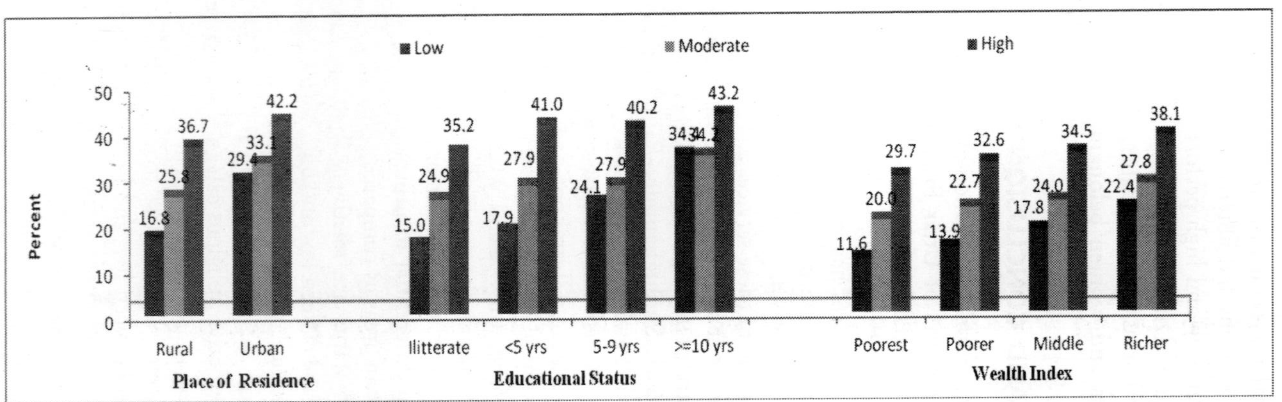

Figure 6.5 : Differences in Contraceptive Use Across Low, Moderate and High Performing Districts Women by their Place of Residence, Educational Status and Wealth Quintile in Uttar Pradesh, 2007-08

category and more educated mothers as compared to older, belonging to rural areas, schedule tribes, Muslims and illiterate mothers. With increase in age, the gap between low and high performing districts increases for contraceptive use. Differentials in utilization of contraceptive was more in rural areas, schedule tribes, Hindus, less than 5 years educated women and women belonging to poorer quintiles.

DISCUSSION AND CONCLUSION

This paper examines the variation in utilization of reproductive and child care services in the districts of Uttar Pradesh. Assessing utilization of maternity care is essential for achieving the MDGs for maternal health in the state of Uttar Pradesh. Though the utilization of reproductive and child health services has improved in the state, there is huge interstate and social group disparity in utilization of these services. The composite index of reproductive and child health reveals large disparities in utilization of these services across districts. Utilization of these services are concentrated in the districts mainly in the western and central part of the state, especially Budaun, Bahraich, Balrampur, Shrawasti, Shahjahanpur, Farrukhabad, Gonda, Sitapur, Kheri, Hardoi, Fatehpur, Etah, Siddharthnagar, Mainpuri, Kannauj, Pilibhit, Kaushambi, Firozabad, Unnao, Auraiya, Banda, Sant Ravidas Nagar, Chitrakoot and Barabanki districts. Differentials in utilization of services are larger across low and high performing districts. The study found wide disparity in post-natal care and safe delivery across the grouped districts. With increase in age, the gap between low and high performing districts decreases for safe delivery. The differential in utilization of ANC visits is more pronounced in urban areas as compared to rural areas. The differences by educational status are relatively high. As the educational status improve the gap between low and high performing districts widens. The pattern is similar in case of wealth quintiles. Utilization of full immunization services is high in urban areas, among the young, schedule castes, other religious category and more educated mothers as compared to rural areas, schedule tribes, Muslims and illiterate mothers, etc. With respect to contraceptive use, with increase in age the gap between low and high performing districts widens. Differences in utilization of contraceptive are more in rural areas, schedule tribes, Hindus, less than 5 years educated women and women belonging to poorer quintiles.

References

Becker, S., H.P. David, H.G. Ronald, G. Connie and R.E. Black (1993), "The Determinants of use of Maternal and Child Health Services in Metro Cebu, the Philippines," *Health Transition Review,* 30(1), 77-89.

Brauner-Otto, Sarah, R. Axinn, William G. and J. Ghimire Dirgha (2007), "The Spread of Health Services and Fertility Transition", *Demography,* 44(4): 747-70.

Chattopadhyay, A. and T.K. Roy (2005), "Are Urban Poor Doing Better than their Rural Counterpart in India? A Study of Fertility, Family Planning and Health", *Demography India,* 34(2): 299-312.

Dholakia, R.H. (2003), "Regional Disparity in Economic and Human Development in India", *Economic and Political Weekly,* 38(39): 4166-72.

Harttgen, K. and S. Vollmer (2011). "Inequality Decomposition without Income or Expenditure Data: Using an Asset Index to Simulate Household Income. mimeo", UNDP Research paper.

International Institute for Population Sciences and Macro Internationals (1992-2006), National Family Health Survey (1-3) data, Ministry of Health and Family Welfare, Government of India.

International Institute for Population Sciences (2010). District Level Household and Facility Survey–III (2008-09). IIPS Mumbai, Ministry of Health and family welfare, Government of India.

Jha, R. (2004), "Reducing poverty and inequality in India: Has the liberalization helped?" In G.A. Cornia (ed.), *Inequality, Growth and Poverty in an Era of Liberalization and Globalization,* UNU-WIDER Studies in Development Economics, Oxford University Press, New York, for UNU-WIDER, Helsinki: 297-327.

Kumar, A. and S.K. Mohanty (2011), "Intra-urban Differentials in the Utilization of Reproductive Healthcare in India, 1992-2006", *Journal of Urban Health,* Bulletin of the New York Academy of Medicine.

Mohanty, S.K. and P.K. Pathak (2009), "Rich-Poor Gap in Utilization of Reproductive and Child Health Services in India, 1992-2005", *Journal of Biosocial Science,* 41(3): 381-98.

O'Donnell, O., E.V. Doorslaer, A. Wagstaff and M. Lindelow (2008), "Analysing Health Equity using Household Survey Data". URL: http://www.worldbank.org/poverty/ health/data/index.htm.

Ram, F. and A. Singh (2006), "Is Antenatal Care Effective in Improving Maternal Health in Rural Uttar Pradesh? Evidence from a District Level Household Survey", *Journal of Biosocial Science,* 38(4): 433-38.

Registrar General of India (2011a), Provisional Population Total: Paper 1 of 2011, India Series 1, Census of India 2011, Office of the Registrar General and Census Commissioner, Government of India.

Registrar General of India (2010), Sample Registration System Statistical Report 2012, Report No. 1 of 2012, Government of India, New Delhi.

Registrar General of India (2011b), Annual Health Survey Bulletins 2010-11, Office of the Registrar General and Census Commissioner, Government of India, Available At: http://www.censusofindia.gov.in

Singh, N., L. Bhandari, A. Chen and A. Khare (2003), "Regional Inequality in India: A Fresh Look", *Economic and Political Weekly*, 38(11): 1069-73.

Singh, L. and C.H. Singh (2007), "Rich-Poor Gap in Maternal Care: The Case of North-East India." *Asian Population Studies* 3(1), 79–94.

Stephenson, R. and A.O. Tsu (2002), "Contextual Influences on Reproductive Health Service Use in Uttar Pradesh, India", *Studies in Family Planning*, 33(4): 309-20.

7

Availability and Accessibility of Maternal and Child Health Services in Odisha

BIDYADHAR DEHURY

INTRODUCTION

The health and well-being of children and mothers are of great concern in developing countries. Many national and international reproductive health agenda continuously focus to improve the health of children and mothers. The International Conference on Population and Development (ICPD) 1994 was a milestone in the history of women's reproductive health and rights. It emphasised to provide universal access to family planning and sexual and reproductive health services and reproductive rights to women. Similarly, in 2000 the Millennium Summit had set out improvement of maternal health and reduction of child mortality as the two important Millennium Development Goals. Goal-5 of the Millennium Declaration 2000 emphasised on the improvement of maternal health by reducing maternal mortality and increasing proportion of births attended by skilled health personnel. Goal-4 targeted to reduce child mortality by two-thirds between 1990 and

2015 by reducing under-five mortality rate (U-5MR), infant mortality rate (IMR) and increasing proportion of one year old children immunised against measles. Despite these efforts, an estimated 68,000 maternal deaths (Hogan, 2010) and 1.8 million child deaths occurred in 2008 (Black *et al.*, 2010) in developing countries. Studies found that maternal deaths are mainly related to labour, delivery, the immediate post-partum period, and obstetric haemorrhage (Rosmans *et al.*, 2006).

Although India experienced substantial improvement in health care since Independence, the health outcomes remain grim compared to the other countries. The progress in maternal and child health services varies across the states in India. Odisha is recognised as one of the poor, high maternal and infant mortality rate states in India. Though it has experienced significant improvement in health condition during the last decade, the reproductive and child health services remaines low in the state. For example, a remarkable reduction in maternal mortality ratio (MMR) from 303 in 2004-06 to 258 in 2007-09 was observed (RGI, 2009; RGI, 2011). However, Odisha yet remains far from meeting the MDG target of reducing MMR to 109 and below by 2015. According to the SRS 2010, the infant mortality rate (IMR) of Odisha was 61 per 1000 live births, which was significantly higher than the national average of 47 per 1000 live births. The relationship of socioeconomic status and utilisation of reproductive and child health services are well established. A number of studies have found that along with other factors, infrastructure, water, sanitation also play important role in determining reproductive and child health (Black *et al.* 2003; Campbell *et al.*, 2006; Lawn *et al.*, 2005; Koblinsky *et al.*, 2003; Pathmanathan *et al.*, 2006; Rosmans *et al.* 2006). However, facility-based care of reproductive health, infants and children has also not been given enough attention. In this case it is interesting to see the available health services for the reproductive and child health and the extent of accessibility of these available services.

The broad objective of the study is to examine the availability and accessibility of maternal and child health care services in Odisha. The specific objectives of the study are to examine (1) the availability of reproductive and child health services at the sub-centres and primary health centres, and (2) the accessibility of reproductive and child health services at the sub-centres and primary health centres in different regions of Odisha. The paper is organised like this. The first part is an introduction. The second part discuses the materials and methods employed in the analysis. Part three presents the results and findings; and lastly the fourth section is a concluding one.

MATERIALS AND METHODS

The study has used the unit data from District Level Household and Facility Survey (DLHS-3), 2007-08. The survey collected data at district level on various aspects of reproductive and child health care utilisation, and accessibility of health facility. The analysis is carried out for the state of Odisha. Facility data (sub-centre and primary health centre) have been used in the analysis. Information about the availability of human resources and physical infrastructure was collected from the sub-centres (SCs) and Primary Health Centres

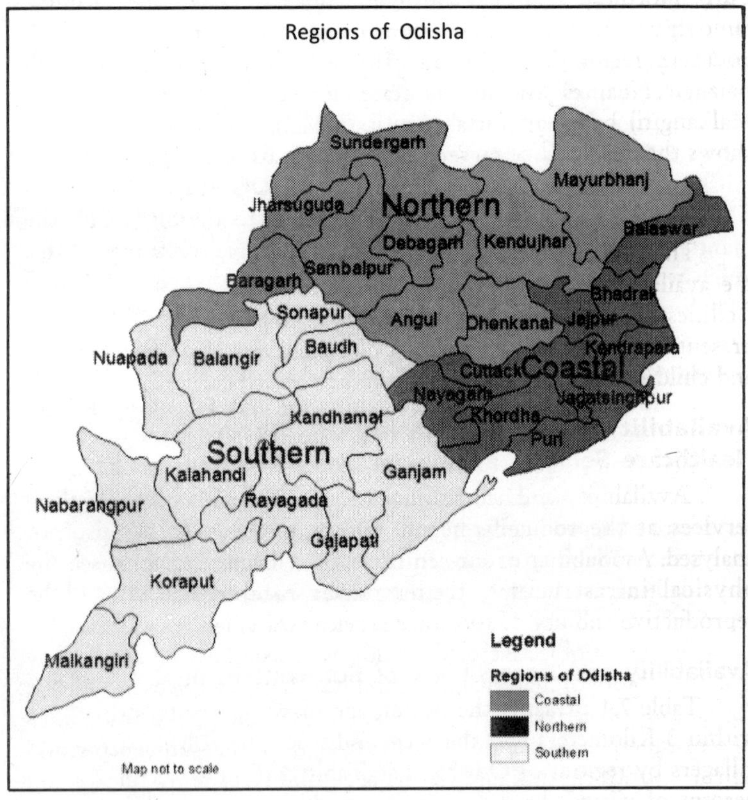

Figure 7.1 : Map Showing Districts and Regional Divisions of Odisha

(PHCs). The data regarding accessibility in terms of transportation facility to the health centres, functionality of the available resources were also collected from SCs and PHCs.

Descriptive statistics are used to present the differentials in availability and accessibility of reproductive and health services by regions of Odisha at sub-centres and primary health centres. Chi-square test and one-way ANOVA are used to compare the significant differences among the regions of the state. We have categorized the districts of Odisha into three regions for comparison purposes (Appendix 1), namely, Coastal region (Balasore, Bhadrak, Kendrapara, Jagatsinghpur, Cuttack, Jajpur, Nayagarh, Khurdha, and Puri), Northern region (Bargarh, Jharsuguda, Sambalpur, Deogarh, Sundargarh, Keonjhar, Mayurbhanj, Dhenkanal, and Anugul), and Southern region (Ganjam, Gajapati, Kandhamal, Baudh, Sonapur, Balangir, Nuapada, Kalahandi, Rayagada, Nowrangpur, Koraput, and Malkangiri) based on the NSS classification of regions. Figure 7.1 shows the districts and the regional classification of Odisha.

RESULTS

The results are presented in two sections. Section one presents the availability and accessibility of maternal and child health care facilities at sub-centres in Odisha and various regions. Section two presents the results about the availability and accessibility of maternal and child health care services at primary health centres in the state.

Availability and Accessibility of Maternal and Child Healthcare Services at Sub-centres by Regions of Odisha

Availability and accessibility of maternal and child healthcare services at the sub-centres and different regions of Odisha are analysed. Availability of sub-centres in the villages, human resources, physical infrastructure, training ever received by the ANM, reproductive and child healthcare services provided are examined.

Availability and Accessibility of Sub-centres in the Villages

Table 7.1 presents the percentage of villages with Sub-centers within 3 Kilometers and the accessibility of the Sub-centers to the villagers by regions of Odisha. The Table depicts that in Odisha 73 percent of villages have Sub-centers within a distance of 3 kms of radius. About one-third of villages could access the sub-centres throughout the year and the other villages have several difficulties in accessing the health centres. Analyzing by various regions of Odisha, it was found that in the northern part a higher percentage of villages (73.5 percent) had sub-centres within 3 kms of distance compared to 73.3 percent in the southern and 71 percent in the coastal regions. However, in the coastal region, the sub-centres were accessible to a higher percentage of villages (48 percent) compared to 26.2 percent in southern and 22.5 percent in northern regions.

TABLE 7.1

Percentage of Villages with Sub-Centers within 3 Kms and the Accessible Throughout the Year by Regions of Odisha, 2006-07

Regions	*Percent of villages within 3 kms from SCs*	*Sub-centres accessible throughout the year to the villages*	*N*
Coastal	70.7	47.9	2588
Northern	73.5	22.5	1947
Southern	73.3	26.2	3493
Odisha	72.5	32.4	8028

Availability of Human Resources in the Sub-centres

Figure 7.2 shows the availability of human resources at the Sub-centres by regions of Odisha. In Odisha, 78 percent of Sub-centres had ANM or female health workers and the male health workers were available in 60 percent of the Sub-centres. The coastal region of Odisha had higher percentage of Sub-centres with an ANM/female

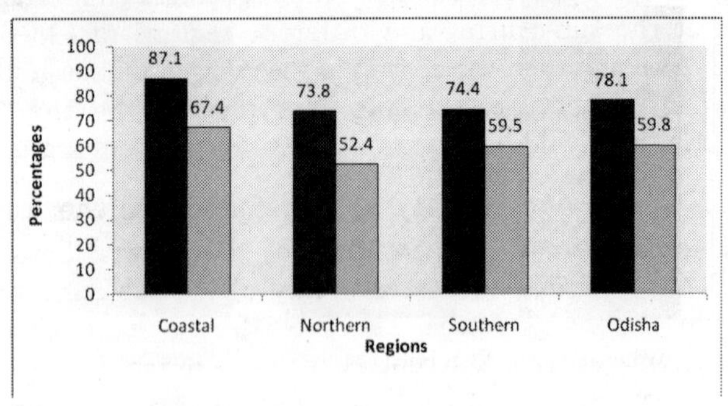

Figure 7.2 : Availability of Human Resources at Sub-centres in different Regions of Odisha, 2006-07

health worker and a male health worker and it was low in the northern region. For example, in the Coastal region more than 87 percent of SCs had an ANM/female health worker compared to 74.4 percent in southern region and 73.8 percent in northern region. Similarly, the coastal region (67.4 percent) had higher percentage of SCs with a male health worker compared to 59.5 percent in southern and 52.4 percent in the northern regions.

Availability of Physical Infrastructures at Sub-Centres

Availability of water supply, sanitation facility and power supply in the sub-centres is shown in Figure 7.3. It is found that in Odisha as whole, three-fourth of the sub-centres have water supply, 30 percent have toilet facility and 67 percent have electricity supply. The provision of sanitation facility in the sub-centres remains low in Odisha. Further, the southern region has higher percentage of sub-centers with water supply (11 percentage points higher compared to the coastal region and 3 percentage points higher compared to the northern region) compared to the other regions. For example, in the southern region, 80 percent of the sub-centers have water supply compared to only 69 and 77 percent in the coastal and northern regions respectively. The southern region has also higher percentage of sub-centers (70 percent) with power supply compared to the coastal (65.2 percent) and northern regions (65.4 percent). However, with regard to the provision of toilet facility in the sub-centres, the southern region lags behind the coastal and northern regions. For

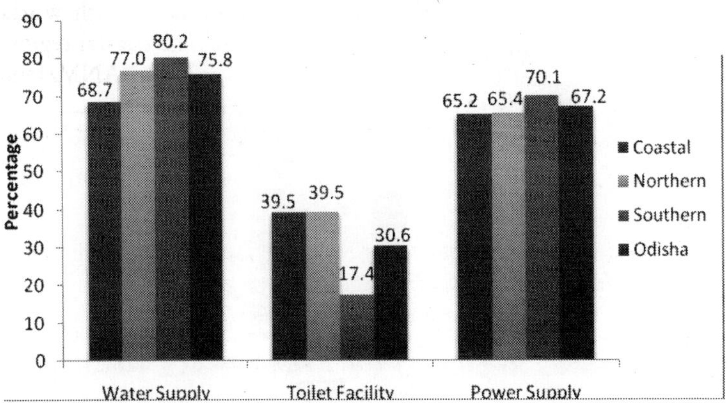

Figure 7.3 : Availability of Water Supply, Sanitation Facility and Power Supply at Sub-Centers by Regions of Odisha, 2006-07

instance, the coastal and northern regions have 39.5 percent of sub-centers with toilet facilities compared to only 17.4 percent in the southern region.

Figure 7.4 presents the percentage of sub-centers having separate labour room and deliveries in labour room by regions of Odisha. In Odisha, only 13.5 percent sub-centers have separate labour room for conducting deliveries. Among these sub-centers only 39.9 percent of sub-centers conducted deliveries in the separate labour room. The northern region has highest percentage of sub-centers that have separate labour room and conducted deliveries in the labour room. For example, in the northern region 27.5 percent of sub-centers have separate labour room compared to 10.3 percent in coastal region and 5.7 percent in southern region. A similar pattern is found in case of deliveries conducted in labour room with highest in northern region and least in southern region. For example, about half of the sub-centers in northern region conducted deliveries in separate labour room compared to 36 percent in coastal region and one-fourth sub-centers in southern region.

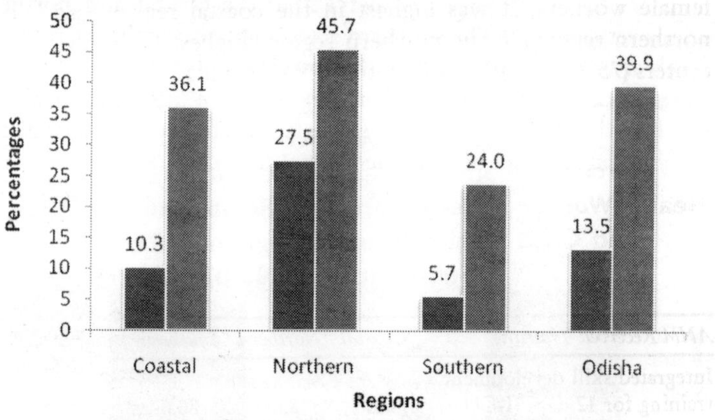

Figure 7.4 : Availability of Separate Labour Room and Conducted Deliveries in Labour Room at Sub-centers by Regions of Odisha, 2006-07

TRAINING RECEIVED BY ANM/FEMALE HEALTH WORKERS

Table 7.2 provides the percentages of sub-centres in which the ANM/female health workers received training on reproductive and child health. It was found that in 87.5 percent sub-centers ANM/ female health workers have received integrated skill development training for 12 days (RCH-1). Among the regions of Odisha, in 91.8 percent of the sub-centers ANM/female health workers have received integrated skill development training for 12 days (RCH-1) in Coastal region compared to 86.6 percent in southern region and 83.4 percent in northern region. The chi square test shows significant differences among the regions in integrated skill development training among ANM/female health workers. In 71 percent sub-centers the ANM/ female health workers received Intra Uterine Device (IUD) insertion training ever. The northern region has highest percentage of sub-centers (76.2 percent) in which the ANM/female health workers received IUD insertion training compared to 70.1 percent in the southern region and 68.5 percent in the coastal region. The chi-square test shows the regional differences are not statistical significant. It was also found that in 86.5 percent of the sub-centers the ANM/female health workers received Integrated Management of Neonatal and Childhood Illness (IMNCI) training. A statistical difference was found among the regions in receiving IMNCI training by ANM/ female workers. It was highest in the coastal region and least in northern region. In the northern region, highest percentage of sub-centers (75.8 percent) in which the ANM/female health workers have

TABLE 7.2

Percentage and Chi-Square Test of ANM/Female Health Worker Received Training Related to Reproductive and Child Health Ever by Regions of Odisha at Sub-Centres, 2006-07

ANM Received Training	*Coastal*	*Northern*	*Southern*	*Odisha*	*Chi2*
Integrated skill development training for 12 days (RCH-1)	91.8	83.4	86.6	87.5	0.015
Intra Uterine Device (IUD) Insertion training	68.5	76.2	70.1	71.2	0.135
Integrated Management of Neonatal and Childhood Illnesses (IMNCI) training	87.8	85.0	86.5	86.5	0.028
Skilled Birth Attendant training	63.1	75.8	72.7	70.3	0.004
Immunization training	87.8	85.0	86.5	86.5	0.646

received skilled birth attendant training compared to 72.7 percent in the southern region and least in coastal region (63.1 percent). The chi-square test shows significant differences among the regions of Odisha. The coastal region has highest percentage (87.8 percent) of sub-centers in which the ANM/female health worker received immunization training compared to 86.5 percent in the southern region and 85 percent in the northern region.

REPRODUCTIVE AND CHILD HEALTH SERVICES PROVIDED AT SUB-CENTRES

Table 7.3 presents the average number of services related to RCH provided during the last one month at sub-centers by regions of Odisha. It was found that the mean number of pregnant women

TABLE 7.3

Average Number of Services Related to RCH Provided in Last One Month and One-Way ANOVA Test at Sub Centers By Regions of Odisha, 2006-07

RCH Services Provided	*Coastal*	*Northern*	*Southern*	*Odisha*	*One way ANOVA*
No. of pregnant women registered for ANC	14.4	14.3	11.6	13.2	F (2.74), P (0.065)
No. of Hemoglobin estimation tests	0.9	8.1	0.9	3.1	F (2.94), P(0.053)
No. of Urine test for presence of Protein	0.5	4.2	0.5	1.6	F(1.52), P(0.220)
No. of Urine test for presence of sugar	0.3	4.1	0.4	1.5	F(1.60), P(0.203)
No. of deliveries conducted at Sub-Centre	0.7	2.1	0.4	1.0	F(5.31), P(0.005)
No. of post-natal care contacts made	7.7	6.2	5.5	6.4	F(10.13), P(0.000)
No. of new-born care provided	7.2	5.5	4.9	5.8	F(14.38), P(0.000)
No. of children treated for Diarrhea	5.8	7.4	8.0	7.2	F(3.13), P(0.044)
No. of Immunization sessions conducted	4.9	3.7	3.5	4.0	F(4.43), P(0.012)
No. of infants and children immunized	73.2	59.8	43.8	57.4	F(7.91), P(0.000)

TABLE 7.4

Average Number of Family Planning and Contraception/ Other Services Provided and One-Way ANOVA Test at Sub-centers by Regions of Odisha, 2006-07

Family planning and contraception services	*Coastal*	*Northern*	*Southern*	*Odisha*	*One-way ANOVA*
No. of Oral Pills users	36.7	26.0	18.5	26.2	F(30.35), P(0.000)
No. of Condom users	38.6	34.3	24.2	31.5	F(4.52), P(0.011)
No. of women given EC Pills	5.7	13.4	5.1	7.7	F(10.24), P(0.000)
No. of IUD insertion cases	6.6	6.4	5.1	5.9	F(0.75), P(0.474)
No. of Sterilization cases accompanied	5.5	9.5	5.5	6.6	F(5.10), P(0.006)
No. of beneficiaries of Janani Suraksha Yojana (JSY)	5.9	10.1	4.5	6.5	F(13.72), P(0.000)

registered for Ante Natal Care (ANC) was 13.2 during the last one month in Odisha. It was highest in the coastal region (14.4) followed by the northern region (14.3) and least in southern region (13.2). The one way ANOVA test (F=2.74, p=0.065) shows a significant difference in the mean differences among the regions of Odisha.

Services related to family planning, contraception and other services provided during the last one month at sub-centers by regions in Odisha are shown in Table 7.4. It is observed that in Odisha the services related to family planning and contraception provided to women at sub-centers was low. For example, the average number of oral pills users were 26 in Odisha. Among the regions, in the coastal region 37 users followed by 26 in the northern region and least in southern region with 19 users of oral pills. Similarly, the average number of condom users was higher in the coastal region (38 users) followed by 34 users in northern region and least in southern region (24 users). However, the northern region had higher number of women given emergency contraceptive pills, and had higher number of beneficiaries of Janani Suraksha Yojana (JSY). The southern region had least average number of family planning and contraception users at sub-centers compared to the other regions. The one way ANOVA test shows significant for all services provided at sub-centers except for IUD insertion.

MATERNAL AND INFANT DEATHS

Table 7.5 provides the average number of maternal, new-born and infant deaths occurred during the last one year at sub-centers by regions of Odisha. During the last one year, the average number of maternal deaths that took place at sub-centers was 1.36. Among the regions, it was found that the southern region had worst experience in these indicators with highest number of maternal and infant deaths at sub-centers. The coastal region had less number of maternal, new-born and infant deaths at sub-centers. The northern region had highest number of new-born deaths during last one year. For example, in the northern region the average number of maternal deaths occurred during last one-year. was 0.95 followed by 1.02 in the coastal part and 2.02 in southern region. Similarly, the average number of infant deaths was 3.33 in the southern regions followed by 2.59 in northern region and least (2.11) in coastal regions. However, the northern region had highest number of new-born deaths with 2.81 compared to 2.7 in southern region and 1.85 in coastal region. One way ANOVA test shows significant among the regions of Odisha in differences of maternal, new-born and infant deaths during the last one year.

TABLE 7.5

Average Number of Maternal Deaths, New-Born Deaths and Infant Deaths Occurred during Last One Year and One-Way ANOVA at Sub-centers by Regions of Odisha, 2006-07

Regions	*Average number of maternal deaths during one year*	*Average number of new born deaths during last year*	*Average number of infant deaths during last year*
Coastal	1.02	1.85	2.11
Northern	0.95	2.81	2.59
Southern	2.02	2.70	3.33
Odisha	1.36	2.47	2.75
One-way ANOVA test	F(2.56), P(0.080)	F(7.22), P(0.001)	F(11.78), P(0.000)

AVAILABILITY AND ACCESSIBILITY OF REPRODUCTIVE AND CHILD HEALTH SERVICES AT PRIMARY HEALTH CENTRES (PHCS)

Availability, Connectivity and Accessibility of PHCs

The availability of PHCs near the villages and the connectivity and accessibility is important for the utilization of health care services, especially for the reproductive and child health care services. Table 7.6 provides the percentage of villages having PHCs within 10 Kms and the connectivity by regions of Odisha. In Odisha, 78 percent of villages had PHC within 10 Kms. The distance varies by regions. In the southern part the highest percentage of villages (78 percent) had PHC with 10 Kms followed by 76 percent in northern region and 75 percent in the coastal region. It shows that the maximum villages in southern region had PHCs nearer to the villages while minimum in the coastal regions. However, the connectivity and accessibility of the PHCs were low. For example, the PHCs in Odisha were accessible throughout the year only to 41 percent of the villages and connected with *pucca* road to only 36 percent of villages. It was found that only 38 percent villages had bus or private vehicles to reach PHCs. It shows that connectivity and accessibility was very low in Odisha. The connectivity and accessibility varies by regions of Odisha. The coastal region stands relatively in a better situation compared to the northern and southern regions. The Table clearly shows that the southern region had worse connectivity and accessibility of the PHCs. For example, the PHCs in southern region were accessible to only 31 percent of villages compared to the 55 percent of villages in coastal region. In the northern region only 24

TABLE 7.6

Percentage of Villages within 10 kms. from PHCs and Connectivity by Different Regions of Odisha, 2006-07

Regions	*Percent of villages within 10 kms. from PHC*	*PHC accessible throughout the year*	*Connected with pucca road*	*Bus/Pvt. Vehicle*	*N*
Coastal	74.8	55.3	51.5	52.5	1,093
Northern	75.7	34.0	24.0	30.6	847
Southern	83.3	30.8	30.5	30.1	1,071
Odisha	78.1	40.6	36.3	38.4	3011

percent were connected with *pucca* road to the PHCs followed by 31 and 52 percent of the villages in the southern and coastal parts of the state respectively.

Availability of Human Resources at PHCs

Table 7.7 provides the availability of human resources at PHCs of Odisha. In Odisha, more than 80 percent of PHCs had a medical officer. About 53 percent and 58 percent of PHCs had a lady medical officer and staff nurse respectively. More than 40 percent of PHCs did not have a male health assistant and laboratory technician. The availability of human resources at the PHCs in Odisha varies region. The southern region had higher percentage of PHCs with the availability of human resources compared to the northern and coastal regions. For instance, in southern region 66 percent of the PHCs had lady medical officers compared to 64 percent in northern region and the lowest in coastal region (32 percent). In northern region 69 percent of PHCs had staff nurse compared to 67 percent in southern region and 40 percent in coastal region. In the southern region 89 percent of PHCs had ANF/female health worker followed by 88 and 86 percent in the coastal regions respectively. The chi-square test shows that the difference in availability of human resources at the PHCs in regions of Odisha are statistically significant.

TABLE 7.7

Availability of Human Resources at PHCs by Regions of Odisha, 2006-07

Availability of human resources at PHC	*Coastal*	*Northern*	*Southern*	*Odisha*	*Chi2*
Medical Officer	68.9	87.4	86.3	80.4	0.000
Lady Medical Officer	31.7	63.7	66.1	53.2	0.000
Staff Nurse	39.5	68.9	67.3	57.9	0.000
Pharmacist	91.6	95.6	98.2	95.1	0.019
LHV/Health Assistant	71.9	83	76.8	76.8	0.075
Male Health Assistant	50.3	65.9	69.6	61.7	0.001
Laboratory Technician	43.1	72.6	71.4	61.7	0.000
ANM/Female Health Worker	86.2	88.1	88.7	87.7	0.774
N	167	135	168	470	

Availability of Physical Infrastructure at PHCs

Table 7.8 presents availability of physical infrastructure in PHCs of Odisha. It was found that 90 percent of the PHCs had designated government building. It varies from 89 percent in coastal region to 92 percent in the southern region. The southern region had the highest percentage of PHCs with the water supply and northern region had highest percentage of PHCs with electricity supply and toilet facilities. For example, in southern 88 percent of PHCs had water supply compared to 82 percent in northern region and 78 percent in coastal region. Similarly, 86 percent, 85 percent, and 82 percent of the PHCs had electric supply in the northern, southern and coastal regions respectively in case of toilet facilities at the PHCs, the southern region was standing far behind compared to the northern and coastal region. For example, in the southern region only 30 percent of PHCs had toilet facilities compared to 44 percent of PHCs in northern and coastal regions. The chi-square test shows that the differences in toilet facilities at PHCs are significant at 95 percent confidence interval.

The availability of labour room at PHCs in Odisha was quite low as only 33 percent of PHCs had labour room and in 85 percent of PHCs the labour rooms were currently in use. The coastal region had highest percentage of PHCs with availability of labour room compared to the northern and southern regions. However, in the southern region the highest percentage of labour rooms were currently in use. For example, in coastal region 36 percent of PHCs had labour room and 80 percent of labour rooms were currently in use. In southern region 29 percent of PHCs had labour room and 92 percent of labour rooms were currently in use. (Table 7.8)

TABLE 7.8

Availability of Physical Infrastructure at PHCs by Regions of Odisha, 2006-07

Physical infrastructure	*Coastal*	*Northern*	*Southern*	*Odisha*	*CHI*
Designated government building	89.2	86.7	92.9	89.8	0.200
Water supply	77.8	81.5	87.5	82.3	0.065
Electricity supply	82.0	85.9	85.1	84.3	0.607
Toilet facility	44.3	44.4	30.4	39.4	0.012
Labour room available	35.9	35.6	28.6	33.2	0.283
Labour room currently in use	79.4	85.7	91.8	85.1	0.183

TRAINING RECEIVED BY MEDICAL OFFICERS AT PHCS

Table 7.9 provides the percentage of PHCs in which any medical officer received training related to reproductive and child health services. The results show that in southern region the highest percentage of PHCs had a medical officer who had received training related to reproductive and child health services as compared to the coastal and northern regions. In southern region 88 percent of PHCs had a medical officer who received integrated skill development training for 12 days compared to 81 percent in coastal region and only 63 percent in northern region. In southern region 82 percent of PHCs had a medical officer who received immunization training compared to 74 percent in coastal region and 68 percent in northern region. Similarly, in southern region 78 percent of PHCs had a medical officer who received medical termination of pregnancy (MTP) training compared to 59 percent in coastal region and 55

TABLE 7.9

Received Training by any Medical Officer Ever at PHC

	Coastal	*Northern*	*Southern*	*Odisha*	*Chi2*
Integrated skill development training for 12 days	80.7	63.2	88.2	78.2	0.000
Immunization training	74.2	67.9	82.0	75.1	0.020
NSV-Non Scalpel Vasectomy training	51.6	54.5	75.6	61.0	0.000
MTP-Medical Termination of Pregnancy training	59.4	55.2	77.6	64.7	0.000
Reproductive Tract Infection/ Sexually Transmitted Infection (RTI/STI) training	76.1	61.2	82.6	74.0	0.000
Management of obstetric complications (BEmOCBasic Emergency Obstetric Care) training	51.6	50.8	74.5	59.6	0.000
IMNCI- Integrated Management of Neonatal and Childhood Illnesses training	60.0	52.2	77.6	64.0	0.000
Skilled Birth Attendant training	60.0	54.5	77.6	64.7	0.000
N	155	134	161	450	

percent in northern region. In southern region 75 percent of PHCs had a medical officer who received integrated management of neonatal and childhood illness training compared to 60 percent in coastal region and 52 percent in northern region. More than 75 percent of PHCs in southern region had a medical officer who received skilled birth attendant training compared to 60 percent in coastal region and less than 55 percent in northern region. The differences in training regarding reproductive and child health at PHCs by any medical officer ever is statistical significant among the different regions of Odisha.

CONCLUSION

The availability of physical infrastructure, human resources and labour room facility for conducting delivery both at the sub-centers and primary health centers was low in Odisha, and it was found very low in the southern region. Accessibility of both sub-centers and PHCs in southern part of Odisha was quite low mainly due to unavailability of *pucca* road connectivity and low transportation facility. As a result a number of PHCs were not accessible throughout the year. Though, the medical officers received training, reproductive and child health services provided at both sub-centers and PHCs were quite low and lowest in southern region compared to other regions. The family planning services provided by sub-centers and primary health centers was low in Odisha and the lowest in southern region. Low level of accessibility of reproductive and child health services leads to a high level of maternal, new born and infant deaths (specially at southern region). It needs to increase the physical infrastructure and human resources as well as improvement of accessing the existing resources at the health center to improve the health of both mothers and children.

REFERENCES

Black, R.E., *et al.* (2010), "Global, Regional and National Causes of Child Mortality in 2008: A Systematic Analysis", *Lancet*; 375: 1969-87.

Black, R.E., S.S. Morris, J. Bryce (2003), "Where and why are 10 Million Children Dying Every Year?" *Lancet*; 361: 2226-34.

Campbell, O.M.R., W.J. Graham (2006), "Strategies for Reducing Maternal Mortality: Getting on with What Works", *Lancet*; 368, 1284-99.

Hogan, M.C., *et al.* (2010), "Maternal Mortality for 181 Countries, 1980-2008: a Systematic thematic of Progress towards Millennium Development Goal 5", *Lancet*; 375: 1609-23.

Koblinsky, M.A. (2003), "Reducing Maternal Mortality: Learning from Bolivia, China, Egypt, Honduras, Indonesia, Jamaica, and Zimbabwe", Washington, DC: World Bank.

Lawn, J.E., S. Cousens and J. Zupan (2005), "4 Million Neonatal Deaths: When? Where? Why?" *Lancet*; 365: 891–900.

Pathmanathan, I.J. Liljestrand and J.M. Martins (2003), "Investing in Maternal Health in Malaysia and Sri Lanka", Washington, DC: World Bank.

Registrar General and Census Commissioner of India (2012), *Sample Registration System Statistical Report, 2010,* New Delhi: Ministry of Home Affairs, Government of India.

Registrar General of India (2011), *Special Bulletin on Maternal Mortality in India, 2007-09*, New Delhi: Ministry of Home Affairs, Government of India.

Registrar General of India (2019), *Special Bulletin on Maternal Mortality in India, 2004-06*, New Delhi: Ministry of Home Affairs, Government of India.

Ronsmans, C., W.J. Graham (2006), "Maternal Mortality: Who, When, Where, and Why", *Lancet*; 368: 1189-200.

APPENDIX I
Regional Divisions of Odisha

Coastal Region	*Northern Region*	*Southern Region*
Balasore	Bargarh	Ganjam
Bhadrak	Jharsuguda	Gajapati
Kendrapara	Sambalpur	Kandhamal
Jagatsinghpur	Deogarh	Baudh
Cuttack	Sundargarh	Sonapur
Jajpur	Keonjhar	Balangir
Nayagarh	Mayurbhanj	Nuapada
Khurdha	Dhenkanal	Kalahandi
Puri	Anugul	Rayagada
		Nowrangpur
		Koraput
		Malkangiri

Note : The regional classification was based on NSS classification of regions.

8

Prevalence of Obstetric Morbidity in Odisha

BINOD BIHARI JENA AND UMA SHANKAR MAJHI

INTRODUCTION

Maternal health issues continues to be at the forefront of global and national health policies. Reduction of maternal death has received high priority especially in view of the increased attention to Millennium Development Goal-5 (MDG-5) which calls for three-fourth reduction in Maternal Mortality Ratio (MMR) by 2015. In spite of all efforts, the progress in reducing maternal mortality is slow. According to an estimate globally about 358,000 mothers die each year from causes related to pregnancy complications, unsafe abortions and childbirth (WHO, 2010). But the reduction in maternal deaths is a major concern in developing countries as almost 99 percent of the maternal deaths occur in these countries. India is also one of the high maternal mortality countries ranking 54th from bottom and the motility level was even higher than many of its neighboring countries such as, Nepal, Bhutan, China and Sri Lanka (CIA, 2010). A current estimate shows that in India more than 56,000 women have died in the year 2010 due to pregnancy related causes (World Bank, 2012). In India, the MDG-5 has set the target to reduce the maternal deaths to 109 per one lakh live births by 2015, but the latest estimate of 2009 shows that maternal mortality ratio was still high at 212 per one lakh live births (RGI, 2011).

The World Health Organization defines maternal death as, "the death of a woman while pregnant or within 42 days of termination of pregnancy, irrespective of the duration and site of the pregnancy, from any cause related to or aggravated by the pregnancy or its management but not from accidental or incidental causes" (WHO, 2005). The causes like haemorrhage and hypertensive disorder are the major contributors to maternal mortality (Khan *et al.*, 2006). There are both direct and indirect causes of maternal mortality and morbidity. A majority of the maternal deaths occur due to direct causes whereas indirect causes account for only one-fifth of the maternal deaths (Ransom and Yinger, 2002). Maternal causes have been found to be more common among women in the reproductive ages in many countries, particularly in the developing world. In the developing countries, pregnancy and child birth-related complications are the leading cause of disability among women aged 15-44 years. It was estimated that 15 to 30 percent of women suffer from chronic illness or injuries as a result of their pregnancy (UNFPA, 2002). The leading cause of death in Africa and Asia was haemorrhage, whereas hypertensive disorders and abortion were responsible for most of the deaths in Latin America and Caribbean countries. Similarly, deaths due to sepsis were higher in Africa, Asia, Latin America and Caribbean countries compared to the developed countries (Khan *et al.*, 2006). Most of the maternal deaths which are caused by hemorrhage, obstructed labour, infection (sepsis), unsafe abortion, and eclampsia (pregnancy induce hypertension) can be saved if affordable and good quality obstetric care is available for them by the health care system (Waterstone *et al.*, 2001).

The World Development Report estimated that 18 percent burden of disease is due to maternal causes and many women suffer from severe morbidities during their pregnancy and child birth (Padma, 2004). The leading cause of maternal deaths is the obstetric morbidity that arises due to pregnancy and child birth. The WHO defines obstetric morbidity as "morbidity in a woman who has been pregnant (regardless of site or duration of the pregnancy) resulting from any cause related to or aggravated by the pregnancy or its management but not from accidental or incidental causes". Pregnancy constitutes a high risk of morbidity and mortality due to associated physiological stress and it is more severe in developing countries where the risk of dying during pregnancy is 10 to 20 times higher than that in the developed countries (Padma, 2004). A small perspective study conducted in a village of India reported that there were 16.5 percent pregnancy-related morbidities for every maternal death (Dutta, *et al.*, 1980). Another study in South India revealed that, the prevalence of maternal morbidities were higher among rural women and these are caused by combination of individual, household, community, medical as well as nutritional factors (Padma, 2004). According to a study, lack of personal hygiene and abortions are major causes of reproductive ill-health and the study suggests the need for strategic intervention to deal with the problem (Garg *et al.*, 2001).

A cross-sectional retrospective study in rural areas of West Bengal revealed the impact of selected socio-demographic factors on reported obstetric morbidity during antepartum and postpartum periods. The study found that more than half of the women during their most recent live births reported at least one morbidity. Mothers with higher levels of education reported fewer overall problems and factors such as age and pregnancy order affect obstetric morbidity differently in different religious groups. More mothers reported postpartum than antepartum problems, and very few sought treatment (Mukhopadhyay *et al*, 2002). The risk factors of severe maternal morbidity include maternal age above 34 years, social exclusion, hypertension, post-partum hemorrhage, induction of labour and caesarian delivery. A Mumbai based study found that working women and women with high income are more likely to report reproductive problems compared to women not working and women with low income (Parikh *et al.*, 1980). Another study shows that age of mother, level of education, religion, and standard of living are significantly related to obstetric morbidity. In Madhya Pradesh, women in the age group of 25-34 and above 35 years were found to be less likely to have obstetric morbidity compared to women in the age group 15-24. In Kerala, Muslim women were found to be having higher likelihood of obstetric morbidity compared to Hindu women. Similarly, educated women reported higher likelihood of obstetric morbidity compared to uneducated women (Sontakke *et al*, 2009).

In India obstetric morbidity also continued to be one of the leading causes of maternal death (Singh, *et al.*, 2012). Millions of women in India suffer from complications associated with child bearing and a large proportion of maternal deaths and morbidities are preventable if proper healthcare, especially obstetric care facilities are made available (Bhatia and Cleland, 1996). Among the various states of India, Odisha continue to remain one of the high maternal mortality states. In 2009, it ranked 6th with a maternal mortality ratio of 258 among the 15 major states of India (RGI, 2011). Similarly, the state's other health indicators are also very low. In 2011, Odisha ranked second in IMR and third in under-five mortality rate among the major states of India, in spite of state's low fertility level (close to replacement level of fertility) both child and maternal mortality rates are very high. In Odisha, maternal morbidity is a serious concern as most of the women delay to treat obstetric morbidity because of lack of better health care facilities and women's ignorance about serious obstetric illness (Planning Commission, Odisha, 2006). Therefore, this backdrop there is a need to study on various aspects of obstetric morbidity in a socio-economically and demographically backward state like Odisha. This study aims to measure the prevalence of obstetric morbidity in Odisha and to study the relationship between socio-economic and demographic factors with obstetric morbidity among the currently married women.

METHODOLOGY

This study is based on the National Family Health Survey-3 (NFHS-3) data which was conducted in 2005-06 by the International Institute for Population Sciences (IIPS), Mumbai and Macro International under the support of the Government of India. It provides important information on fertility, family planning, maternal and child health, morbidity and mortality, and socio-economic conditions for India and all states. The survey is based on nationally representative sample of 124,385 women in the age group of 15-49 years. The present study focuses on only currently married women having at least one birth during the last five years preceding the survey. For obstetric morbidity, NFHS-3 collected information on various health problems faced by the women during pregnancy and two months after delivery for the most recent birth during five years preceding the survey. Mothers were asked whether at any time during the pregnancy they have experienced problems such as, difficulty with vision during daylight; night blindness; convulsions not from fever; swelling of legs, body, or face; excessive fatigue; and vaginal bleeding. Similarly, women were asked if they had excessive vaginal bleeding or very high fever (both are symptoms of possible post-partum complications) at any time during last two months after birth of her most recent child.

The variables 'pregnancy complications' and 'post-partum complications' are computed by clubbing six pregnancy related problems and two post-partum related problems mentioned above. The outcome variable 'obstetric morbidity' is computed by clubbing both the variables 'pregnancy complications' and 'post partum complications'. In order to get a clear picture about the pattern of obstetric morbidity, the mean number of obstetric morbidity corresponding to women's background characteristics is also calculated. A logistic regression analysis has been carried out to study the net effect of various socio-economic and demographic factors on obstetric morbidity. The dependent variable 'obstetric morbidity' is dichotomously categorized ('obstetric morbidity'=1, 'no obstetric morbidity'=0). The independent variables taken into the regression analysis are age of mother at the time of child's birth, number of children ever born, religion, caste, educational status, place of residence, working status, wealth quintile and status of antenatal care utilization.

RESULTS AND DISCUSSIONS

Types of Obstetric Morbidity and their Prevalence

Obstetric morbidity is one of the major causes of maternal death. In India, every year a large number of women suffer from obstetric problems due to lack of education and low economic status as they affect significantly women's health (Bhatia and Cleland, 1996). These apart, there are many other factors at individual, household and community level responsible for high prevalence of obstetric morbidity. An analysis has been carried out from NFHS-3 data set to show the prevalence of various types of obstetric morbidity in India as well as in Odisha (Figure 8.1 and Table 8.1).

Table 8.1 shows the various types of obstetric morbidity and their prevalence in Odisha and India. From the Table 8.1 it is clear that 'excessive fatigue' was the most common problem during pregnancy accounting for 50 percent of the total women in Odisha. Similarly, swelling of the legs, body or face was the next common problem faced by nearly one-fourth of total women in Odisha. The corresponding figures for India were more or less same. Like as, in Odisha nearly 60 percent of women had any pregnancy-related problem compared with 57.5 percent in India. The prevalence of both the post-partum complication problems was also lower in Odisha compared to India. Similarly, in Odisha the prevalence of any

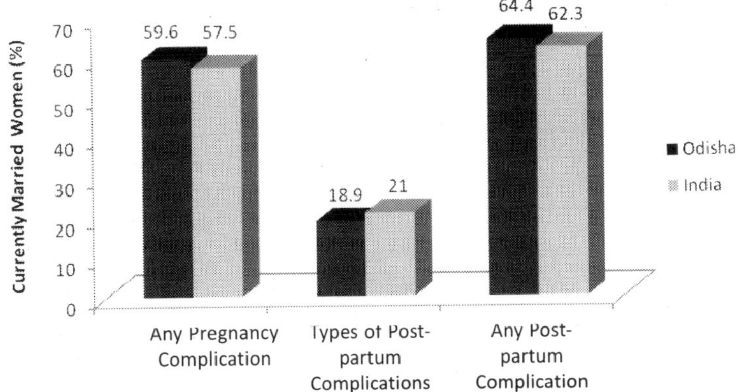

Figure 8.1 : Prevalence of Obstetric Morbidity in India and Odisha, 2005-06

TABLE 8.1

Prevalence of Obstetric Morbidity among Currently Married Women in Odisha and India, 2005-06

Types of Obstetric Complication	*Odisha (N=1355)*	*India (N=39677)*
Types of Pregnancy Complications		
Difficulty with vision during daylight	4.10	6.3
Night blindness	9.90	8.9
Convulsions not from fever	14.5	10.3
Swelling of the legs, body, or face	24.2	25.2
Excessive fatigue	50.0	47.8
Vaginal bleeding	2.70	4.40
Any Pregnancy Complication	59.6	57.5
Types of Post-partum Complications		
Massive vaginal bleeding	10.9	12.4
Very high fever	11.5	13.5
Any Post-partum Complication	18.9	21.0
Any Obstetric Morbidity	64.4	62.3

postpartum complication problem (18.9 percent) was lower than India (21 percent). But, the prevalence of any obstetric morbidity which includes either pregnancy complication or postpartum complication was higher in Odisha (64.4 percent) as compared to national average (62.3 percent).

TABLE 8.2
Mean Number of Obstetric Morbidity among Currently Married Women by Background Characteristics

Background Characteristics	*Mean number of obstetric morbidity (all women)*	*No. of women*	*Mean number of obstetric morbidity (women with at least one morbidity)*	*No. of women*
Age of Mother at Child's Birth				
<15-25 yrs	1.28	838	1.98	543
25-35 yrs	1.24	452	1.98	282
35-49 yrs	1.57	48	2.30	33
Children Ever Born				
1	1.25	416	1.86	279
2	1.19	384	1.86	245
3	1.27	234	2.10	141
4 & above	1.42	305	2.25	195
Religion				
Hindu	1.27	1289	1.98	824
Others	1.52	42	2.24	29
Caste				
SC	1.54	243	2.22	168
ST	1.15	352	2.02	200
BC	1.14	362	1.83	226
General	1.35	368	1.94	256
Education				
No education	1.24	601	2.13	349
Primary	1.48	235	2.11	166
Secondary & above	1.22	502	1.79	343
Place of Residence				
Rural	1.31	1138	2.02	735
Urban	1.01	200	1.78	123
Working Status				

Not working	1.25	892	1.90	591
Primary sector	1.29	380	2.23	219
Service sector	1.48	66	2.03	48
Wealth Index				
Lower	1.35	832	2.11	531
Middle	1.23	235	1.92	151
Upper	1.07	272	1.65	177
ANC Utilisation				
No utilisation	1.13	107	2.25	54
Partial utilisation	1.28	874	2.02	555
Full utilisation	1.22	249	1.74	174
Total	1.25	1338	1.96	858

Table 8.2 shows the mean number of obstetric morbidity according to women's background characteristics. The mean number of obstetric morbidity is separately shown for all currently married women as well as women with at least one morbidity according to their background characteristics. In Odisha, for all currently married women the number of obstetric morbidities varies from minimum zero to maximum seven. The overall mean number of obstetric morbidity varies from 1.25 for all currently married women to 1.96 for currently married women with at least one complication. It was observed that aged women experienced a higher mean number of obstetric morbidity compared to younger women. The mean number of obstetric morbidity was 2.30 and 1.98 for women whose age at the time of child's birth was in the age group 35-49 years and 15-35 years, respectively. The mean number of obstetric morbidity was higher for women with larger number of children ever born compared to fewer number of children ever born. Similarly, the mean number of obstetric morbidity was higher for other religious groups, schedule tribe and schedule caste women, women without education and with primary education, women residing in rural areas, working in primary and service sectors and having lower wealth index. The mean number of obstetric morbidity among the currently married women with at least one complication declines as the utilization of antenatal care increases. The mean number of obstetric morbidity for women with no antenatal care utilization was 2.25, whereas for women with partial and full antenatal care utilization it was 2.02 and 1.74, respectively. Hence, there exists an

inverse relationship between the status of antenatal care utilization and mean number of obstetric morbidity.

RESULT FROM LOGISTIC REGRESSION

Table 8.3 shows the result of the logistic regression analysis. The logistic regression is carried out to identify the determinants of obstetric morbidity in Odisha. Since, obstetric morbidity is the outcome of not only biological factors but also of demographic and socio-economic conditions, and availability of health facilities, so these factors are included in the regression analysis. From the analysis the factors like caste, education, place of residence and wealth index are found to have significant effect on obstetric morbidity. The likelihood of obstetric morbidity was significantly lower for schedule tribe women (Odds Ratio = 0.693, P < 0.10) compared to the schedule caste women.

TABLE 8.3
Determinants of Obstetric Morbidity in Odisha, 2005-06

Background Characteristics	*Odds Ratio Exp(B)*
Age of Mother at Child's Birth	
< 15-25 yrs®	
25-35 yrs	0.840
35-49 yrs	1.385
Children Ever Born	
1®	
2	0.846
3	0.855
4 & above	1.166
Religion	
Hindu®	
Others	1.501
Caste	
SCs®	
STs	0.693*
OBCs	0.790
General	0.097

Education	
No Education ®	
Primary	1.445**
Secondary & Above	1.492***
Place of Residence	
Rural®	
Urban	0.741*
Working Status	
Not working®	
Primary sector	0.778
Secondary sector	1.366
Wealth Index	
Lower®	
Middle	0.716*
Upper	0.630***
ANC Utilisation	
No utilisation®	
Partial utilisation	1.645*
Full utilisation	2.131***

Note : Dependent variable is Obstetric Morbidity (0= No Obstetric Morbidity and 1= Any Obstetric Morbidity)
* 10 percent level of Significance
** 5 percent level of Significance
*** 1 percent level of Significance
® Reference category

Similarly, women with primary education (Odds Ratio =1.445, $P<0.05$) and secondary and above education (Odds Ratio =1.492, $P<0.01$) have experienced obstetric morbidity more likely compared to non-educated women. Therefore, the educational level of women shows an inverse causal relationship with obstetric morbidity. Those women who are educated up to primary level and secondary and above, the chances of their obstetric morbidity increased by 1.445 and 1.492 times respectively compared to non-educated women. This contradictory result may be due to higher chances of reporting obstetric morbidity by the educated women.

Women belonging to urban areas have less likelihood of obstetric morbidity (Odds Ratio=0.741, $P<0.10$) compared to rural women. This may be because women in rural areas marry at an early age and at this age girls' reproductive physiology is still in formative stage and pregnancy during this period may become detrimental to their health leading to more obstetric complications. Like as, the likelihood of obstetric morbidity was lower for women belonging to middle (Odds Ratio=0.716, $P<0.10$) and upper wealth quintiles (Odds Ratio=0.630, $P<0.01$) as compared to women from poor wealth quintile. This is because economic status has positive impact on women's health.

The other variables such as woman's age at child birth, number of children ever born, working status and religion have shown no significant effect on obstetric morbidity. But, the likelihood of obstetric morbidity was lower for middle-aged women (25-35 yrs), women belonging to OBCs and general category, women working in primary sector and belonging to Hindu religion, though they are not significant. Analysis shows that utilization of antenatal care has negative impact on obstetric morbidity. Women with partial and full utilisation of antenatal care have shown significantly higher chances of obstetric morbidity compared to women who have never gone for any antenatal care. The odds ratio is 1.645 and 2.131 for partial ANC and full ANC, respectively and they are highly significant. Generally, women who have taken ANC care should have less chance of having obstetric morbidity than those who have never taken any ANC. This contradictory result may be due to the fact that, women who have received antenatal care have better reporting of morbidities compared to women with no antenatal care utilization.

CONCLUSION

The present study provides an insight into the prevalence of obstetric morbidity and the various factors associated with it in a backward state like Odisha. The finding of the study revealed that in Odisha about two-thirds of the currently married women reported some kind of obstetric complication during their pregnancy and child birth. But more than half of the women reported many kind of pregnancy complications and the reported pregnancy-related problems were concerning excessive fatigue and swelling of legs, body and face. The study also revealed that the mean number of obstetric morbidity was higher for aged women, women with larger number of children ever born, women belonging to SC and ST categories, women residing in rural areas, women with low education and low wealth quintile, and women without and with partial utilization of antenatal care. Further it reveals that women's age at the time of child's birth, residence, caste, birth order and level of education are important factors influencing obstetric morbidity. Since, a severe obstetric morbidity can significantly affect women's health and well-being, therefore early prevention and appropriate management are essential. Greater attention should be given to the health care needs among women especially rural uneducated poor women during the period of pregnancy, child birth and post-partum. Therefore, there is a need to strengthen the maternal care programmes and improve health care facilities so that every expectant mother will get the necessary care. Further the government need to improve the awareness level among women about various obstetric complications so that they would be able to take necessary precautions and timely use of medical care.

REFERENCES

Bhatia, J.C. and J. Cleland (1996), "Obstetric Morbidity in South India: Results from a Community Survey." *Social Science and Medicine,* 43(10), 1507-16.

Datta, K.K. *et al.* (1980), "Morbidity Pattern among Rural Pregnant Women in Alwar, Rajasthan—A Cohort Study", *Health and Population Perspectives and Issues,* 3, 282-92.

Garg, S. *et al.* (2001), "Perceived Reproductive Morbidity and Health Care Behavior among Women in Urban Slum", *Health and Population—Perspectives and Issues,* 24(4): 178-88.

International Institute for Population Sciences, *National Family Health Survey (NFHS-3), 2005-06,* India. Mumbai: International Institute for Population Sciences, 208-14 and 436-46.

Jain, K. *et al.* (2012), "Are Self-Reported Morbidities Deceptive In Measuring Socio-Economic Inequalities", *Indian Journal of Medical Research,* 136: 750-57.

Khan, K.S. *et al.* (2006), "WHO Analysis of Causes of Maternal Death: A Systematic Review", *The Lancet,* 367, 1066-74.

Mukhopadhyay, S. *et al.* (2002), "Obstetric Morbidity and Socio-Demographic Factors in Rural West Bengal, India", 7(1), 41-52.

Padma, G.R.; (2004), 'Maternal Morbidity in Rural Andhra Pradesh, Centre for Economic and Social Studies, Hyderabad, *Working Paper No. 63.*

Ram, F. *et al.* (2006), "Maternal Mortality: Is the Indian Programme Prepared to Meet the Challenges?" *Health and Development,* 2 (1 &2), 67-80.

Ransom, E.I. and N.V. Yinger (2002), "Making Motherhood Safer", *Population Reference Bureau,* Washington, D.C.

Say, L. *et al.* (2004), "WHO Systematic Review of Maternal Morbidity and Mortality: The Prevalence of Severe Acute Maternal Morbidity (near miss)", *Reproductive Health,* 1(3).

Singh, R. *et al. (2012)* "Morbidity Profile of Women during Pregnancy: A Hospital Record Based Study in Western UP", *Indian Journal of Community Health,* 24 (4).

Sontakke, P. *et al.* (2009), "Obstetric Morbidity among Currently Married Women in Selected States of India," *The Journal of Family Welfare*, 55(2), 17-26.

United Nations Fund for Population Agency. Emergency Obstetric Care, *UNFPA, 2006.* http://www.unfpa.org/public/home/mothers/pid/4385.

Waterstone, M. *et al.* (2001), "Incidence and Predictors of Severe Obstetric Morbidity: Case Control Study," *Bio-Medical Journal*, 322, 1089-94.

World Health Organisation (2005), *Maternal Mortality in 2005: Estimates Developed by WHO, UNICEF and UNFP,* Geneva: World Health Organisation.

World Health Organization (2010), *Trends in Maternal Mortality: 1990 to 2008*, Geneva: World Health Organization.

9

Expenditure Pattern and Gender Disparity in Health in Odisha

Sudhakar Patra and Kabita Kumari Sahu

INTRODUCTION

The inadequacy in public health expenditure in India has received the attention of researchers and policy makers for quite some time now. No state has ever committed more than 3.5 percent of its resources to the health sector. It is a fact that from the 1970s there has been a steady decline in public sector investment on health. The average health expenditure in our country is only 2.6 percent of total government expenditure. The health care expenditure has not kept pace with increase in total government expenditure. The share of public health expenditure in national income peaked at 1.3 percent of per capita GNP in the mid-1980s; but since then has declined. The Central Government-sponsored health programmes were severely affected after the reform measures initiated in 1991. The share of the central grants for public health declined from 27.92 percent in 1984-85 to 17.17 percent in 1992-93, and that for the disease control programme from 41.47 percent in 1984-85 to 18.5 percent in 1992-93. There is rural-urban hiatus in terms of investment, infrastructure development and availability of health care. The expenditure by the states accounts for around 90 percent of all public health expenditures. Usually the developed states like Goa, Haryana, Karnataka, Maharashtra, Gujarat, and Punjab have higher per capita expenditure as compared to the states of Bihar, Rajasthan, Odisha, and Madhya Pradesh. The exception being Kerala, which despite being economically not very prosperous has a higher expenditure on health. In the analysis, the state financing and infrastructure data were supplemented by the data gathered from various national and small sample studies. They show that there is an overwhelming domination of the private sector in health care, brought about by the gross underdevelopment of the public sector and by the complete lack of regulation and planning for the private sector. In this context, the objective of the study is to present a comprehensive picture of public spending on health care in Odisha after 1996-97 with special focus on expenditure on reproductive and child health which indicate gender dimension in health care expenditure. It focuses on the pattern of and trends in public expenditure on health care in Odisha. Specifically, it describes the magnitude of public expenditure on health and health related aspects in general and on reproductive and child health services in particular.

LITERATURE REVIEW

There is a plethora of literature dealing with issues related to health care expenditure. The first study was R.B. Lal's Singapore study of private household expenditure, which focused on private expenditure on health in Singapore and also on the government healthcare expenditure for the same area (GOI, 1946). The Indian Institute of Management, Ahmadabad had carried out a study of health finance covering all the levels of health expenditure—state, municipal, corporate and household (IIM, 1987). Another study of state health financing in India is that by Roger Jefferey. He looked at state health expenditure from the perspective of planning—the administrative process involved in making allocations—and in the context of policy changes. Tulasidhar and Sarma (1993) did a comparative study of different states of India with respect to public expenditure, medical care at birth and infant mortality. They found that in all the states per capita real public spending grew faster than real per capita state domestic product. Of late, a number of studies have been done on the healthcare financing in India. Duggal (1996) discusses public-private participation in health sector and how this can be optimised for best results. Bhat (1996, 2000) discusses about the importance of regulating the private sector in India and how public-private partnership can bring needed resources while also taking care that the vulnerable groups—the poor and rural populations—have access to health facilities. These studies suggest that India's dependence on private sector in healthcare is very high. Utilisation studies show that a third of in-patients and three-fourth of out-patients utilise private healthcare facilities (Duggal and Amin, 1989; Yesudian, 1990; Visaria and Gumber, 1994). Dreze and Sen, (1995) analysed life expectations at birth and they found substantial differences at birth across states. States such as Madhya Pradesh and Odisha have mortality rates of well over 100 per 1000 live births in rural areas (Dreze and Sen, 1995; Mahal, Srivastava and Sanan, 2000).

In another study Mahal *et al.* (2000) tried to find the distribution of public health subsidies in India in different states. Despite a considerable desire for "equity" in public policy documents, they found that public subsidies on health are distributed quite unequally across different socio-economic groups in India. At the all-India level, the share of the richest 20 percent of the population in total public sector subsidies is nearly 31 percent, nearly three times the share of the poorest 20 percent of the population. In rural areas this inequality was much greater where the share of the top 20 percent in public subsidies was nearly four times that of the poorest 20 percent. Mahal *et al.* (2000) find that 31 percent of public subsidies on health accrued to urban residents, somewhat higher than their share in the total population of about 25 percent. If we look at the state level picture, substantial differences in the degree of inequality are also found. The southern states such as Kerala, Tamil Nadu and Andhra Pradesh, and the western states of Maharashtra and Gujarat are enjoying a much more equal distribution than the north Indian states. Some of these inequality in the allocation of public health subsidies can be explained by income-related differences in utilisation patterns of public facilities, with the rich using more care, if health care is a normal good. When promoting equity is a key objective of the state, there is no doubt that there remains substantial scope for improvement, either in terms of interstate equity or distributions of public subsidies within state.

There are very few studies, which take states of India as the unit of analysis. For example, Mitra and Varoudakis (2002) examined the effect of infrastructure on manufacturing industries' total factor productivity and technical efficiency in the case of Indian states. They showed that differences in infrastructure endowments across Indian states explain in a significant way their differences in industrial performances. Datt and Ravallion (1998) explain the elimination of rural poverty in different states of India. They found that the speed of rural poverty elimination has been diverse across different states. But there are few studies of this kind.

PUBLIC EXPENDITURE ON HEALTH IN SELECTED ASIAN COUNTRIES

It is criticised that human development index and health index are low in India as the government expenditure on health is abysmally low. The comparison of health expenditure with other Asian countries suggests that India's public health expenditure is only 17.9 percent of the total expenditure on health care while it is close to 90 percent in case of smaller countries like Bhutan and Maldives (Table 9.1). In Sri Lanka and Bangladesh, the percentages of public health expenditure to total health expenditure are 48.90 and 44.20 respectively which is more than 2.5 times that of India.

TABLE 9.1

Public Expenditure on Health as Percent of Total Expenditure on Health, 2011

Country	*Percent of Public Expenditure*
Bhutan	90.6
Maldives	83.5
Korea	73.4
Thailand	57.1
Sri Lanka	48.90
Bangladesh	44.2
Nepal	29.70
Indonesia	25.10
India	17.90
Myanmar	17.80

Source : World Bank Data.

HEALTH STATUS IN ODISHA

Odisha is a major state in eastern India where the annual population growth is 1.83 percent, which is lower than the all-India percentage of 2.14. Scheduled Tribes and Scheduled Castes, mostly

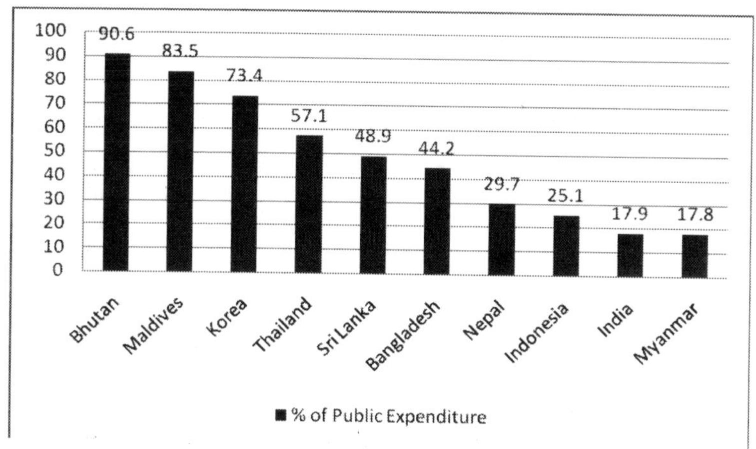

Figure 9.1 : International Comparison of Public Health Expenditure

living below the poverty line, constitute nearly 38 percent of the population. About half of the state's population live below the poverty line, with limited access to exploitable resources due to a complex interplay of social, economic, and cultural dynamics. Frequent droughts, floods, and other natural calamities not only impoverish the people, but also make them morbidly stoic towards the pace of development. Despite some attempts by successive governments, fairness in resource distribution has evaded the disadvantaged groups. The inability of these groups to demand their own rights has not improved the situation. The disease burden is high. Communicable, pregnancy-related, and childhood ailments account for about 65 percent of the diseases. The infant mortality rate was 9.7 in 1999, 97 (Sample Registration System, 1999), the highest in the country. This ofcourse came down to 65 in 2009. The publicly provided health service outlets are available, more or less in accordance with the all-India norms, but factors such as low population density (203), geographic inaccessibility, cultural barriers, ignorance, poor service quality, and the deep-rooted influence of traditional healers make the overall outcome of service system unsatisfactory. Public sector expenditure on health is about 1.2 percent of the Gross State Domestic Product, and about 3 percent of the annual budget. A large portion of the funds is spent in the tertiary sector. Allocation to health has remained low during the 1990s, and the sustained increase in the wage and salary component has made the non-salary portion shrink over the years. Coverage of preventive services, particularly immunisation, has been generally satisfactory during the last decade. Medical care is mainly publicly provided (90 percent), and the organised private sector is very thin.

Health Care in Odisha is a major concern of the Government and the population as a whole. Being a poor state it has not been possible to allocate a large sum for health care. However, Odisha has made significant progress in health development. The expenditure on health which was Rs. 567.28 crore in 2003-04 has gone up to Rs. 630.90 crore in 2004-05 and Rs. 1559.60 crore has been allocated in the Budget Estimate for the year 2011-12. The average annual allocation for health is around 4 to 5 percent of the total expenditure of the State. Per capita health expenditure has gone up from Rs. 147.73 in 2003-04 to Rs. 378.53 in 2010-11. Besides, the allocation made by the Government of Odisha a substantial amount is being spent on EAPs outside the budget for health sector every year. While Rs. 37.18 crore was spent in 2003-04, it went up to Rs. 523.16 crore in 2009-10 outside the budget. The number of health care institutions in the government sector has remained stagnant over the years. From 2675 in 2001-02 it has gone up to 2927 in 2008-09. In addition to these public institutions, a plethora of private health care institutions have also come up in the State.

Life expectancy at birth in Odisha has gone up from 51.93 years during 1971-1981 to 62.13 years during 1996-2001 and 62.3 years for the period 2006-10 (projected) in respect of males and from 49.59 years to 61.15 years in 1996-01 and 64.8 years for the period 2006-10 (projected) for females. The all India life expectancy during the corresponding periods were 50.90 years, 62.80 years and 65.8 years (projected) for males and 50.00, 64.20 and 68.1 years (projected) for females. Infant Mortality Rate (IMR) for 1000 live births in the State has plummeted from 124 in 1991 to 83 in 2003 and to 65 in 2009. During the same period the all India figure declined from 80 to 60 and 50 respectively. The health expenditure in Odisha from 1996 to 2013 is presented in Table 9.2.

An attempt is made here to know the least square trend of health expenditure and percentage to total expenditure. The least square coefficient is found to be 80.67 which indicates that the health expenditure is increasing on an average by Rs. 80 crore every year (Table 9.2). But the time series of health expenditure is not stationary as per augmented Dicky Fuller test. It implies that there is wide fluctuation in health expenditure every year over 17 years of study.

TABLE 9.2
Health Expenditure in Odisha from 1996 to 2013

Year	*Total health expenditure (in Rs. crore)*	*Percent of total State expenditure*	*Percent of GSDP*	*Growth rate of health expenditure*
1996-97	293.83	4.66	2.03	10.61
1997-98	328.71	4.79	1.82	22.05
1998-99	421.71	4.88	2.11	7.54
1999-00	456.10	4.50	1.90	10.87
2000-01	511.74	4.62	2.03	-1.65
2001-02	503.42	4.17	1.91	7.95
2002-03	546.92	4.11	1.97	11.32
2003-04	616.79	3.95	1.74	10.43
2004-05	688.67	4.41	1.87	-9.04
2005-06	631.56	3.98	1.96	28.06
2006-07	877.98	4.28	2.31	-4.26
2007-08	842.03	3.58	2.02	5.87
2008-09	894.57	3.32	2.12	25.38
2009-10	1198.86	3.93	2.42	24.44
2010-11	1586.78	4.07	2.56	-1.76
2011-12	1559.27	3.96	2.31	0.021
2012-13(P)	1559.60	3.48	2.13	—
Mean	795.21	4.16	2.07	9.24
S.D	432.80	0.45	0.22	11.18
ADF	Non-stationary	Stationary	Stationary	Non-stationary

Source : Government of Odisha, *Economic Survey of Odisha*, Various years.

Similarly, percentage of health expenditure to total state expenditure is 4.16. It implies that health expenditure in Odisha is below 5 percent. The growth rate of health expenditure is negative in 2000-01, 2006-07 and 2010-11. There is wide fluctuation in growth rate for which the series is non-stationary.

Least Square equation of total health expenditure in Odisha is

$$Y = a + b\,t$$
$$Y = 74.58 + 80.67\,t \;(SE = 7.89,\; R^2 = 0.87,\; N = 17)$$

Trend of percentage of health expenditure to total expenditure

$Y = a_1 + a_2 t$
$Y = 4.81-0.07\ t$ (SE= 0.01, t = -5.37, R^2 = 0.65)

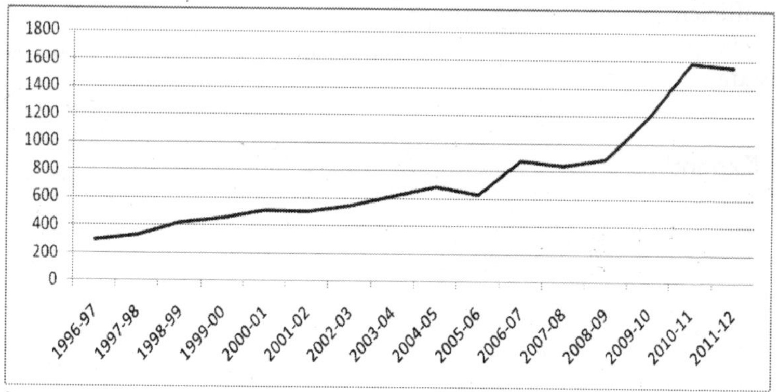

Figure 9.2 : Trend of Health Expenditure in Odisha from 1996 to 2013 (in Rs. crore)

GENDER DISPARITY IN HEALTH EXPENDITURE

Gender disparity in health can be studied only on the basis of household health expenditure data. Since the present study is based on secondary data, expenditure on reproductive and child health was taken as indicator for examining gender disparity. The public expenditure on reproductive and child health services has tripled from Rs. 108 crore in 1996-97 to Rs. 336 crore in 2007-08. In real terms, however, the increase was only 5.09 percent. While the expenditure fluctuated from 1996-97 to 2004-05, it increased thereafter largely due to the increase in allocations routed outside the state budget and in the expenditure on nutrition. Contributions from the Health and Family Welfare Department accounted for between almost half and two-thirds of the total expenditure on reproductive and child health services during 1996-97 to 2004-05, but declined thereafter to between one-quarter and two-fifths of the total as a result of an increase in off-budget spending particularly after the allocation of NRHM funds which comprise a substantial share of RCH expenditure. The expenditure on reproductive and child health services fluctuated considerably during the 12-year study period. Between 13 and 26 percent of the total health and health-related expenditure was allocated for reproductive and child health services;

in the most recent year, 2007-08, it was 21 percent (Table 9.3). Nonetheless, as a share of gross state domestic product, expenditure on reproductive and child health services remained below one percent throughout this period. Female health has not been accorded sufficient priority in public expenditure in Odisha as is evident from the expenditure of 20 percent on reproductive and child health in the state.

TABLE 9.3

Expenditure on Reproductive and Child Health in Odisha

Year	*Expenditure on Reproductive and Child Health*	*Percent of Total Health Expenditure*	*Percent Expenditure on Maternal and Child Health*
1996-97	62.71	20.16	0.41
1997-98	64.53	17.11	0.37
1998-99	86.90	18.67	0.39
1999-00	79.57	17.55	0.30
2000-01	80.06	14.73	0.25
2001-02	66.65	13.36	0.35
2002-03	76.43	17.76	0.25
2003-04	73.92	14.36	0.34
2004-05	94.21	18.38	0.51
2005-06	81.92	25.77	0.55
2006-07	126.39	23.25	0.42
2007-08	137.46	20.65	0.37
2008-09	142.67	21.23	0.39
2009-10	152.15	22.21	0.40
2010-11	163.23	23.07	0.42
Mean	99.25	19.21	0.38
S.D	34.81	3.56	0.08

Source : Finance Dept., Govt. of Odisha.

ASSESSMENT OF HEALTH SYSTEMS IN ODISHA

There has been a significant change in the health scenario over the past two decades. Infant mortality has decreased from 143 to 97

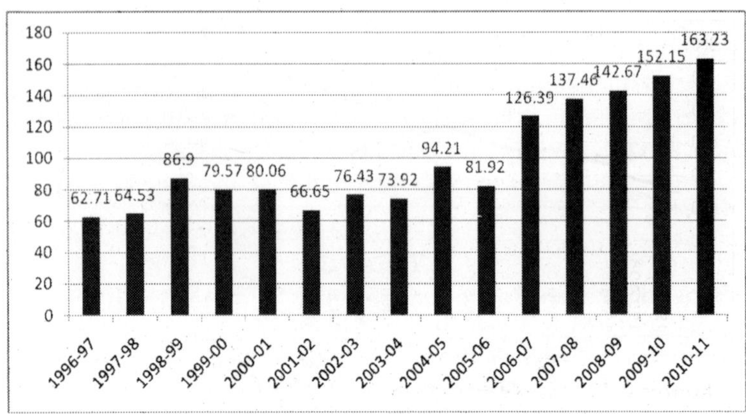

Figure 9.3 : Trend of Expenditure on Reproductive and Child Health

TABLE 9.4

Per Capita Health Expenditure in Odisha

Year	*Per Capita Health Expenditure at Current Price*	*Per Capita Health Expenditure at Constant Price (WPI deflator, 1999)*
1996-97	84.80	66.66
1997-98	93.44	70.36
1998-99	118.09	83.93
1999-2000	125.81	86.58
2000-01	139.04	89.30
2001-02	134.85	86.44
2002-03	144.17	91.07
2003-04	160.18	94.06
2004-05	176.18	81.38
2005-06	159.18	105.69
2006-07	217.94	94.69
2007-08	205.90	86.15
2008-09	225.33	92.32
2009-10	234.34	93.08
2010-11	255.56	97.36

Source : Government of Odisha (2012), *Odisha Budget at a Glance, 2011-12.*

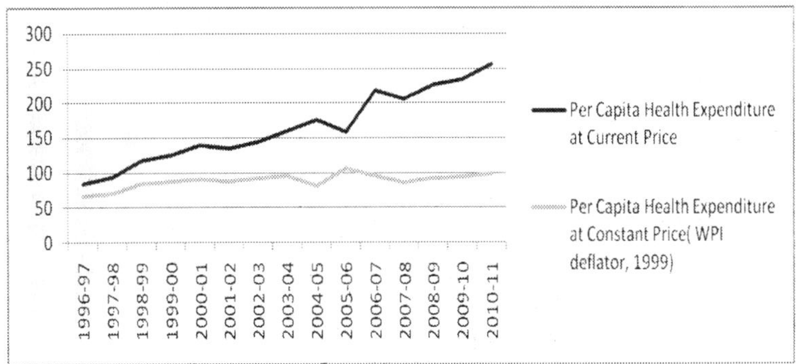

Figure 9.4 : Trend in per Capita Health Expenditure in Odisha

during 1980 to 2000, a reduction of 46, which is not a small achievement. However, it is a matter of concern that over the last four years the Infant Mortality Rate (IMR) has stagnated. Institutional delivery has not increased much, but the deliveries are now taking place in better surroundings than before due to increased awareness of the people supported by the trained birth attendants, anganwadi workers, and Auxiliary Nurse Midwives (ANMs). The institutional arrangements for medical care have also improved. The network of sub-centres, primary health centres, and community health centres has been giving comprehensive health care in a meaningful manner over the years. The introduction of the multi-purpose health worker scheme has increased the number of sub-centres, thereby reducing the population load of each basic health worker. The maternal and child health services show visible improvement in quality and coverage, but the continuing pattern of a high percentage of domiciliary delivery has been a matter of concern. Alternate way of addressing the issue have been tried by making the Trained Birth-attendants (TBAs) capable of conducting deliveries in a hygienic condition, making available clean delivery kits, and making the public more aware of the importance of sanitation and cleanliness. Attempts at improving hospital services, and making doctors available at more peripheral level have given mixed results. The high proportion of doctors' vacancies in the rural areas continues to be a grave problem, but there has been some earnest attempt under the reform process to address this issue. The monetary incentive given for rural service earlier and currently introduced in a limited fashion is not attractive to doctors, as the money involved is too small. Compulsory rural or tribal service though incorporated in the rules, does not always work efficiently, as the implementation is not strict. However, the recent introduction of one year's mandatory service in difficult areas for all doctors selected for the post-graduate courses has helped in filling up a large number of positions in the remote districts.

FACTORS RESPONSIBLE FOR CHANGES IN HEALTH STATUS IN ODISHA

Multiple factors have been responsible for the changes in the health indicators in the state. Some of these were within the purview of the Health Department; others were outside:

(a) The improved network of primary health institutions—health sub-centres, primary health centres (PHCs), and block hospitals—along with the improved skills of staff, better equipment, and more availability of drugs.
(b) Focused campaigns and programmes on major communicable diseases such as leprosy, TB, polio, etc. and on conditions such as cataract blindness.
(c) Improved facilities at secondary and tertiary care centres.
(d) Sustained efforts at health education that have resulted in increased awareness of issues like safe drinking water, Oral Rehydration Therapy (ORT), contraception, prevention and control of diarrhoea, early treatment of leprosy and TB, etc.
(e) Various health reforms introduced from time to time.
(f) Availability of donor funding for various health activities, primarily from international donors.

INITIATIVES IN HEALTH SECTOR REFORM AND THEIR IMPACT

Interest in health sector reform began in Odisha in the mid-1990s. Two events heralded the beginning of this interest: (1) the formation of a Committee of the Odisha Legislature chaired by the Health Minister (called the House Committee) which looked into three important aspects of health care and advised the raising of additional resources for health care activities by the introduction and retention of user charges in the medical colleges and district hospitals, granting greater autonomy to the major hospitals, and the abolition of private practice by government doctors; (2) the evaluation done by the British Government's Department for International

Development (DFID) of its two health and family welfare projects in Odisha found that further capital investment in the health sector would be inadvisable unless certain systemic changes were undertaken. The evaluation suggested that reforms were needed in three main areas, viz. maintenance (of buildings and equipment), medicine, and mobility, (the three 'M's) if past and future investment in the health sector were to show results. In the five years or so following these two events, a number of reforms, both large and small, have been introduced in the health sector in Odisha. Some of them relate to changes in administrative and operational systems, some to changes in personnel policies including skill development for better service delivery, and some were aimed at giving a minimum health guarantee to the people. The reforms have had varying degrees of success. Some of the principal reform measures are described below.

(a) Essential Drug List

The essential drug list in generic names cuts down the purchase of unnecessary drugs, and results in rational drug prescription; bulk purchase, central payment, and adherence to a strict schedule of payment results in economies of scale and value for money (for example, IV fluids earlier supplied at Rs. 16 per bottle, now costs Rs. 6). Strip packing has increased the acceptability of the drugs by the public; quality testing and black listing of substandard drug suppliers has resulted in supply of good quality drugs. The institutions have the freedom to select their own drugs; and most important of all, drugs are available in plenty in all the institutions. A great deal of advocacy was necessary in the initial stages to overcome the resistance of vested interest groups. The system got stabilised only after about a year or so. However, there is now wide acceptability in the state. Further improvements that are underway are the adoption of a computerised online inventory control system, training in rational drug use, etc.

(b) User Charges

The department used to charge a nominal fee from 1997 for certain facilities in the hospitals, principally for X-rays and rooms. The fee was extremely low, only a fraction of the cost or market prices of the corresponding service. Moreover the amount paid went to the government coffers and not to the hospital, hence there was little motivation to collect it. Under the new system, user charges were introduced for three categories of service; viz. diagnostics, special accommodation and transportation, in the tertiary, district, and district level hospitals. The districts were also divided into three categories on the basis of their economic prosperity and slightly varying rates were fixed for the different categories. Registered societies were set up for each hospital and the user charges collected are retained by the society for use in the hospital. People below the poverty line are exempted from payment. Similarly, tests relating to the national programmes are not charged (viz. leprosy, TB, malaria, etc.). The societies have been given the freedom to enhance the existing rates or introduce rates for new activities. They also have the authority to utilise the funds as they think fit, subject only to general guidelines (viz. no spending on construction, on major equipment, or on hiring of personnel). By making funds available at the hospital level for day-to-day working capital and emergency needs, the scheme has greatly benefited the public. Financial decisions are taken at the district level, thereby ensuring greater autonomy, high motivation, and increased interest in improving the hospitals.

(c) Privatization of Cleaning in Hospitals

Though most government hospitals have a fair number of regular government employees to do the cleaning work, lack of cleanliness is a common feature. Yet cleanliness is an essential requirement of every hospital and it was necessary to find a way to ensure this. An experiment was therefore attempted in 1998 to contract out the cleaning work of a major hospital in Odisha to private agencies. Sulabh International, who has been a pioneer in the field of public sanitation, was contracted at a negotiated price for undertaking the cleaning services of the state's Capital Hospital, Bhubaneswar, in July 1997. It was agreed that the existing cleaning staff (i.e. the government employees) would be engaged in other work in the hospital. The State Government's Finance Department required that while no retrenchment need take place, existing vacancies of cleaning staff should be abolished and any new vacancy occurring as a result of retirement or death should not be filled up. Initially there were some protests from the Class IV employees union, but since no retrenchment of staff was involved, the protests did not gather momentum. The difference to the hospital in about two month's time was remarkable. Bathrooms, which earlier stank and had been unapproachable most of the time were clean, the corridors were without litter, the window grills and ceiling fixtures were dust and cobweb free. Public response to the change was also extremely positive, with surprise being expressed at how a government hospital could be so clean. Demands started coming in from other hospitals to contract out the cleaning in those institutions as well. Since funds were a constraint, this could not be done, at once, in a large number of hospitals.

(d) Mandatory Pre-PG Rural Service

The state has a large number of vacancies of doctors in tribal and 'difficult' areas. Several efforts made earlier to ensure the presence of doctors in these areas did not meet with success. At the same time, young doctors got hardly any rural orientation and made efforts to remain in urban areas all the time. Under this scheme, 11 districts, to which doctors were generally unwilling to go and which have consistently had a large number of vacancies were selected and health institutions in them identified. The entrance examination for the medical post-graduate (PG) courses is held one year ahead of the date of admission. Those who qualify are advised about the medical college and the discipline they will get and thereafter assigned to one of the institutions in the 11 districts. Those who are not already in government employment are given contract appointments and assigned to these districts. The doctors are to work in these institutions for one year and only after obtaining a certificate regarding completion of the period are allowed admission into the PG course. The initiative has been extremely successful, ensuring the presence of doctors in difficult and remote areas. One major reason why this initiative has succeeded where others have failed is that the assignment is for a limited period only and it is linked to something that is highly desired (a PG degree). It is understood that other states like Kerala are also adopting this practice.

(e) Internship Training

Prior to the change, medical interns were given community health training in three training centres (under the control of medical college) and their attached health institutions. They were trained in large groups of 25 or more, they got hardly any exposure to real community health problems and the quality of the training was poor with little or no hands on training. The supervision was done entirely by the medical college teachers, who are themselves not very much in touch with community health conditions and developments. Under the new scheme, the interns are sent in groups of two and three to community health centres under the control of the CDMOs. They are exposed to real community health situations and get 'hands on' training. They are supervised both by the Medical Officers in charge of the institutions as well as the medical college teachers. The benefit of this scheme are several: it produces better trained doctors; it exposes young doctors to the rural health scenario; and it is expected to promote better attendance of doctors in rural health institutions if, and when, these doctors join the state health service in future.

CONCLUSION

The resources allocated for health remained more or less at 4-5 percent of the state's total expenditure and just one percent of the gross state domestic product (GSDP) from 1996-97 to 2011-12. These public spendings are clearly less than those articulated in the Health Policy of 2002, and would definitely influence service delivery by affecting capital expenditure and health inputs. As discussed, the outlay on capital expenditure was abysmally low compared to the vast infrastructure requirements in the state. Although contributions from the state's own resources accounted for most of the public expenditure on health, its share has declined in recent years and concomitantly contributions from the Central Government and external sources have increased. For example, contribution from externally-funded projects and central assistance routed outside the state budget comprised 20-28 percent of the total public expenditure on health during 2005-07. With regard to allocations by type of health care functions such as primary, secondary and tertiary, the findings indicate that the spending on secondary care (17 percent, on average), spending on primary care had not reached the prescribed limit of 55 percent in most of the years under study. With a substantially higher administrative expenditure, the state is constrained to allocate more resources to these heads. Again, low spending on primary and secondary care reflects wrong priority setting which affects equity issues in the health system. Per capita health expenditure at current prices increased from Rs. 85 in 1996-97 to Rs. 206 in 2007-08 . However, at constant prices, it was Rs. 95 in 2007-08. While it increased by almost 8 percent at current prices during the 12-year study period, at constant prices it increased by only 3 percent. Findings, moreover, indicate that the state recorded one of the lowest per capita expenditures on health among the major states in the country. With an average real per capita expenditure of Rs. 74 during 1991-92 to 2006-07, the state ranked eleventh position among the major states. Although maternal and child health situation in Odisha is characterised by considerable mortality and morbidity, health expenditure on maternal and child health is limited. For example, over the period from 1996-97 to 2007-08, only 18 percent of health expenditure was on the provision of maternal and child health services. While expenditure on reproductive and child health services increased at a modest pace till 2004-05, it increased sharply thereafter, an increase that can be attributed largely to the increase in allocations routed outside the state budget. Of the total expenditure on reproductive and child health services, a major share—between 12 to 13 percent—was allocated for rural family welfare services and centres. In contrast, urban family welfare services and facilities received only 2 percent or less of the total expenditure on reproductive and child health services, and maternal and child health services received just 2 to 7 percent. It is also notable that only 3 percent or less was allocated for training. Further, although increased donor funding for reproductive and child health brings more flexibility in funding based upon planning, it raises questions of programme sustainability after funding ceases. It is also suggested that the actual spending fell short of budget estimates every year, and this was largely due to low utilisation of plan expenditure, thereby raising doubt about the absorbing capacity and efficiency of the executing agencies in planning and implementing different programmes.

Financial transparency and management practices have a major bearing on the efficiency of public spending. Certain procurement related practices need to be changed to bring in greater transparency and involvement of technical experts. Age-old practices of drug procurement result in the supply of poor quality drugs and often, in their untimely supply, leading to poor results. This urgently calls for the introduction of reforms to enhance the effectiveness of public spending. Most of the earlier reform efforts were donor-driven and introduced as a part of programme implementation strategies and therefore could not be sustained. Major policy issues such as the transfer of power to panchayati raj institutions and those involving health administration and management, human resource related subjects, particularly promotion and transfer policies and leadership issues have adversely affected service delivery in the state. Concerted efforts need to be initiated in these areas in order to improve planning, monitoring and utilisation of funds so as to improve maternal and child health services in Odisha.

REFERENCES

Ahluwalia, Montek S. (2000), "Economic Performance of States in Post-Reforms Period," *Economic and Political Weekly*, May 6.

Bhat, Ramesh and Nishant Jain (2004), *Time Series Analysis of Private Healthcare Expenditures and GDP: Co-Integration Results with Structural Break*, Ahmedabad: Indian Institute of Management.

Bhat, Ramesh (1996), "Regulation of the Private Health Sector in India," *International Journal of Health Planning and Management*, Vol. 11, pp. 253-74.

Choudhary, U.D.R. (1993), "Interstate and Intra-State Variations in Economic Development and Standard of Living," *Journal of Indian School of Political Economy*, 5

Government of Odisha (2012), *Economic Survey*, 2005-06 to 2011-12, Bhubaneswar: Government of Odisha, Directorate of Economics and Statistics.

Duggal, Ravi (2001), "Health Policy in India," *Health Action*, October.

Duggal, Ravi, Sunil Nandraj and Asha Vadair, (1995) "Health Expenditure across States Part-I," *Economic and Political Weekly*, Vol. XXX, No. 15, April 15, pp. 834-44.

Mahal, Ajay, Vivek Srivastava and Deepak Sanan. (2000), *Decentralisation, Democratisation and Public Sector Delivery of Services: Evidence from Rural India*, New Delhi: National Council of Applied Economic Research.

Mitra, Arup, Varoudakis Aristomene and Veganzones-Varoudakis Marie-Ange (2002), "Productivity and Technical Efficiency in Indian States' Manufacturing: The Röle of Infrastructure," *Economic Development and Cultural Change*, Vol. 50, Issue 2.

Nayyar, R., *Rural Poverty in India: An analysis of Interstate Differences*, Bombay: Oxford University Press.

Newhouse, J.P. (1977), "Medicare Expenditure: A Cross-National Survey," *Journal of Human Resources*, 12, pp. 115-25.

Satia, J.K. *et al.* (1987), *Study of Health Care Financing in India*, Ahmedabad: Indian Institute of Management.

Tulsidhar, V.B. (1993), "Expenditure Compression and Health Sector Outlays", *Economic and Political Weekly*, November.

Visaria, P. and A. Gumber (1994), *Utilisation of and Expenditure on Health Care in India: 1986-87*, Gujarat Institute of Development Research, Gota, Gujarat.

Yesudian, C.A.K. (1990), 'Utilisation Pattern of Health Services and Its Implications for Urban Health Policy', Takemi Program in International Health, Harvard School of Public Health.

10

Gender and Health Enhancement in Tamil Nadu

P. ANBALAGAN

INTRODUCTION

Health is one of the sectors which can stimulate the economy in a great way. Many developing nations pay higher attention to the health sector in order to strengthen social development through the provision of health care facilities. The Alma Ata Conference of 1978 also recognized WHO's 'Health for all' objectives. The goal 'Health for all' was initially accepted by the member countries of WHO in 1981. The Conference declared that 'primary health care is essential to make health care universally accessible. The Conference also laid emphasis on equitable distribution of health service. Of late, the Government of India considered the provision of health facilities and basic safety to the people especially the downtrodden. Consequent upon the realization of this fact the Government of India initiated the National Rural Health Mission (NRHM) in 2005 and then National Urban Health Mission (NUHM) in order to achieve the goals of the National Health Policy and the Millennium Development Goals (MDGs). These two programmes aim at addressing the gap in the provision of effective healthcare to the rural and the urban population especially the poor, women and children within the time frame. In short, the aim is to have inclusive growth through the provision of healthcare to all. All the south Indian states are in the forefront in making provision for health care facilities for the common people.

Tamil Nadu occupies a dominant position in the implementation of many social sector reforms. It has witnessed a high level of literacy, significant fall in poverty, generation of employment opportunities, and increase in the per capita income. It is documented that 90 percent of investment on infrastructure is obtained mainly from the state budget. Fund allocation through budget on social sector has been substantially increased during the Five Year Plans in Tamil Nadu. Consequently, Tamil Nadu ranked 7th in Human Development Index (HDI) in 1981 which improved to 3rd rank in 1991 and it maintained the same position in 2001 too. However, the state of Tamil Nadu has achieved desired progress in many fields viz. literacy, student enrolment rate, reduction of birth rate, death rate, infant mortality rate and increase in life expectancy. In this context, the study has identified health as the most important parameter for knowledge-based development. Even though there are several social sectors viz. education, health, housing, sanitation, family planning and population control, this study considers health as an important ingredient for human development. Hence, it focuses on health sector development. The paper specifically attempts to examine the budgetary allocation for the health sector during the planning era and also to analyse the performance of various health indicators in Tamil Nadu. The study also attempts to analyse various health related performance of women in the recent decades in the state. The study is mainly based on data published in the documents of the Government of Tamil Nadu and the Government of India.

SURVEY OF LITERATURE

Good health is a basic requirement for determining the quality of life and a healthy population can contribute to productivity and overall economic growth of the society. Health performance and economic growth are positively associated. The role of health in influencing economic outcomes has been reported by several economists (Kaushik *et al.*, 2006). Preston (1975) examined the distributional aspect of income and health relationship using cross country evidence and found that improvements in income distribution have relatively large impact on poor countries. Adler *et al.* (1994) examine the relationship between income and health expenditure across the countries. They found that there is positive correlation between them. Gupta and Mitra (2004) examined the relationship among health, poverty and economic growth in India for the 15 Indian states. The study found that per capita public health expenditure positively influences the health status of people.

Duraisamy *et al.* (2005) also examined the determinant of economic growth and health, using panel data of 14 major Indian states. It is found that the per capita income and per capita expenditure on health exerted a positive effect on the life expectancy at birth. It is very clear that health is the important parameter to determine the economic growth of the country. Malthora *et al. (*2006) examined the relationship between public health expenditure and level of economic development of various states in India. The empirical result of this study shows that there is significant relation between per capita health expenditure and per capita income. It is also found that higher income permits individuals and society to afford for better health care and ultimately better health increases productivity and enhances the ability to earn more income.

Maya (2011) analyses healthcare expenditure and its performance in different states in India. This study found that the share of health expenditure in the total expenditure of different states has declined. Even though there is a significant achievement in health performance in different states in India, there are wide disparities among the states. Singh (2011) attempted to analyse the health situation in India, particularly health expenditure by public, private and other agencies. The study found that almost three-fourth of the total health expenditure is borne by the households as out-of-pocket expenditure. It is seen that health expenditure of the major states is declining in recent years. Providing health services to the public by the government is inadequate both in terms of quantity and quality. Hence, improved health services and access to government health facilities will have to continue as a major thrust area in policy making.

Anbalagan (2011) studied healthcare development and examined various health insurance schemes in India. The study found that healthcare expenditure in India is way behind the developed and even some of the developing countries. Out-of-pocket expenditure has increased considerably in recent years mainly due to declining public expenditure on health. Consequently, the poor are the most vulnerable group to meet the growing healthcare expenditure. Though several health insurance schemes have been introduced for the poor people in India, there is no universal coverage.

Eapen *et al.* (2012) study reveals that the most glaring form of gender discrimination is found in the health sector, where it is visibly manifested in the form of low sex ratio, high level of sex differentials in morbidity and mortality as well as differential access to treatment and care. Data show that mortality is higher among women than man.

Prasad (2010) in her study discusses about the Dr. Muthulakshmi Maternity assistance scheme in Tamil Nadu. The study found that a large number of women who received benefits were SC, STs and OBCs. The study hardly found any evidence of corruption and leakage. The foregoing section analyses how health sector plays a predominant role in promoting the socioeconomic development of the nation and its current situation in Tamil Nadu.

INVESTMENT ON SOCIAL AND HEALTH SECTORS

Development of infrastructure in India so far has been the responsibility of the government and the sector is beeing financed primarily through budgetary allocation. The philosophy of planning in India was governed by the consideration that the state has to play a leading role in initiating and directing the process of economic development. One of the main thrusts of Indian planning is to facilitate strong infrastructure for attaining the target level of growth in each plan. Hence, infrastructure has been assigned a key role in the Five Year Plans in India. The social sector expenditure in India at the state and the Central level was 28.73 percent of the GDP in 1990-91, which decreased to 27.72 percent in 2007-08. The share of budget allocation on education was 3 percent and 2.84 percent, and health accounted for 1.28 percent and 1.39 percent in the corresponding periods (*Economic and Political Weekly*, March 2008, p. 79). Tamil Nadu is one of the leading states in the country to develop social infrastructure during the past decades.

Table 10.1 shows budgetary allocation on social infrastructure in Tamil Nadu and India. When the budgetary allocation for social sector development in Tamil Nadu is compared with that of the all India picture, it is ascertained that it has registered significant surge from the First to the Tenth Five Year Plan. Further, when we present a comparative picture of Tamil Nadu and the all India figures, it indicates that the social sector in total budget allocation in Tamil

Nadu is much higher than the all India figure. In Tamil Nadu, social sector share to the total budget allocation has increased considerably to 35 percent during the Tenth Plan as against 19.96 percent during the First Plan. It is documented that the state of Tamil Nadu has focused on the development of social infrastructure development in the post-liberalization period (Anbalagan, 2005). Therefore, investment on social infrastructure like health and education constitutes the core of human resource development.

TABLE 10.1
Budget Allocation for Social and Community Sectors in Tamil Nadu

(*Rs. in Crore*)

Five Year Plans	*Tamil Nadu*			*Share of Social Sector allocation to Total Budget in India (in percent)*
	Social and Community Sectors	*Total Budget allocation*	*Share of Social sector allocation to Total Budget (in percent)*	
I Plan	16.05	80.39	19.96	14.3
II Plan	37.96	187.76	20.21	12.6
III Plan	82.05	347.15	23.12	12.5
IV Plan	142.82	558.96	25.55	13.4
V Plan	237.68	833.52	28.52	12.1
VI Plan	1108.68	3644.61	30.42	12.9
VII Plan	2292.84	6317.44	36.29	11.8
VIII Plan	3779.65	10200.00	37.10	10.2
IX Plan	8606.00	25000.00	34.40	14.7
X Plan	13654.00	40000.00	35.00	16.0

Source : Compiled from various budget documents of Government of Tamil Nadu and Government of India.

Health is a priority sector for Tamil Nadu Government. Apart from allocation of funds by the public sector the state has also access to funds for health expenditure through private unilateral and multilateral grants and/or loans. The state has shown rapid progress across different aspects of its health system. The growth of population has drastically come down during the last few decades,

TABLE 10.2

Health Infrastructure Facilities in Tamil Nadu (in numbers)

Year	*Hospitals*	*Dispensaries*	*PHCs*	*HSC*	*Beds*	*Doctors*	*Nurses*
(1)	*(2)*	*(3)*	*(4)*	*(5)*	*(6)*	*(7)*	*(8)*
1993-94	427	484	1693	8681	46128	9754	19463
1994-95	382	314	1697	8681	47638	10380	19976
1995-96	612	357	1779	8700	47638	10308	19976
1996-97	489	357	1698	8684	49340	10361	19692
1997-98	309	187	1408	8681	50703	8601	19571
1998-99	310	188	1409	8681	50703	8757	19578
1999-2000	323	202	1410	8682	52237	8872	17746
2000-01	326	208	1410	8682	49057	8719	9835
2001-02	324	214	1411	8682	47892	9133	0539
2002-03	324	214	1411	8682	NA	NA	NA
2003-04	323	213	1413	8682	51472	9464	20839
2004-05	315	213	1415	8682	.51765	9543	9757
2005-06	315	213	1417	8683	52487	10011	23466
2006-07	329	215	1417	8683	52536	10882	24504
2007-08	318	215	1421	8706	55013	11014	24270
2010-11	323	216	1533	8706	60684	14113	14800

Source : Various issues of *Statistical Hand Book of Tamil Nadu*, Chennai: Government of Tamil Nadu.

which can be attributed largely to huge investment on education and health. Expenditure on health increased from Rs. 3.89 crore in 1990-91 to Rs. 2298.83 crore in 2005-06 in Tamil Nadu, an increase of 600 times. The percentage share of health expenditure to total budgetary allocation has decreased from 9.50 percent in 1993-94 to 6.91 percent in 2005-06. Between these periods the share of health sector in the total budget witnessed fluctuation. Public expenditure as a share of GSDP was 0.71 percent in 2004-05. During the Eleventh Plan the estimated expenditure on health in the state was Rs. 27.3 million. The per capita government expenditure on health in Tamil Nadu has increased from Rs. 36.25 in 1985 to Rs. 100.75 in 1995, which further increased to Rs. 352.90 in 2005-06.

Tamil Nadu is endowed with well established health infrastructure both in the government and private sectors giving rise to increased availability of medical facilities for the people. The daily average in-patient and out-patient strength has substantially increased in the state. Table 10.2 shows the development of health infrastructure in Tamil Nadu between 1993-94 and 2010-11. The Table 10.2 also indicates that there are no major changes in the availability of hospitals, dispensaries, primary health centres and health sub-centres between 1993-94 and 2010-11. However, availability of bed strength has increased from 46,128 in 1993-94 to 60684 in 2010-11. Even though the number of doctors and nurses in the different health institutions exhibited fluctuation between 1993-94 and 2010-11, it recorded considerable increase in its strength in 2010-11.

The emphasis laid on the health sector by Tamil Nadu during the various five-year plans shows the increasing priority given to this sector over time. The Second Five-Year Plan concentrated on expanding health facilities in Tamil Nadu and in the subsequent Plans the targets were fixed for complete eradication of small box. The Fifth Plan decided to ensure primary health centres for every panchyat union with one sub-centre for every 10,000 population. The Ninth Plan envisaged health care for all and better access to health. The Tenth Plan outlay for the improvement of health infrastructure facilities was Rs. 800 crore and the National Population Policy 2000 was vigorously implemented in the state. The Eleventh Plan ensured universal access of quality health care to the poor and it is one of the major objectives of the State Government now. The Plan also took steps for the prevention and control of specific diseases, prevention of food and drug adulteration as well as dissemination of health promoting information and behaviour. The total plan outlay of the Eleventh Plan of the state was Rs. 1503.50 crore (GoTN, 2008).

The National Sample Survey 60th Round (2004) has revealed that the cost of treatment in Tamil Nadu is very low when compared to other states in India. The average medical expenditure for non-hospitalised treatment per ailing person during a period of 15 days in rural Tamil Nadu was only Rs. 184. It was the second lowest among all the states in India. In urban areas it occupied fourth place with regard to low expenditure in India. In Tamil Nadu, the Government, voluntary and private sectors play a pivotal role in providing health infrastructure which has resulted in improvement in various health indicators. However, disparities among the districts have widened. Hence, private sector, voluntary organizations and government have to concentrate more on backward and remote regions.

PERFORMANCE OF HEALTH SECTOR

Health indicators like life expectancy, birth rate, death rate, infant mortality rate (IMR) and maternal mortality rate (MMR) show impressive improvement in the state. Table 10.3 reflects the performance of health indicators in Tamil Nadu. The IMR reveals that there has been a drastic reduction from 113 in 1971 to 28 per

TABLE 10.3

Performance of Health Indicators in Tamil Nadu

Year	*Infant Mortality Rate (per 1000 population)*	*Crude Birth Rate (per 1000 population)*	*Crude Death Rate (per 1000 population)*
1971	113	31.4	12.7
1981	93	28.0	11.8
1991	57	20.7	8.8
2001	49	19.1	7.9
2005	37	16.5	7.4
2006	37	16.2	7.5
2007	35	15.8	7.2
2008	31	16.0	7.4
2009	28	16.3	7.6

Source : Government of Tamil Nadu, Various issues of Tamil Nadu Economic Appraisal, Chennai.

1000 population in 2009. Birth and death rates also recorded a declining trend during the same reference period. Crude Birth Rate has come down from 31.4 per 1000 population to 16.3 in the state. Improvement in health facilities also have major influence on the reduction of Crude Death Rate in Tamil Nadu, which has come down from 12.7 per 1000 in 1971 to 7.6 per 1000 in 2009. The life expectancy rate is an important indicator of the overall health status of the population. The major effects of better health infrastructure on life expectancy at birth are positive. Life expectancy at birth for males and females in Tamil Nadu was 67 and 69.75 respectively during 2000-06, which was as low as 41 and 39.24 in 1951.

Table 10.4 presents the different types of health services provided by the various health institutions in Tamil Nadu during the period from 2003-04 to 2011-12. When the average number of in-patients treated every day in 2003-04 stood at 0.17 lakh, it marginally increased to 0.18 lakh in 2011-12. The treatment of out-patient has not registered significant improvement as it increased from 1.91 lakh to only 2 lakh during this period. The conduct of minor operations, however, has gone up significantly as it went up from the average of 8.39 lakh to 10.07 lakh. (Table 10.4)

TABLE 10.4

Services Provided by the Medical Institutions in Tamil Nadu

(*in Lakh*)

Service Rendered	*2003-04*	*2006-07*	*2011-12*
Average no. of in-patients treated daily	0.17	0.17	0.18
Average no. of out-patients treated daily	1.91	2.04	2.00
No. of major operations during the year	1.75	1.79	1.84
No. of minor operations during the year	6.64	6.02	8.40
No. of deliveries conducted	1.15	2.14	1.67

Source : Government of Tamil Nadu, Various issues of Tamil Nadu Economic Appraisal.

CHILD DELIVERY

Globally 5 lakh women die of pregnancy-related causes every year and 99 percent of these occur in the developing countries. In India less than a half of the women (47 percent) have institutional delivery and 53 percent had their births assisted by a skilled birth attendant. As many as 49 percent of pregnant women still do not have the minimum requirement of even three antenatal visits during pregnancy and only 46.6 percent of mothers receive iron and folic acid for at least 100 days during their pregnancy. Among the Indian states, institutional delivery has significantly improved in Tamil Nadu along with Kerala.

Age at marriage is one of the important indicators of health status of people. In Tamil Nadu the mean age at marriage for boys was 26.8 years in 2007-08 while it was 26.4 years in 2002-04. This shows that the mean age at marriage has not increased in the recent years. On the contrary, the mean age at marriage for girls has marginally increased from 20.7 years to 21.4 years respectively during the same period. In case of girls below 18 years of age, it has improved from 15.5 years in 2002-04 to 19.4 years in 2007-08. In Tamil Nadu, the average number of births of a woman in the age group of 15-19 was 3.2 percent of the total in 2007-08. The noteworthy fact is that institutional delivery has improved from 86.2 percent in 2002-04 to 94.1 percent in 2007-08 in the state. Delivery at home conducted by skilled health personnel has also improved from 23.2 percent to 26.4 percent during the same period. With regard to sterilization it is always higher in case of females. Safe delivery accounted for 95.6 percent in 2007-08 in the state as per DLHS II and III.

It is noteworthy that deliveries conducted by the Government medical institutions have significantly increased in recent decades. The deliveries undertaken by the various bodies in Tamil Nadu are presented in Table 10.5. Among the government medical institutions, government hospitals conducted 39.7 percent of the deliveries in

Table 10.5
Deliveries in Tamil Nadu

(In percent)

Delivery undertaken	*2004-05*	*2005-06*	*2006-07*	*2007-08*	*2008-09*
Sub Centres	7.4	7.2	6.1	5.8	2.3
Primary Health Centres	7.8	7.9	7.9	13.1	22.9
Government hospitals	42.1	42.5	43.3	42.2	39.7
Private hospitals	42.8	42.5	42.7	32.2	34.6
At home	5.7	4.4	3.4	1.7	0.5

2008-09. There has been phenomenal increase in institutional delivery undertaken by the Primary Health Centres (PHCs) as it increased from 7.8 percent in 2004-05 to 22.9 percent in 2008-09. It is also observed that delivery at home has significantly come down from 5.7 percent to 0.5 percent during this period. On the other hand, the percentage of sterilization went up from 64 percent in 2001-02 to 76.9 percent in 2010-11 in the state.

MATERNAL MORTALITY RATE

Maternal mortality is considered to be one of the vital indicators of health status of women. Maternal short stature and iron deficiency (anemia) increase the risk of death of a mother at delivery which account for about 20 percent of maternal mortality. The Millennium Development Goals (MDGs) had set the target to reduce maternal death to 200 per one lakh live births by 2007 and 109 per one lakh live births by 2015. At the national level maternal mortality rate was quite high with 254 per one lakh live births in 2004-06. It reveals the neglect of women during their most vulnerable period of pregnancy and child birth. Data also show that maternal mortality rate is estimated to be quite high among women belonging to scheduled castes and scheduled tribes (Lingam, 2011). As the Government of Tamil Nadu took several measures to reduce maternal mortality rate in the state, it resulted in significant reduction to 79 per one lakh live births in 2008-09. The state has achieved the objective before the target period.

Dr. Muthulakshmi Reddy Maternity Assistance Scheme has been in operation in Tamil Nadu since 1989-90. The Scheme gives priority to maternal and child welfare and realized the importance of maternal nutrition. After the increase of financial assistance under the scheme in 2006-07, a woman receives monetary assistance of Rs. 6000. This amount is paid at the rate of Rs.1000 per month for a total period of 6 months covering 3 months in antenatal care and 3 months in post-natal period up to two children. A total of 2.41 lakh pregnant women have been benefited in Tamil Nadu under this scheme.

Provision of health care facilities is an important determinant of life expectancy of people. As the Government of Tamil Nadu has taken several policy measures to strengthen health facilities in the state, life expectancy at birth has significantly improved during the last six decades. Since 1981 female life expectancy has been higher than their male counterpart and it has increased from 39.24 years in

TABLE 10.6

Trend in Maternal Mortality Rate in Tamil Nadu

Year	*MMR*	*Year*	*MMR*
1995-96	127	2002-03	123
1996-97	126	2003-04	114
1997-98	114	2004-05	109
1998-99	123	2005-06	94
1999-2000	126	2006-07	95
2000-01	133	2007-08	91
2001-02	145	2008-09	79

Source : www.esdproj.org/site/DocServer/MAT-P1_Vaidyanathan_3.7.10.ppt.

TABLE 10.7

Expectation of Life at Birth in Tamil Nadu

Year	*Male*	*Female*
1951-61	41.09	39.24
1961-71	47.50	46.50
1971-81	52.50	51.90
1981-91	57.40	58.50
1991-96	62.85	63.05
1996-01	64.85	65.20
2001-06	67.00	69.75

Source : Government of Tamil Nadu (2008), *Annual Statistical Abstract of Tamil Nadu,* Chennai: Government of Tamil Nadu.

1951-61 to 69.75 years in 2001-06. Similarly, male life expectancy has also improved from 41.09 years to 67 years during the same period. (Table 10.7)

The *Approach Paper of the Twelfth Five-Year Plan* of Tamil Nadu has a host of objectives. Its aim is to make public health care comprehensive, universal, transparent, accountable and participatory that delivers quality, rational, appropriate care with protection of patients' rights, patients choice and health equity, that is non-exclusive and non-discriminative. The vision of the Twelfth Five-Year Plan ensures that the quality of healthcare service in the public sector should be user-friendly especially for women and children.

CONCLUSION

The Government of Tamil Nadu gives considerable attention to health development to improve human capital especially among the weaker sections, viz. women and children. Despite this, health infrastructure in the hospitals, dispensaries, primary health centres and health sub-centres has not shown significant improvement in absolute number. The promotional measures taken at different stages like installation of modern medical equipments, upgradation of medical institutions and encouragement of private health facilities have largely benefited the people in the state. The state has also shown considerable improvement in institutional delivery particularly in government health institutions. The inferences of the study are that MMR has drastically come down due to serious implementation of maternal care programmes. This has given rise to perceptible increase in female life expectancy during the last two and a half decade.

Notwithstanding the fact that the health indicators of the state have significant position compared to the national level, still there are many parts of the state which are struggling to receive better medical facilities in their regions and localities. Though government hospitals provide low-cost or free medical services to the people, usually people prefer private health care centres to public ones. Absence of proper health care facilities in rural health centres, high cost of treatment in the private institutions, shortage of doctors and supporting staff and lack of access to medical care are the major hurdles in achieving universal healthcare.

Compared to other states of India, Tamil Nadu has a distinct place in implementing government schemes by instituting strong accountability measures and incentives at the grassroot level. The *Vision of Tamil Nadu 2023* has set the objective of universal access to healthcare. It seeks an ambitious goal in key parameters such as crude birth and death rates, MMR, IMR and under-5 MR. If the goals enshrined in the Vision are realized, Tamil Nadu will further improve in all the health indicators.

REFERENCES

Adler, N., *et al.* (1994), "Socioeconomic Status and Health, the Challenges of the Gradient," *American Psychologist*, 49, pp. 15-24.

Anbalagan, P. (2011), "Equity Aspects of Healthcare with Reference to Health Insurance for the Poor in India", *Indian Economic Journal*, (Special Issue) December.

Aschauer, D.A. (1990), *Public Investment and Private Sector Growth*, Washington, D.C: World Bank, Economic Policy Institute.

Duraisamy, P., and A. Mahal (2005), "Health, Poverty and Economic Growth in India," in *Financing and Delivery of Health Care Services in India*, NCMC Background Paper, Commission on Macroeconomics and Health, Ministry of Health and Family Welfare, New Delhi: Government of India.

Eapen, Mridul and Aashu Kupur Metha (2012), "Gendering the Twelfth Plan—A Feminist Perspective, *Economic and Political Weekly*, Vol. XLVII, No. 17, April 28.

Government of India (2004), *National Sample Survey Organization (*60th Round), New Delhi: Government of India.

Government of Tamil Nadu (2004), *Annual Statistical Abstract of Tamil Nadu, 2002-03,* Chennai: Department of Economics and Statistics.

Government of Tamil Nadu (2005), *Statistical Hand Book of Tamil Nadu, 2005,* Chennai: Department of Economics and Statistics.

Government of Tamil Nadu (2007), *Tamil Nadu Economic Appraisal*, Chennai: Evaluation and Applied Research Department.

Government of Tamil Nadu (2008), *Eleventh Five Year Plan Tamil Nadu 2007-2012*, Chennai: State Planning Commission.

Government of Tamil Nadu, (2012), *Vision Tamil Nadu 2023*, Chennai.

Gupta, I. and Arup Mitra (2004), "Economic Growth, Health and Poverty: An Exploratory Study for India, *Development Policy Review*, 22, pp. 193-206.

Kaushik, K.K.K.K. Klein and Lawrence, N. Arbenser (2006), *The Relationship Between Health Status and Health Care Expenditure in a Developing Hill Economy: An Econometric Approach,* IEA Annual Conference Volume, Kurukshetra University, Haryana.

Kuznets, Simon (1966), *Modern Economic Growth: Rate Structure and Spread*, New Delhi: Oxford & IBH Publishing, p. 490.

Leonard, A.G. (2006), *Tamil Nadu Economy*, Chennai: Macmillan.

Lingam, Lakshmi Vaidehi Yelamanchili (2011), "Reproductive Rights and Exclusionary Wrongs: Maternity Benefits", *Economic & Political Weekly*, Vol. XLVI, No. 43, October 22.

Malthora, Neena *et al.* (2006), *Health and Development: Inter-Links in India,* IEA Annual Conference Volume, Kurukshetra University.

Maya, (2011), "Financing Healthcare in India", *Indian Economic Journal*, Special Issue (Challenges of Inclusive Growth), December.

Mitra, Arup (1999), "Infrastructural Development for Competitiveness", *Productivity*, Vol. 40 (2), July-September 1999.

Munnel, A.H. (1992), "Policy Watch: Infrastructure Investment and Economic Growth", *Journal of Economic Perspectives*, Vol. 6 (4), pp. 189-98.

Pai Malaney (2000), *Health Sector Reform in Tamil Nadu: Understanding the Role of the Public Sector*, Centre for International Development, Harvard University.

Preston, S.H. (1975), "The Changing Relation between Mortality and Level of Economic Development," *Population Studies*, 29, pp. 231-48.

Reserve Bank of India (2004), *Hand Book of Statistics on State Government Finances*, Mumbai: Reserve Bank of India.

Schultz, T.N. (1971), *Investment in Human Capital: Role of Education and of Research*, New York: Free Press.

Singh, Bishwa Nath (2011), "Human Resource Development and Inclusive Growth: The Route through Health Services", *Indian Economic Journal*, Special Issue (Challenges of Inclusive Growth), December.

World Bank (1994), *World Development Report, 1994: Infrastructure for Development*, New York: Oxford University Press.

11

Health Status of Women in Goa

FERNANDA ANDRADE AND DIVYA SINGH

INTRODUCTION

Health is regarded as the most crucial aspect of human well-being. It is also seen among the basic capabilities that gives value to human life (Sen, 1999) and serves as an economic growth engine (David, 2002). *The World Development Report, 2012* considers investment in health as crucial to enrich human capital endowment which in turn shapes the ability of men and women to reach their full potential (World Bank, 2012) Health should be seen as an integral part of the development agenda. Good health is sought not just for pleasure and not only for reducing pain; but for expanding a person's capabilities and freedoms (Sen, 1999).

A woman's health not only influences the household economic well-being (Vellcoff and Adlakha 1997) but is also viewed as an investment in society's welfare (Rios, no date). A number of studies stress that women's health contributes to development generally in two ways: first as mothers they give birth to children and nurture them, and secondly as a means of their potential participation in the development of health programs and services to benefit the entire population. As per the 2011 Census, women constitute about 48.5 percent of the country's population. It is important to note that the health of Indian women is intrinsically linked to their status in society. *The World Development Report 2012: Gender Equality and Development* assessed global gender gap among 58 countries and placed India at rank 53 in overall ranking and in health and well-being its position is only 34th rank.

OBJECTIVES

This paper attempts to provide a profile of women's health in Goa state in the following ways:

(i) To examine the state's primary health care approach in terms of services offered and its accessibility to women in Goa.
(ii) To examine the health concerns of women in the state.
(iii) To map the various initiatives and health policies of Goa in order to assess the state's responsiveness towards gender sensitivity.

THE SETTING

Goa is the 25th state in India which was liberated from Portuguese rule in 1961. It was part of the Union territory of Goa, Daman & Diu till it was carved out to form a separate state in 1987. Goa covers an area of 3702 sq kms and comprises of two revenue districts viz. North Goa and South Goa. The boundaries of Goa state are defined by the North Terekhol River which separates it from Maharashtra in the east and Karnataka in the south and by Arabian Sea in the west. The population of the state is 14,57,723 and it ranks fifth in terms of literacy with a literacy rate of 87.40 percent, according to the 2011 Census. Though female literacy rate increased to 81.84 percent, it is still below male literacy rate of 92.81 percent. The female population is nearly 49 percent of the total population. In all, there are 334 revenue villages of which 194 are in North Goa district and 140 in South Goa district.

Goa is largely an urbanized state with 62.17 percent of the population living in urban areas. On an average Goa's NSDP per capita income during 2004-05 to 2009-10 (at Constant prices) has been the highest in the country (Govt. of Goa, MOSPI 2011). Goa was ranked as the best placed state by the Eleventh Finance Commission for its infrastructure and was also ranked at top for best quality of life in India by the National Commission on Population based on 12 indicators (Wikipedia).

TABLE 11.1
Health Infrastructure in Goa

Item	*Units*	*Pre-liberation or immediately after liberation*	*1987*	*2010-11*
Government hospitals	Nos.	17	31	32
Beds in government hospitals	Nos.	1,098	2,371	2,884
Private hospitals	Nos.	85	83	129
Beds in private hospitals	Nos.	1,405	1,312	2,760
Population served per bed	Nos.	211	31	
Health centres including maternity, dental, sub-centres and medical dispensaries (Govt.)	Nos.	20	214	254
Area served per hospital	Per sq. km	34.27	32.19	22.71
Patients treated indoor (Govt.)	No. in lakh	0.12	0.6	1.71(P)
Patients treated outdoor	No. in lakh	0.55	8.32	12.75(P)
Population served per hospital	Nos.	10,316	9,943	8,984

Note : *Indoor patients have been considered.
Source : Govt. of Goa, DPSE, 2011.

SNAPSHOT OF GOA'S HEALTH STATUS

Goa is known to have the most extensive health care system in India and is often rated one of the better performing state in India with regard to general health indicators. Goa has been credited with the model state for healthcare during 2007-10. (Parulekar, A. and Parulekar, M., no date) Good performance on indicators such as per capita income and literacy rate are reasons often attributed to the better position of women in Goa. In the rural areas, health services are provided through a network of integrated health and family welfare delivery system comprising of sub-centers, Primary Health Centers, Community Health Centers and district hospitals. Most of the indices seem to have improved since Goa attained statehood. For most households in Goa, the private medical sector is the main source of health care (71 percent of urban households and 68 percent of rural households) (NFHS-3). The Government of Goa has attained the goal of "Health for All" by the year 2000 A.D. through its various health and medical care programmes. Thus, it is considered as one of the best performing states in the matter of health and medical care.

There are biologically determined physiological differences that manifest in variations in needs and vulnerabilities between male and female. The gender effect varies across male and female based on the roles, access, power and sex. The type of health care need also varies by gender such as the accessibility of health care, empowerment with regard to health and sex.

Women's Health

This section presents the various indicators primarily responsible for women's health such as sex ratio, life expectancy and death rate. Birth rate of Goa state (13.6) is the lowest in the country. Life expectancy for males is 68 and for females it is 72 in 2004 as against the national life expectancy figure of 65.4, according to the 2011 Census. Kumar and Radha Devi (2010) describe that since women are genetically programmed to have a comparatively lower mortality, life expectancy at birth should be high for them compared to that of men. Death rate also helps to estimate the extent of need for health services. Table 11.2 shows that as compared to males, female death rate is less which depicts better health status of women.

TABLE 11.2

Death Rate by Sex and Residence, 2010

	Death Rate			*Rural*			*Urban*		
	Total	*Male*	*Female*	*Total*	*Male*	*Female*	*Total*	*Male*	*Female*
India	7.2	7.7	6.7	7.7	8.3	7.2	5.8	6.2	5.3
Goa	6.6	7.6	5.6	8.1	9.0	7.2	5.7	6.7	4.7

Source : *SRS Bulletin*, 2011.

Sex Ratio

Sex ratio is also the basic indicator of gender inequality. Though Goa stands at a better footing as compared to the national picture with regard to sex ratio, the serious issue is the declining trend in sex ratio in the State (except for 2011). The declining sex ratio in Goa reflects that like the rest of the country, there is male child preference in the state. This declining trend demolishes the myth that all is well for women in the State. (Desouza, 2011). The important reasons for the declining sex are primarily due to male child preference, sex determination of the unborn child, feticide/selective abortion, infanticide and migration of women, etc. (*Gender Profile of Goa*, no date).

TABLE 11.3

Sex Ratio in Goa and India

Year	*Goa*	*India*
1901	1091	972
1911	1108	964
1921	1120	955
1931	1088	950
1941	1084	945
1951	1128	946
1961	1066	941
1971	981	930
1981	975	934
1991	967	927
2001	960	933
2011	968	940

Source : Data book for DCH, 10 April 2012.

Infant Mortality Rate

Infant and child mortality rates reflect a country's level of socioeconomic development and quality of life. The two are also used for monitoring and evaluating population and health programmes and policies. The state of Goa has the lowest infant mortality (IMR) rates in India. In 2009, it recorded the least number of infant deaths per 1000 live births i.e. 10 (Table 11.4). It was followed by Kerala (12), Manipur (16) and Puducherry (22). Goa has a scheme to screen all newborn delivered in the Government hospitals for any inborn errors of metabolism introduced in 2008. This shows that Goa has surpassed the MDG goal as well.

Birth Intervals

Research shows that waiting at least three years between children reduces the risk of infant mortality. The median interval between births in Goa is 37 months, six months longer than the

TABLE 11.4

Indicators and Goals on Infant Mortality : Goa and India

Item	*IMR*
Goa (at the time of statehood in 1987)	24.88
Goa (in 2010)	10
India	47
MDG Goal (by 2015)	42

Source : National Rural Health Mission, PIP, Goa, 2011-12.

national average. The median birth interval is longer in Goa than in all other states in India except Kerala and Tripura.

REPRODUCTIVE HEALTH

Maternal Mortality Rate (MMR)

Maternal Mortality Ratio (MMR) is defined as the number of maternal deaths per 100,000 live births due to causes related to pregnancy. It is a useful indicator to capture the reproductive health status of women as well as the reach and adequacy of maternal health services available and utilised by women. Maternal mortality and morbidity are two major health concerns that are interwoven with high levels of fertility. In India, MMR is 56 times the ratio in the United States. (Kumar & Khan, 2010) The high levels of maternal mortality are highly distressing because the majority of these deaths could be prevented if women had availed adequate health care services. Lack of accessibility to health care facility is the most important factor contributing to high MMR. (World Bank, 1996)

Goa Development Report, 2011 pointed out that thirty-nine percent of married women in Goa experience at least one reproductive health problem, and this is one area where Goa is on par with the rest of India. The current Maternal Mortality Rate (MMR) of India is 212 per one lakh live births, whereas the country's MDG in this respect is 109 by 2015. Goa comparatively has a low MMR (<40 in 2011) and performing much better than India and had attained the MDG goal. (Dhar, 2012). At national level, social factors like illiteracy, low socio-economic conditions, and poor access to health facilities are the contributing factors to high maternal mortality. The MMR is only partial indicator of maternal health situation in any given country. Hence, the other indicators of maternal health status like antenatal check-up, institutional delivery and delivery by trained personnel are taken to get an overall picture of maternal health status.

TABLE 11.5

Maternal Mortality : Goa and India

Item	*Maternal Mortality Rate*
Goa (Pre-liberation 1961)	144
Goa (At the time of statehood 1987)	48
Goa (in 2011)	<40
India	212
Millennium Development Goal (by 2015)	109

Source : NRHM Goa presentation, 2012.

ANTENATAL CARE (ANC)

Since the Portugal times, Goan population has been made aware of the importance of ANC and other positive health seeking behaviour. This acts as an important contributor towards positive health seeking behaviour which in turn contributes in a great way to fewer maternal and infant deaths. (Ministry of Health and Family Welfare, 2011). Among women who gave birth in the five years preceding the NFHS-3 survey, almost all women (98 percent) received antenatal care from a health professional (97 percent from a doctor and 1 percent from any other health professional). Ninety-five percent of women in Goa had three or more antenatal care visits, the second highest percentage in India and well above India's figure of 52 percent. In Goa for 87 percent of births mothers received iron and folic acid supplements (IFA), and for 69 percent of births mothers consumed IFA for the recommended 90 days or more. Eighty-seven percent of mothers received two or more doses of tetanus toxoid vaccine. The WHO conducted a Maternal and Neonatal Tetanus Elimination (MNTE) Survey in North Goa district for three days. It was found that there were no neonatal deaths due to tetanus. (Goa Charter, 2008) Ninety-four percent of births in Goa during the five years preceding the Survey took place with the assistance from a health professional. Ninety-two percent of births (second highest after Kerala) during five years preceding the NFHS-3 Survey in Goa took place in a health facility (93 percent in urban areas and 92 percent in rural areas) as compared to 39 percent for India. Though the government sector caters to only 45.9 percent of deliveries, the most complicated cases are handled at Goa Medical College which is a government institution. There were no instances of out-of-pocket expenditures at least for maternal and child health facilities. (Ministry of Health and Family Welfare, 2011) The early postnatal care helps safeguard a mother's health and it also helps to reduce maternal mortality. Despite the high proportion of institutional deliveries, only 76 percent of mothers in Goa had a postnatal checkup within 2 days of their last birth, as is recommended. (NFHS-3).

MARRIAGE AND FERTILITY

Early age at first birth and a higher number of total pregnancies have adverse impact on women's health. In Goa at current fertility levels a woman has an average of 1.8 children in her lifetime compared to 2.7 for India. Goa is one of the 7 states in India where fertility is below the replacement level. This is despite the fact that contraceptive prevalence rate is much lower than the national average of 56 percent and knowledge of contraception is universal in Goa. This can be attributed to the highest age at marriage of Goa in the country, both for women and men. In fact, in the age group 15-19 only 6 percent of women in Goa are married, compared to the national average of 30 percent. (NFHS-3)

NUTRITIONAL STATUS

Women's nutrition assumes additional importance due to its critical but complex association with their well-being and the implication it has for human development (Jose & Navanneetham, 2008). It is, therefore, necessary to assess the nutritional status of women in Goa. Thus, this part of the paper tries to examine the different aspects of women's nutritional status in Goa.

Food Intake: A major determinant of the nutritional and health status is the average intake of energy (calorie), protein and iron. Adequate amounts of protein, fat, carbohydrates, vitamins and minerals are required for a well-balanced diet. Table 11.6 depicts the percentage of ever married women aged 15-24 years consuming specific food at least once a week. It is seen that only 30.8 percent of women aged 15-24 are consuming fruits at least once in a week. However, only 6.9 percent women daily consume fruits in India. Goa has a better performance in terms of milk/curd, fruits, egg and chicken/meat/fish consumption than the national percentages. However, pulses/bean or vegetable consumption in Goa is less than the national percentage.

Table 11.6
Percentage of Ever Married Women Aged 15-24 Years Consuming Specific Foods at Least Once a Week

	Type of food							
	Milk or curd	*Pulses or beans*	*Green leafy vegetables*	*Other vegetables*	*Fruits*	*Eggs*	*Chicken, meat or fish*	*Number of women*
India	53.3	88.1	85.5	92.7	30.8	28.2	31.3	24,571
Goa	66.2	85.7	74.3	83.9	56.8	40.0	79.8	126

Source : Computed from report *Reproductive and Sexual Health of Young People in India*, Government of India: Ministry of Health and Family Welfare, July 2009.

Body Mass Index: Malnutrition in adults can be assessed using the body mass index (BMI), which is defined as weight in kilograms divided by height in metres squared (kg/m^2). Adults with a BMI below 18.5 are considered to be too thin for their height. Adults with a BMI of 25 or higher are considered to be overweight or obese. A normal weight for height is indicated by a BMI of 18.5-24.9. The mean BMI for adolescent girls aged 15-19 years is 19, a little above the normal range of 18.5 - 24.9. Almost 12 percent women in the age group 15-19 years were found to be less than 145 cm in height, thus faced the risk in pregnancy and health of their babies.

Anaemia: Anaemia is a major killer in India. Statistics reveal that every second an Indian woman falls into the category of anaemic and one in every five maternal deaths is directly due to anaemia (Nayan Tara, 2011). It also results in an increased risk of premature delivery and low birth weight. Table 11.7 depicts the low BMI and anaemia percentage in Goa compared with national scores. It shows that Goa is performing better than the Indian averages in these two indicators. However, it is noteworthy to mention that there is an increase in the percentage from NFHS-2 to NFHS-3. In 2005-6, 27.9 percent women had low BMI and 38 percent were anaemic. The NFHS-3 also reveals that 56 percent of the women, more so in rural areas, were anaemic in all age groups. The mean body mass index among ever married women aged 15-24 years in India was 19.2 in 1998-99 while Goa had 19.3 mean BMI score. Further, 44.7 percent of ever married women in India aged 15-24 years were with low BMI (below 18.5 kg/m^2) while the figure stood at 47.8 percent in case of

Goa. However, Goa has a higher prevalence of overweight and obesity as 20.2 percent of the women in Goa are obese.

TABLE 11.7

Low Body Mass Index (BMI) and Anaemia in Women

(*Percent*)

Status	*Women with BMI below normal*		*Men with BMI below normal*	*Anaemia in ever married women (aged 15-49)*		*Women who are obese*	*Men who are obese*
	NFHS-2 (1998-99)	*NFHS-3 (2005-06)*	*NFHS-3 (2005-06)*	*NFHS-2 (1998-99)*	*NFHS-3*	*NFHS-3*	*NHFS-3*
India	35.8	35.6	34.2	51.8	55.3	12.6	9.3
Goa	27.1	27.9	24.6	36.4	38	20.2	15.4

Source : Data book for DCH; 10 April 2012 & http://cbhidghs.nic.in.

Table 11.8 depicts the percentage of ever married women aged 15-24 classified as having iron deficiency anaemia in India and Goa in 1998-99. It shows that 1.7 percent of women aged 15-24 in India suffer from severe anaemia while in Goa it is 1.6. In terms of women with any anaemia Kerala is the best in performance where only 25.4 percent women aged 15-24 years have any kind of anaemia, while this percent is highest in Assam with 72.0 percent. In Goa 42.8 percent of women in the age group of 15 to 24 suffer from any kind of anaemia. Jose and Navaneethan (2006) in their study concluded that malnutrition amounts to deprivation in one of the most elementary and central aspects of well-being and has implications for human development which are large and cumulative. They argued that women's malnutrition be viewed as an important issue of human development, rather than as an isolated issue of health specific to women. Nutritional anaemia is a common condition and a major public health problem that needs special attention. Iron deficiency in food intake is the most common cause of nutritional anaemia in human beings (Dabade *et. al.*, 2006). Agarwal *et. al.* (2006) suggested that screening for anaemia, treatment of anaemic women, and availability of food fortification, milk sugar and salt with iron to build long term iron stores remains the key to reduce anaemia. Dietary modification and proper awareness are the key to prevent anaemia.

Table 11.8
Anaemia among Women

	Percent of women with any anaemia	*Percent of women with mild anaemia*	*Percent of women with moderate anaemia*	*Percent of women with severe anaemia*
India	58.0	39.1	17.2	1.7
Goa	42.8	34.7	6.5	1.6
Highest in India	72.0 (Assam)	48.6 (West Bengal)	26.9 (Assam)	3.9 (Meghalaya)
Lowest in India	25.4 (Kerala)	22.4 (Kerala)	2.3 (Kerala)	0.0 (Himachal Pradesh)

Source : Computed from the report *Reproductive and Sexual Health of Young People in India*, New Delhi: Government of India, Ministry of Health and Family Welfare, July 2009.

MEASURES UNDERTAKEN BY THE GOVERNMENT OF GOA FOR HEALTHCARE DEVELOPMENT

Equity in access to health care and securing a prominent place for health in the overall developmental framework is one of the major concerns. (Government of Goa Citizen Charter, 2008). In Goa all patients admitted in Government hospitals are provided diet, basic diagnostics including doctors services free by the State Government. (Ministry of Health and Family Welfare, 2011). Goa has also a unique Mediclaim scheme wherein Rs. 1.5 lakh per illness is provided for availing super specialist treatment that is not available in Government hospitals whose income is less than Rs. 1.50 lakh per annum. Some of the Central Government schemes that are in force in Goa are the National Rural Health Mission (NRHM), Integrated Child Development Scheme (ICDS), Janani Suraksha Yojana (JSY), Reproductive and Child Health Programme (RCH-II), Jananishishu Suraksha Karyakaram, etc.

SOME OTHER INITIATIVES TAKEN UP BY THE STATE

Health awareness especially relating to female health is one of the prime focuses of health initiatives in the state. The State Health Department is giving health tips in five local newspapers, giving cinema theater slides on a regular basis and conducting awareness programme in schools. Regarding awareness on PC and PNDT, there was a short film contest on Save the Girl Child (PC & PNDT Act) in 2011 where 23 entries were received in the state of Goa. Mother and Child Protection (MCP) cards are provided to all pregnant women. Presence of an MCH card has been made mandatory for availing State Government schemes for girl child. This has helped to increase antenatal care registration. (NRHM, PIP Goa 2011-12)

Goa has a special mammography unit launched in 2010. This is important to note that for the first time in the country this unit has been set up in the government sector. Two mobile clinic vans with mammography ultrasound and pathology unit are already launched and operational for early detection and prompt treatment of breast cancer. Various camps were organized at Margao, Vasco, Mapusa, Ponda, Canacona, Valpoi, Curchorem, Pernem, Bicholim, Shiroda, Sanquelim, Sanguem, Siolim, Curtorim, Aldona and Panaji in which a total of 2871 patients participated.

An initiative very unique to Goa is the screening of infant metabolic disorders. All infants born in the government hospitals are tested through blood for metabolic disorders to benefit the defective children in their early stages. The program began in June 2008 and so far more than 30,000 babies have been screened (as reported by NeoGen labs, 2011). Counseling cells have been initiated for breast feeding promotion in Goa's district hospitals which conduct sessions for pregnant mothers through films on the importance of breast feeding and antenatal classes. The Government of Goa also launched Measles Mumps Rubella (MMR) and Rubella Vaccines programme in May 2009 as a result of which the vaccine is provided as a part of immunization. (Government of Goa Citizen Charter, 2008). Care of sick children and severe malnutrition is another important programme. Provision of Rs. 10 lakh is made at the ward levels for complementary feeding, feeding tubes etc. Infant Death Audits are conducted for assessment of medical and socio-cultural factors related to perinatal, infant and child deaths in Goa maternal death review is conducted wherein maternal deaths among all women between 15- 49 years are identified, their cause of death is analysed and required remedial action taken. These apart, state level workshops are organized in collaboration with partners like Federation of Obstetric and Gynecological Societies of India and Indian Medical Association to discuss issues related to maternal mortality. Decisions taken at the workshop are disseminated to districts for corrective action. (NRHM, PIP Goa, 2011-12) Gestational diabetes Programme has also been initiated in Goa which is meant to focus on meal planning, blood glucose monitoring and insulin for pregnant women with diabetes. (NRHM, PIP Goa 2011-12).

RCH outreach camps are conducted in underserved areas for detection of congenital anomalies in children and detection of malignancies in women with the involvement of private sector. Pap-Smear Examination is also undertaken by all Primary Health Centers in collaboration with Goa Medical College for early detection of Carcinoma cervix in female population with specific complaints. This is carried on a regular basis. Skilled birth attendant training is conducted in the district hospitals for doctors and nurses. (Government of Goa Citizen Charter, 2008) Assured referral transport through 108 ambulances is available for all pregnant women in the state. As there is no facility for drop back provision for these women, the state is in the process of collaborating with Goa State Transport buses to provide drop back facilities for pregnant women. (NRHM, PIP Goa 2011-12)

The healthcare facilities in Goa can be ranked well in respect of general neatness and cleanliness. The function of cleaning in major government health centers has been outsourced to ensure cleanliness. (Ministry of Health and Family Welfare, 2011). In Goa, involvement of the political leaders in the public health care sector is high. For instance, the absence of doctors in health care facilities is reported by the local Panchayat to the local or state level politicians, sometimes even to the Health Minister. The political involvement and in-built community monitoring mechanism in Goa ensures that the system performs well and there is minimum absenteeism in public health institutions. (Ministry of Health and Family Welfare, 2011)

CONCLUSION

Goa has been ranked high among all the states in India in terms of not only its general health condition but also in terms of women's health indicators. Good performance in terms of high per-capita income and high literacy rates have often been sighted as an important factor. Provision of free medical services especially for maternal health and child care and easy accessibility through state emergency services have resulted in increase in institutional deliveries and healthcare. Added to all these, the other important factors that have given fruit are the awareness creation amongst women belonging to lower income category about the importance of professional health care facilities. The continuous monitoring by community and local leaders has made the Government accountable in terms of healthcare provision. Though the State is performing well in terms of health and infrastructure indicators, it needs to lay stress on improving quality of healthcare at all levels of service delivery by implementing quality certification of hospitals and employing professional hospital managers. The State should also ensure the provision of continuous medical education to enhance the capacities of staff employed under the public health sector.

References

Agarwal, K.N. *et al.* (2004), "Prevalence of Anaemia in Pregnant and Lactating Women in India," *Indian J Med Res,* 124, August 2006, pp. 173-84.

Dabade, Gopal. *et. al.* (N.A.), "A Study on Drugs for Treating Anaemia," Retrieved from http://fkilp.iimb.ernet.in/pdf/Healthcare_Anaemia/Diagnosis_and_Treatment_of_Anaemia/Accuracy_effectivness_and_saftety_of_treatment_options/Dabade_A_Study_on_Drugs_for_Treating_Anaemia_campaign.pdf

David, M.M., and F.C. Cyril (2002), "Health as an Economic Engine: How Better Health Leads to Economic Development," *Business Perspectives,* 14(4), 12-15. Retrieved from http://search.proquest.com/docview/228761216?accountid=45979

Desouza, Shaila (2011), *Organising Women for Empowerment: A study of an Experiment in Goa,* Retrieved from http://hdl.handle.net/10603/2722

har, Arti (2012), *U.N.: India Likely to Miss MDG on Maternal Health*, Retrieved from http://www.thehindu.com/health/policy-and-issues/article3595095.ece

Government of Goa Citizen Charter (2008), *Health Intelligence Bureau*, Directorate of Health Services.

Gender Profile of Goa (No date) available at: http://ncw.nic.in/pdfreports/Gender percent20Profile-Goa.pdf

Government of Goa (2011), *Indicators of Socioeconomic Development*, Goa: Directorate of Planning Statistics & Evaluation (DPSE).

Government of India (2011), State Domestic Product and Other Aggregates: Various Base Years, Ministry of Statistics and Programme Implementation (MOSPI), Available at: http://mospi.nic.in/Mospi_New/site/inner.aspx?status=3&menu_id=82

Jose, Sunny. and Navaneetham K. (2008), "A Factsheet on Women's Malnutrition in India," *Economic & Political Weekly*, Retrieved from http://environmentportal.in/files/6_20.pdf

Kumar, Ajith N. and D. Radha Devi (2010), 'Health of Women in Kerala: Current Status and Emerging Issues,' Working Paper 23, Centre for Social-Economic and Environment Studies, Kochi.

Government of India, Ministry of Health and Family Welfare, (2005-06), *Goa National Family Health Survey (NFHS-3), India (2005-06*), Mumbai: International Institute for Population Sciences.

Mediclaim Scheme http://india.gov.in/citizen/health/viewscheme.php?schemeid=487.

Ministry of Health and Family Welfare (2011), Fifth Common Review Mission Goa http://nhsrcindia.org/pdf_files/resources_thematic/Health_Sector_Overview/NHSRC_Contribution/Goa_474.pdf.

National Rural Health Mission (NRHM), *PIP Goa* 2011-12.

Nayan Tara, S. (2011), *India's Anaemia Woes- A study*, Retrieved from http://tejas-iimb.org/articles/59.php.

NeoGen labs (2011), available at: http://neogenlabs.com/wordpress/?p=216

Parulekar, A. and M Parulekar (No date) Future of Healthcare in India and Goa, Goa Institute of Management.

Rios Rebecca De Los (No date) *Gender, Health and Development: An approach in the Making*, Retrieved from http://www.amro.who.int/English/DD/PUB/SP541-3-17.pdf

Sen, Amartya Kumar (1999), *Development as Freedom*, Oxford University Press.

Sen, Amrtya, (No date) *Health: the Perspective of Knowledge*, Retrieved from http://www.institut.veolia.org/en/cahiers/sustainable-development-knowledge/ideas-broadening/sen.aspx.

SRS Bulletin (2011), http://pib.nic.in/archieve/others/2012/feb/d2012020102.pdf

United Nations Development Programme available at: Millennium Development Goals: Eight Goals for 2015. http://www.undp.org/content/undp/en/home/mdgoverview.html

Velcoff, Victoria and Arjun Adalkha (1998), *Woman's Health in India*, U.S. Department of Commerce, Economics and Statistics Administration.

Wikipedia Goa http://en.wikipedia.org/wiki/Goa. Original source: *Reports of the Finance Commissions of India: First Finance Commission to the Twelfth Finance Commission: the complete report. India,* Finance Commission. Academic Foundation, 2005, p. 268.

World Bank (2012), *World Development Report 2012: Gender Equality and Development,* Washington, D.C.: World Bank.

12

Gender Differentials in the Prevalence of Fever and Reporting Pattern through Emergency Medical Services in Andhra Pradesh

BIRANCHI JENA AND M.N.V. PRASAD

INTRODUCTION

Women's health issues have received higher international focus and renewed political commitment in recent decades. While targeted policies and programmes have enabled women to lead healthier lives, significant gender-based health disparities remain a major issue in many developing countries. With limited access to education and employment, high illiteracy rates and increasing poverty levels are making health improvements for women exceedingly difficult. (UN, 2005) Basic health care, family planning and obstetric services are essential for women—yet they are not within reach for millions. Gender equity approach to health is essential to enable women's full participation in the planning and delivery of health services. It is a well-known fact that men and women have dissimilar rates of different diseases and thus seek medical care differently and in differing amounts. Understanding gender difference is a prerequisite to recognize the basis of existing gaps in health and health seeking behaviour of men and women. This will enable health service providers to effectively address gender inequality in health. (Kaur, 2009) Gender is also significantly associated with differentials in illness patterns as well as with differences in health seeking behaviour. There is a difference between sex and gender. While sex is biological, gender is a social and cultural construct that describes norms of behaviour for men and women, i.e. masculinity for men and feminity for women. (Sagar, 2004) A number of studies indicate that social or gender factors often play a major role in the ill-health of women. Gender factors influence the extent to which women are able to have control over their own circumstances affecting their health and the quality of life. (Sekhar, 2007) Communicable disease is still a major health burden in developing countries.

Developing country populations, particularly in small island states, arid and high mountain zones, and in densely-populated coastal areas are considered to be vulnerable especially for vector-borne diseases including malaria and dengue. (Majra and Gaur, 2009) As accessibility to health care centre has been a major challenge in developing countries, free ambulance service would improve the treatment rates at designated health care centres. Patients' requirement of ambulance service is fairly accurate in predicting fever where the complaint is subjective fever. (Buckley and Conine, 1996)

Andhra Pradesh is the fifth largest state in India, both in area and population. It is situated in the Deccan plateau and is sprawled over an area of 276,754 sq. km. With generally hot and humid climate and frequent changes in climate, seasonal ailment like fever has been a major challenge for Andhra Pradesh. (*Andhra Pradesh Human Development Report 2007*) As per the National Sample Survey Organization (NSSO) data, the prevalence of morbidity has declined by 7.3 percent between 1995 and 2004 in the state. However, the prevalence among females has gone up by 7 percent and it has declined by 19 percent among males in the same period. Fever is still a major health problem in Andhra Pradesh and the NSSO 60th Round found that prevalence of fever of unknown origin was 1340 per one lakh population in 15 days preceding the Survey. The prevalence was found to be higher among females (1450 per one lakh population) than males. (1225 per one lakh population) (NSSO, 2004)

The GVK Emergency Management and Research Institute (GVK EMRI) is a pioneer in providing emergency management services in Andhra Pradesh. There are many emergencies in which the public health agency plays a central role in defining the scope of risk, highly infectious disease such as fever. Keeping the above points in view an attempt is made to examine gender differences in accessing health services through GVK EMRI services and thus the main objective of this paper is to study gender differentials with respect to prevalence and reporting of fever to GVK EMRI.

DATA AND METHODOLOGY

A community-level household survey was conducted during 15 Dec. 2008 to 15 Jan. 2009 to find out the prevalence of fever among individuals of the households in the selected three districts of Andhra Pradesh based on a sample drawn on the basis of systematic random sampling method. The three districts were selected based on the level of infant mortality rate, female literacy, urbanization and proportion of the scheduled caste/tribes population to ensure representative sampling units for the study. Data regarding morbidity status with respect to fever were collected for a period of three months preceding the Survey using a questionnaire for 408 households on different socio-economic-demographic characteristics in 21 primary sampling units (villages/urban wards). The selected 408 households have 1067 males and 1060 females and information about their disease status was collected from the head of the household.

For the purpose of the study, fever was defined as a condition when the human body temperature is more than 38°C (100.4°F). During data collection the prevalence of fever was subjectively evaluated based on the response of the respondents (head of the household) about the household members. The response was recorded irrespective of a device (thermometer) being used or not used by the members of the household to measure the temperature of the person who was reported as suffering from fever at least once in three months preceding the Survey. However, necessary probing was made during the Survey to record the correct answer. Diagnosed cases of malaria, chikungunya, dengue fever etc. were also included in this study.

GVK Emergency Management and Research Institute (GVK EMRI) started running the first professional and comprehensive free emergency services in India since August 2005 under the Public-Private Partnership (PPP) programme by running a single toll free number 108. Currently 108 services are available in 10 states in India and Andhra Pradesh is one of the leading states in implementing this programme more than three years ago. This service in Andhra

Pradesh is aimed at a population of over 80 million spread across an area of 276,754 square kilometer accounting to nearly 8.4 percent of India's territory with a fleet of nearly 750 mobile emergency units.

GVK EMRI maintains a database including details of the emergency for which the service is used. The current study also compiled data pertaining to emergency related to fever being reported to GVK EMRI during August 2007- July 2008. The reported cases of such emergency to GVK EMRI were 18,747 in the three selected districts, of which 12,010 were male and 6737 were female. The analysis of gender-wise differentials of reporting cases of fever using reported cases to GVK EMRI and the results from household survey were carried out. Data analysis was performed using the calculated prevalence rates, odds ratio and Chi-square test. The test of significance were two-tailed, with a probability (p) value <0.05 being considered significant.

RESULTS

The Survey result shows that 55 percent of the victims, who suffered from fever, required emergency medical services. Although the proportion of male victims (55.6 percent) who required emergency medical services for the sick was more than the proportion of female victims (54.9 percent), the difference was found to be statistically insignificant.

The overall prevalence rate of fever was found to be 11.5 percent in the three months preceding the Survey in the study areas. The prevalence rate was higher among females (13.2 percent) as compared to their male counterparts (9.8 percent). The absolute difference in the female and male prevalence rate was 3.4 percent and a relative difference of 25 percent for fever indicated that females are more prone to fever in the study area. As far as the risk of suffering from fever is concerned, the analysis shows that females were 1.39 times more vulnerable in suffering from the sickness ($p<0.001$) than the males.

As far as the reporting of such emergency is concerned, the odds ratio method is applied to find out the likelihood of female victims reporting for emergency health services in comparison to the male victims for fever. For this purpose of the analysis, reporting of emergencies other than fever was considered as the reference group. All the emergencies pertaining to pregnancy was excluded from the present analysis. The results show that females were 1.12 times more likely seek medical emergency services for fever in comparison to other medical emergency ($p < 0.001$) than their male counterparts.

The gender-wise differential in the prevalence rate is more evident when age is taken into consideration. The prevalence rate of fever was more among the male population at an early age and declines with progress of age and on the other hand the prevalence of such morbidity among females was less among the lower age group and increases with age. The prevalence of fever was almost double among males of less than five years of age (17.5 percent) as compared to the females of the same age group (9.5 percent). Similarly, the prevalence rate was almost four times more among the female population in the age group of 35-44 (19.5 percent) than the male population of the same age group (5.7 percent) (Figure 12.1).

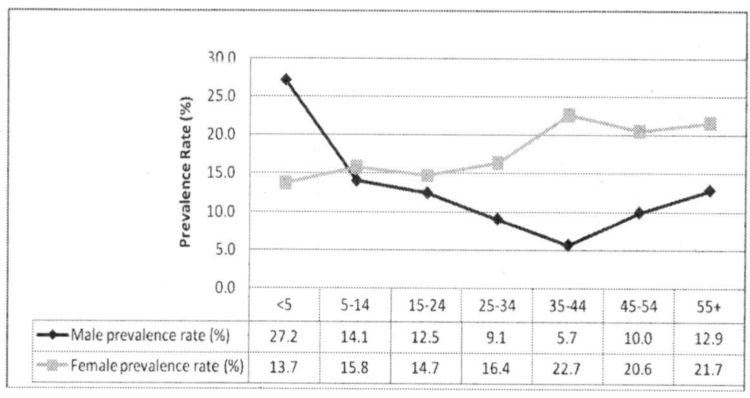

Figure 12.1 : Age-wise Prevalence Rate of Fever—All Types in the Study Population

GVK EMRI being the sole free emergency service provider in Andhra Pradesh and the community level study showed that around 55 percent need emergency medical services including emergency transport. It is important to compare the prevalence rate with the reporting of such cases to GVK EMRI by taking age and gender into consideration. Since the prevalence rate cannot be compared directly with the reporting of the cases to GVK EMRI, the age-wise proportion of victims from the survey was compared with the age-wise reporting of cases to GVK EMRI.

Those who suffered from fever during the Survey period, more than 61 percent of the male victims were below 24 years of age whereas females in the age group of 15-44 contributed the major proportion (53 percent). It is worth mentioning that there was a significant variation in the proportion of prevalent cases between males and females who were below 5 years of age. Again the proportion of prevalent cases was more for males in the age group 5-14 years (22 percent) as compared to the females of the same age group (16 percent). In the age group of 15 and above, the proportion of prevalence cases were more for females than the males. GVK EMRI data revealed that there was no significant variation in the age-wise reporting of cases by male and female victims.

If we compare the age-wise proportion of prevalent cases with the proportion of reported cases, it is revealed that the reporting of cases for fever was significantly low for the age group up to 24 years and the proportion of reporting of such sickness to GVK EMRI is more for the age-group of 25 and above when compared with the prevalence rate. Therefore, it is evident that GVK EMRI services were less effective for the victims of less than 24 years of age. The variation in the proportion of prevalent cases and the proportion of reported cases to GVK EMRI was more evident for male victims than female victims (Figure 12.2). The proportion of prevalent cases in the age group of under five male victims were found to be 21 percent where as the proportion of victims reporting to GVK EMRI for emergency service was as low as 4 percent. On the contrary, for under-five female victims the proportion of prevalent cases was 7 percent as against the reporting cases of 5 percent. Similar is the case with male and female victims of age group of 5-14 years. Thus, the

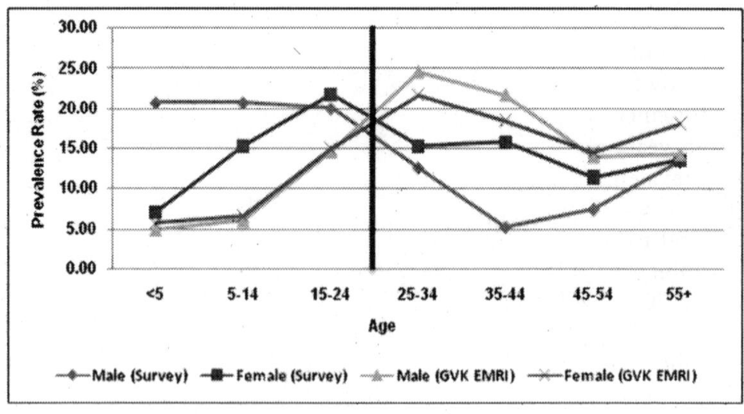

Figure 12.2 : Age-wise Prevalent Cases of Fever

GVK EMRI services were more effective for female victims in the age-group of less than 15 years than their male counterparts. On the other hand, GVK EMRI services were proved to be quite effective for victims in the age-group of more than 25, though it was more effective for male victims.

DISCUSSION

The study reveals that there was a significant difference in the prevalence rate of fever among females than that of males. Earlier research in the present geographical study area revealed that the chance of being suffered by typhoid, malaria and jaundice diseases in females was more when compared to males in areas both covered and not covered by the water supply project. (Nagavara Prasad, 2007) Another study discussed that women may be more susceptible than men to diseases which cause death. Comparisons of the morbidity of men and women in the same households usually show female morbidity to be higher, possibly due to lack of health care facilities. Differential morbidity by gender is partly due to the different health hazards to which men and women are exposed. (ODA, 1995)

A study of GVK EMRI indicates that the demand for emergency services for communicable diseases in Andhra Pradesh has increased from 7 percent in 2006 to 29 percent in 2007 and further to 43 percent in 2008. (Agarwal and Jena, 2008) Therefore. reporting of morbid conditions like fever to GVK EMRI is continuously increasing to GVK EMRI. The present study indicates that 63 percent of the victims reporting for fever were male. Chihiro *et al.* reported that when facing no serious situation, males were more likely to call an ambulance than the females. (Chihiro *et al.*, 2007) The present study found that the proportion of victims reporting to GVK EMRI for emergency services for fever are more the age group of more than 25 years for both male and female victims than the proportion of prevalent cases. Again, it is also found that seeking emergency services from GVK EMRI increases with age. Elderly persons would tend to call an ambulance more than the younger persons and age influenced the hypothetical ambulance call rate linearly. (Chihiro *et al.*, 2007)

The study found a higher prevalence rate of fever among male children of less than five years than those of the female children of the same age group. However, the proportion of reporting to GVK EMRI is significantly less for the male children with morbid conditions like fever. Such variation is expected due to the perception of quicker access to medical attention and the amount spent in accessing medical care including transportation. Accessing definite medical care through GVK EMRI ambulance are often perceived as a late service as it takes around 40 minutes to reach the victim from getting the call in case of fever disease. The marginal benefit of providing medical care is higher for sons than for daughters, where as the marginal costs are same. Thus, a larger proportion of sons get medical care than daughters. This bias would not have occurred if all the families coordinated their actions and took more of their sick daughters to hospitals/doctors. (Lahiri, 2005) Son preference can lead to higher value being placed on the health of male children. There is evidence that male children receive better health care in some cases. (Madhiwalla, 2000) The results of the present study with low variation in the proportion of prevalence and reporting for emergency services for female children below five years ensured better health seeking behavior for the female children. Thus, a free EMS for the community like services provided by GVK EMRI would increase better health access for female children and ensure a reduction in child mortality, especially female child mortality rate.

There is wide disparity in the utilization of public health facilities at different levels. While the tertiary hospitals were overloaded, the first referral systems like health posts were underutilized. Utilization of the formal health sector is lower among women than men. More than 12 percent of the reasons for not seeking health care by women related to the lack of physical access to health facilities. Access to health care facilities in terms of distance and who provided health care were the major factors which influenced utilization. In case of nearly two-third of the illness episodes, health facilities with less than 10 minutes distance from home were approached. (Madhiwalla, 2000) This indicates that provision of transportation facility plays a vital role in community health seeking behaviour as well as utilization of the health facilities. Cases handled by GVK EMRI for fever shows an average time of transportation of a patient from the spot to the hospital is around 30 minutes. This clearly signifies the role of GVK EMRI intervention in improving the health seeking behaviour among females and overall utilization of healthcare facilities.

Unwell men received equal treatment irrespective of age, whereas among women, those in the age-group of 0-11 years have a higher number of treated illnesses. (Madhiwalla, 2000) The results of the present study revealed that there was a significant variation in proportion of prevalence and reporting of diseases like fever between male and female aged below 15 years. The absolute difference in the proportion of prevalent cases and proportion of reported cases of fever for females below 15 years were found to be 10 percent where as this difference in case of male victims was 31 percent. This indicates that most of the female victims were using health care facilities through GVK EMRI services whereas in case of male victims the health care facilities were used without much dependency on GVK EMRI's free EMS system.

CONCLUSION

The study concludes that there is wide gender variation in the prevalence and reporting of fever. The results further reveal that the intervention in terms of free EMS services has been quite effective for the age group of 25 years and above. The results suggest that reporting from the lower age group is less as compared to the prevalence rate in such age group. It implies that free emergency medical service is less effective for lower age groups. However, GVK EMRI's intervention has proved significantly effective for female victims of less than 5 years than the male victims of this age group. Considering high child mortality under 5 years, GVK EMRI's intervention in terms of free EMS has helped especially the female child to utilise the health care system more effectively. Lower utilization of this service was observed among the male victims at lower age. Thus, it is important to increase awareness among the parents to enhance the usage of EMS services especially for the male child to improve the status of survival further for the male child.

References

Agrawal, Gopal and Biranchi, N. Jena (2008), Project Report on 'Health Transition in India: Raising Demand for Emergency Health Care Services', Emergency Management and Research Institute, Andhra Pradesh, India.

Buckley, R. and M. Conine (1996), "Reliability of Subjective Fever in Triage of Adult Patients", *Annals of Emergency Medicine*, Volume 27, Issue 6, pp. 693-95.

Chihiro, Kawakami *et al.* (2007), 'Influence of Socioeconomic factors on medically unnecessary calls', BMC Health Services Research, 7:120, http://www.biomedcentral.com/1472-6963/7/120. Accessed on 13 March 2009.

GVK Emergency Management and Research Institute (GVK EMRI), Andhra Pradesh State of India. http://emri.in/. Accessed on 09 March 2009.

Kaur, Manmeet (2005-07 to 2005-09), "CME; Mainstreaming Gender in Health", *Indian Journal of Community Medicine*, Vol. 30, No. 3.

Lahiri , Sajal and Sharmistha Self, "Exogamy and Bias against Daughters in Health-care Provision: A Theory and Evidence from Two Northern States in India" posted at OpenSIUC, http://opensiuc.lib.siu.edu/econ dp/39. Accessed on 13 March 2009.

Madhiwalla, Neha *et al.* (2000), *Health, Households and Women's Lives: A Study of Illness and Childbearing among Women in Nasik District, Maharashtra*, Mumbai: CEHAT, June 2000, p. 141.

Majra, J.P.A. Gur (2009), "Climate Change and Health: Why Should India be Concerned?" *Indian J. Occup Environ Med.*, 13:11-6.

Nagavara Prasad, M. (2007), "Access to Safe Drinking Water and its Effect on Health; A Statistical Approach", Ph.D. thesis, Sri Krishnadevaraya University, Anantapur.

NSSO (2004), National Sample Survey Organization (NSSO) — 52nd and 60th Round', New Delhi.

Okojie (1994), Gender Norms and Values on Health Seeking Treatment, http://www.liv.ac.uk/lstm/hsr/GG-7.html. Accessed on 09 March 2009.

Overseas Development Administration (ODA), (1995), 'Gender issues in India: Key findings and recommendations', Short report-32, February 1995 (revised) Report commissioned by the Overseas Development Administration (DFID), UK.

Sagar, A. (2004), "Gender Concepts—Using Gender to Examine Ill-health in Women". http://www.indmedica.com/journals/pdf/iapsm/Alpana percent20Sagar.pdf. Accessed on 13 March 2009.

Sekhar, Himanshu *et. al.* (2007), 'Gender and Development: Dimensions and Strategies—Introduction and Overview', India. http://mpra.ub.uni-muenchen.de/6559/ MPRA Paper No. 6559, posted 03. January 2008. Accessed on 13 March 2009.

United Nations Population Division (2005), *The Promise of Equality: Gender Equity, Reproductive Health and the Millennium Development Goals*, New York: UNFPA. http:// www.unfpa.org/swp/2005/pdf/en_swp05.pdf. Accessed on 09 March 2009.

Website http://www.whereincity.com/india/andhra-pradesh/. Accessed on 26 August 2009.

Websitehttp://www.aponline.gov.in/Apportal/HumanDevelopment Report2007/APHDR_2007_ Chapter7.pdf. Accessed on dated 26 August 2009.

13

Nutritional Status of Women in Punjab

An Analysis

BHARTI KAPUR

INTRODUCTION

Eliminating hunger and malnutrition is one of the fundamental challenges facing humanity (Lomborg, 2004). Malnutrition and its associated disease conditions can be caused by eating too little, eating too much, or eating an unbalanced diet that lacks necessary nutrients. Malnutrition is one of the most devastating problems worldwide and is inextricably linked with poverty. The oppression of women socially and culturally means they have less access to everything, including food, resources, health care, community support and information. The problems arise from cultural, political and economic realities that must be addressed in tandem (Dewan Manju, 2008).

Poor nutrition in infancy and early childhood increases the risk of perinatal, infant, and child morbidity and mortality, long-term physical growth, cognitive development and future learning capacity, school performance and educational outcomes, work performance, and reproductive outcome. These are outcomes of an intergenerational cycle of ill-health and growth failure, which are compounded by gender discrimination in childcare, feeding, and health care. Securing adequate nutrition for women is, therefore, a socially and economically important goal for developing countries (Nestel, 2000).

Nutrition has a central role in human well-being. It is both an essential element of, and also a critical input to other aspects of well-being. Adequate nutritional attainment is equally essential both for men and women. However, women's nutrition assumes additional importance due to its critical but complex association with their well-being and the implication it has for human development. Yet, it is women's nutrition—to that extent their well-being—which has often been subsumed under the umbrella of "family welfare" and ignored ostensibly due to "constraints from culture" in India and other South Asian countries.

Undernutrition would denote a deprivation of the basic aspect of well-being: the lack of freedom to lead a minimal healthy life. The implication that women's malnutrition have for human development are multiple and cumulative. For instance, maternal malnutrition tends to increase the risk of maternal mortality. Maternal short stature and iron deficiency anaemia, which increase the risk of death of the mother at delivery account for at least 20 percent of maternal mortality (Black *et al.*, 2008). Additionally, maternal malnutrition impinges significantly on such important but interconnected aspects as intrauterine growth retardation, child malnutrition and rising emergence of chronic diseases, among others (Osmani and Sen, 2003; Victora *et al.*, 2008). Therefore, analysis of the nutritional attainment of women assumes significance and relevance.

The present paper endeavours to provide an analysis on the level of malnutrition among women in India. An inter-state difference in women's malnutrition has also been examined. As the study mainly concerns the state of Punjab, it examines the extent of women's malnutrition in Punjab and determines the spatial, social and economic disparities in women's malnutrition within the state. These issues are addressed by analysing the National Family Health Survey-3 (NFHS-3) data, 2005-06. It is important to state, at the outset, that the focus of the paper is limited in scope. It does not deal with the issues of causation or provides an explanation, but rather presents a preliminary factsheet on women's malnutrition in Punjab.

Before getting on with the analysis, a note on the indicators of nutrition used here is in order. The body mass index (BMI) measures the weight to squared height (w/h^2) and a BMI of less than 18.5 indicates undernutrition, referred to as chronic energy deficiency (CED). On the contrary, BMI above 25 and 30 refers to overweight and obesity respectively, which are also indicative of poor nutrition. However, chronic energy deficiency tends to indicate the absence of freedom to lead a minimally healthy life, and hence is structurally different from overweight and obesity, which relate to *inter alia* an unhealthy lifestyle. Iron deficiency anaemia which is one of the widespread forms of women's malnutrition in developing countries is indicated usually by 11.9 grams/decilitre of haemoglobin in the blood. Haemoglobin below 9.0 and 7.0 grams/decilitre denotes moderate and severe anaemia respectively.

LEVELS OF MALNUTRITION AMONG WOMEN (15-49 YEARS) IN INDIA

Table 13.1 presents the level of malnutrition among women (15-49 years) in India during 2005-06. While more than one-third of women suffer from chronic energy deficiency (CED), around 10 percent are overweight or obese. Thus, close to 50 percent of women in India suffer from malnutrition of one form or the other. Chronic energy deficiency (CED) persists as the dominant form of malnutrition in rural India affecting around 40 percent of women, which is about 15 percentage points more than the incidence among urban women. On the contrary, overweight or obesity, from which

TABLE 13.1

Levels of Malnutrition among Women in India (15-49 Years) (2005-06)

(*in percentage*)

BMI	*All India*	*Rural*	*Urban*
CED	35.6	40.6	25.0
Overweight or Obese	12.6	7.4	23.5
Anaemia			
Any Anaemia	55.3	57.4	50.9
Moderate or Severe	16.8	17.5	15.1

Source : Computed from NFHS-3 data.

nearly one-fourth of urban women suffer, is slowly emerging as an important nutritional problem in urban India. Again, about 50 percent of women in both rural and urban India suffer from malnutrition, though its nature varies between rural and urban regions. Equally, over half the women in the age group of 15-49 years suffer from anaemia. Unlike in CED where the gap between rural and urban regions is significantly large, the regional gap is relatively lower in anaemia. Thus, more than 50 percent of women irrespective of their place of residence are anaemic, whether mild, moderate or severe. The last two, the serious forms of anaemia, afflict more than 15 percent of women in both rural and urban India.

INTER-STATE DIFFERENCE IN WOMEN'S MALNUTRITION

Table 13.2 provides the level of women's malnutrition in 18 major states. To begin with, chronic energy deficiency (CED) affects half of the women in Bihar (45 percent), which is followed by Chhattisgarh, Jharkhand (43 percent each), Madhya Pradesh and Odisha (41 percent each). West Bengal, with an incidence of around 39 percent, is not far from these states. These states tend to have more than twice the proportion of undernourished women in states such as Kerala and Punjab, which are at the other end of the spectrum. Rather than CED, what seems to be an important issue in these two states is overweight or obesity: nearly 30 percent of women suffer from overweight and obesity taken together. However, what these states have in common with others is that in all these states about 50 percent of women suffer from malnutrition of one form or other. Assam and Jharkhand, with nearly 70 percent of women suffering from some form of anaemia, remain at the top among these states. Close on their heels come Bihar (67 percent), West Bengal (63 percent), Andhra Pradesh (63 percent) and Odisha (61 percent). In Assam and Andhra Pradesh, nearly one-fourth of women suffer from moderate and severe anaemia. Here too, Kerala and Punjab remain at the lower end, both in terms of overall incidence as well as moderate and severe anaemia. Thus, the incidence of anaemia in Assam is over two times more than that in Kerala. It becomes essential at this stage to point out that Punjab is a much better state in so far as nutrition among women is concerned. But there is no point in deriving complacency as a large proportion of women in Punjab is suffering from malnutrition. Thus, a mere comparison with other states would usher in a false sense of complacency, which would divert attention from some of the significant issues at hand. Therefore, the present study primarily focuses on examining the extent of women's malnutrition in Punjab and also the existing social and economic disparities in women's malnutrition.

TABLE 13.2

Women's Malnutrition Across Major States in India (2005-06)

(*in percentage*)

States	*BMI*		*Anaemia*	
	CED	*Overweight or Obese*	*Moderate or Severe*	*Any*
Kerala	18.0	28.1	7.1	32.8
Punjab	18.9	29.9	11.8	38.0
Tamil Nadu	28.4	20.9	15.8	53.2
Uttaranchal	30.0	12.8	14.8	55.2
Haryana	31.3	17.4	18.5	56.1
Andhra Pradesh	33.5	15.6	23.9	62.9
Karnataka	35.5	15.3	17.1	51.5
Uttar Pradesh	36.0	9.2	14.7	49.9
Maharashtra	36.2	14.5	15.6	48.4
Gujarat	36.3	16.7	19.1	55.3
Assam	36.5	7.8	24.7	69.5
Rajasthan	36.7	8.9	17.9	53.1
West Bengal	39.1	11.3	17.4	63.2
Odisha	41.4	6.6	16.3	61.2
Madhya Pradesh	41.7	7.6	15.1	56.0
Jharkhand	43.0	5.3	19.9	69.4
Chhattisgarh	43.4	5.6	17.6	57.5
Bihar	45.1	4.6	16.9	67.4
India	35.6	12.6	16.8	55.3

Source : Computed from NFHS-3 data.

LEVEL OF MALNUTRITION AMONG WOMEN (15-49 YEARS) IN PUNJAB

The level of malnutrition among women (15-49 years) in Punjab during 2005-06 is presented in Table 13.3. It reveals that 18.9 percent of women suffer from chronic energy deficiency (CED) while 29.9 percent are overweight or obese. Women in the rural areas (19.9 percent) are a little more affected by CED as compared to urban women (17.2 percent). This reflects an insignificant gap between rural and urban areas. Overweight or obesity persists as the dominant form of malnutrition in urban Punjab affecting around 36 percent of women, which is about 10 percentage points more than the incidence among rural women. On observing the levels of anaemia among women in the age group of 15-49 years, it is found that more than one-third of women suffer from anaemia in one form or the other irrespective of their place of residence and around 12 percent are afflicted with moderate or severe form of anaemia. It is interesting to observe that the incidence of anaemia among women is higher among urban women. Unlike in overweight or obesity where the gap between rural and urban regions is significantly large, the gap is relatively lower in anaemia, as only 2 percent points difference has been observed in rural and urban areas. (Table 13.3)

TABLE 13.3

Levels of Malnutrition among Women in Punjab (15-49 Years) (2005-06)

(*in percentage*)

BMI	*All Punjab*	*Rural*	*Urban*
CED	18.9	19.9	17.2
Overweight or Obese	29.9	26.2	36.3
Anaemia			
Any Anaemia	38	37.4	39.1
Moderate or Severe	11.8	12.3	11.0

Source : Computed from NFHS-3 data.

Considering women in the age group of 15-49 years as a single group may lead to cloaking the variation in the incidence of malnutrition across age groups. Also, they may have different marital status. Given their economic or social disadvantages, for instance, it is likely that widows or separated women suffer from malnutrition more than others. It may be useful, therefore, to look at the levels of nutrition among women of different age groups and marital status.

An age-wise analysis in Table 13.4 reveals that chronic energy deficiency (CED) persists as a dominant form of malnutrition among women in the age group of 15-19 years affecting around 39.2 percent of women, which is 22.6 percentage points higher than the incidence among women in the age group of 40-49 years. On the contrary, overweight or obesity is dominant among women belonging to older age group (40-49 years) affecting 52.7 percent of women while only 5.3 percent women in the age group of 15-19 is affected by overweight or obesity. Thus, the incidence of CED goes down with an increase in age and the reverse holds good for overweight or obesity. Age does not appear to be a deterrent to anaemia as about 36-41 percent of all women are anaemic in one form or other. Further, the incidence of moderate or severe anaemia does not vary much with age. An age-wise analysis of anemia reveals that the highest percentage

TABLE 13.4

Women's Malnutrition in Punjab, 2005-06
Age and Marital Status

(*in percentage*)

Age/Marital Status	*BMI*		*Anaemia*	
	CED	*Overweight or Obese*	*Moderate or Severe*	*Any*
Age				
15-19	39.2	5.3	13.9	41.4
20-29	22.1	18.0	12.1	38.8
30-39	11.2	43.3	10.7	36.2
40-49	6.6	52.7	10.8	36.0
Marital Status				
Never Married	34.0	10.1	11.1	37.2
Currently Married	13.5	30.8	12.2	38.4
Widowed/divorced/ separated/deserted	13.6	*	7.6	34.7

Note : * Percentage not shown; based on fewer than 25 unweighted cases.
Source : Computed from NFHS-3 data.

of anaemic women are found in the age group of 15-19 years (41.4 percent), while the lowest are in the age group of 40-49 years (36.0 percent). The women in the age group of 15-19 years also indicate the highest incidence of moderate and severe anaemia (13.9 percent).

Surprisingly, the incidence of CED is higher among never married women (34 percent), which is 20 percentage points higher than currently married women (13.5 percent) and also among widowed/divorced/deserted/separated women considered together (13.6 percent). On further observation it is found that recently married women (30.8 percent) as compared to never married women (10.1 percent) are overweight or obese, reflecting a considerable difference between the two groups. On the contrary, marital status does not seem to have much impact on the degree of anaemia. However, the incidence of anaemia is highest among currently married women (38.4 percent) followed by never married women (37.2 percent) and widowed/divorced/deserted/separated women considered together (34.7 percent).

TABLE 13.5

Women's Malnutrition in Punjab, Social and Economic Groups (2005-06)

(in percentage)

Age/Marital Status	*BMI*		*Anaemia*	
	CED	*Overweight or Obese*	*Moderate or Severe*	*Any*
Social Groups				
Scheduled Caste	26.8	22.6	13.4	42.6
Other Backward Classes	19.8	31.7	12.6	32.8
Others*	14.3	33.6	11.0	36.3
Wealth Groups				
Lowest	30.5	13.8	10.7	38.0
Second	35.8	11.5	14.9	41.2
Middle	29.0	17.6	13.4	42.0
Fourth	21.7	23.3	14.4	40.9
Highest	12.7	39.2	9.5	34.9

Note : * Not belonging to scheduled castes or other backward classes.
Source : Computed from NFHS-3 data.

The earlier discussed disparity in women's nutrition induces us to look at other forms of disparities as well, mainly social and economic. Table 13.5 depicts women's malnutrition in Punjab during the period 2005-06 based on social and economic groups. It indicates that 26.8 percent women (15-49 years) from scheduled caste are inflicted with chronic energy deficiency (CED) followed by women belonging to the OBC (19.8 percent) category and others (14.3 percent). The maximum incidence of overweight or obesity falls on women belonging to the group categorised as other (33.6 percent), followed by women belonging to OBC (31.7 percent) and SC (22.6 percent). Thus, the incidence of malnutrition declines with the so-called rise in social status. On observing anaemia among women belonging to different social groups a major gap is noticed, as 42.6 percent of women from SC suffer from anaemia while the corresponding figures for others and OBC are 36.3 percent and 32.8 percent. Such difference reflects huge disparities between social groups.

Before discussing the disparity between wealth groups, a methodological note on the construction of wealth groups used for the analysis needs to be mentioned. Since NFHS-3 data do not contain information on income or expenditure, information related to household assets and durables were combined to create household wealth, based on which households were grouped into five quintiles with the help of the approach developed by Filmer and Pritchett (1998). As per this methodology, nearly 20 percent of all households that form the bottom quintile would qualify as the poorest followed by yet another 20 percent of households as the second quintile or the poor. By contrast, 20 percent of households constitute the upper quintile (IIPS and ORC Macro, 2007).

The highest incidence of chronic energy deficiency (CED) has been found in the second quintile group (35.8 percent) while the least incidence has been observed for the highest quintile group (12.7 percent). In case of overweight or obesity it is found that women belonging to the second quintile group (11.5 percent) accounted for the least infliction of obesity and those belonging to the highest quintile group (39.2 percent) recorded the maximum infliction of obesity. About 40 percent of women in various wealth groups suffer from anaemia and its least incidence falls on the women of highest income group (34.9 percent). Thus, it has been observed that malnutrition among women goes down drastically with a rise in the household wealth status, creating equally large disparity between the wealth groups. It is also important to add here that the proportion of women suffering from anaemia is not low even within the richest quintile. This suggests that a substantially large proportion of women in India irrespective of the household wealth status suffer from malnutrition.

CONCLUSION

The above analysis brings to the fore some disquieting observations and thereby raises a number of important issues. Not only do the levels of malnutrition among women in India and Punjab continue to be quite high, but the level among women from disadvantaged social and economic groups are much higher. While social disadvantage tends to go with a higher incidence of malnutrition among women, economic disadvantage does more so.

It has been found that close to 50 percent of women in India suffer from some kind of malnutrition. Chronic energy deficiency (CED) persists as the dominant form of malnutrition in rural India affecting around 40 percent of women. Overweight or obesity is slowly emerging as an important nutritional problem among women in urban India. More than 50 percent of women irrespective of their place of residence are anaemic, whether mild, moderate or severe. Inter-state difference in women's malnutrition in India is also prominently visible. A much higher incidence of malnutrition is noticed in the eastern states, such as Bihar, Jharkhand, Odisha and West Bengal. On the other hand, Kerala and Punjab fare better as compared to other states. Yet a large proportion of women in Punjab are suffering from malnutrition.

Women in the rural areas of Punjab are affected more by chronic energy deficiency (CED) as compared to urban women while overweight or obesity persists as the dominant form of malnutrition in urban Punjab. The incidence of anaemia among women is higher in urban women. An age-wise analysis of malnutrition among women reveals that the incidence of CED goes down with an increase in age and the reverse holds good for overweight or obesity. An age-wise analysis for anaemia shows that the highest percentage of anaemic women are found in the youngest age group of 15-19 years while the lowest are in the oldest age group of 40-49 years. The incidence of CED is higher among never married women while marital status does not seem to have much impact on the degree of anaemia.

Huge disparities in levels of malnutrition have been reflected between various social groups. The incidence of malnutrition declines with the so-called rise in social status. Further, it has been noticed that malnutrition among women goes down significantly with rise in household wealth status. The proportion of women suffering from anaemia is not low even within the richest quintile.

The increase in malnutrition among women in Punjab, whether it is due to the failure of the market or the state or due to gender inequality or because of changing food habits, does not augur well for various reasons. Malnutrition amounts to deprivation of the basic and central aspects of well-being. It also has implications for human development which are large and cumulative. For instance, the adverse influence of maternal malnutrition extends beyond maternal mortality to intrauterine growth retardation, child malnutrition and rising emergence of chronic diseases, among others (Osmani and Sen, 2003; Victora *et al.*, 2008). Therefore, it is important that women's malnutrition be viewed as an important issue of human development rather than as an isolated health issue specific to women. Construing women's malnutrition as an issue of human development would entail both immediate measures to address malnutrition as well placing women's well-being firmly on the development agenda.

References

Black, Robert E. *et al.* (2008), "Maternal and Child Undernutrition: Global andRegional Exposures and Health Consequences", *Lancet*, published online January 17. DOI: 10.1016/S0140-736(07) 61690-0.

Dewan, Manju (2008), "Malnutrition in Women", *Stud. Home Comm. Sci.*, 2(1): 7-10.

Government of India (2008), *National Family Health Survey-3*, 2005-06, Ministry of Health and Family Welfare.

Filmer, Deon. and Lant Pritchett (1988), 'Estimating Wealth Effects without Expenditure Data or Tears: An Application to Educational Enrolments in States of India', Policy Research Working Paper No 1994, Development Economics Research Group, Washington, DC.: World Bank.

International Institute for Population Sciences (IIPS) and ORC Macro (2007), *National Family Health Survey-3, 2005-06, India: Volume-I*, IIPS, Mumbai.

———, (2007a): *Key Findings from National Family Health Survey-3, 2005-06: Various States of India*, IIPS, Mumbai.

Lomborg, B. (2004), *Global Crises, Global Solutions*, Cambridge: Cambridge University Press.

Osmani, Siddiq and Amartya Sen (2003), "The Hidden Penalties of Gender Inequality: Foetal Origins of Ill-health", *Economics and Human Biology*, Vol. 1, No. 1, pp. 105-21.

Nestel, Penelope (2000), "Strategies, Policies and Programmes to Improve the Nutrition of Women and Girls," Food and Nutrition Technical Assistance Project (FANTA), Washington, DC.

Victora, Cesar G. *et al.* (2008), "Maternal and Child Undernutrition: Consequences for Adult Health and Human Capital", *Lancet*, published online on January 17. DOI:10.1016/S0140-6736(07)61692-4.

14

Awareness of Health Insurance Scheme among Working Women in Unorganized Sector : A Study of Rural Women in Coimbatore of Tamil Nadu

SHERLY THOMAS AND V.L. LAVANYA

INTRODUCTION

Better health translates into greater and more equitable distribution of wealth by building human and social capital that increases national productivity (Bloom, 2004; WHO, 2001). Sen (1999) indicates that health like education is among the basic capabilities that gives value to human life. Health contributes to both social and economic development. Recent empirical work has sought to assess the association between human capital and aggregate economic performance and found that given labour and capital, improvement in health status and education of the population lead to a higher output (Barro and Sala-i-Martin, 2004). The role of health in influencing economic outcomes has been well understood at the micro -level. Healthier workers are able to work longer, generally more productive and consequently able to secure higher earnings. On the contrary, illness and disease shorten the working lives of people, thereby reducing their lifetime earnings. Better health also has a positive effect on the learning abilities of children and leads to better educational outcomes (school completion rates, higher mean years of schooling, achievements) and increases the efficiency of human capital formation by individuals and households (Strauss and Thomas1998; Schultz, 1999).

India's healthcare system is mostly served by the private sector and consequently the burden of healthcare expenditure falls directly on households which has adverse implications for the poor India. The healthcare expenditure is steadily increasing for the last five years but it is in-form of public-private mix. The concept of health insurance is gaining popularity in India because of financial burden on 85 percent of the working population in the country. In case of critical illness and instant need of huge amount of cash money, it is imperative to have health insurance.

WOMEN'S EMPLOYMENT IN THE UNORGANIZED SECTOR

Amongst those who are left out of any social protection system in India and amongst those who are poor, women form a major group. Women dominate those forms of work that are unregulated and unregistered and found mostly in the informal sector. In many regions, women's participation in remunerated work in the formal and non-formal labour market has increased significantly and has changed during the past decade. While women continue to work in agriculture and fisheries, they have also become increasingly involved in micro, small and medium sized enterprises. Women's share in the labour force continues to rise and almost everywhere women are working in large numbers outside the households.

Women's occupations are fluid and multi-dimensional. It is important to know the types of work women are involved in to identify health risks. Agricultural workers perform a variety of tasks and there are also gender specific occupations in agriculture. The gender segregation of work gives rise to different health implications for women and men. The tasks which men and women undertake also vary from culture to culture and at different times in different places. Poor nutrition, for example, may be a more important factor in some types of occupational health impairment than simply being female. The effects of potential occupational hazards on women's reproductive health have received special attention in recent years as more and more women are entering the paid work force. In this context women should be aware about the health insurance schemes and their benefits. In this situation they must know about the health insurance scheme and its benefits.

The condition of health insurance in India is deplorable. Around 85 percent of Indian population does not use health insurance to finance their medical expenditure. These people pay for their medical expenditure from their pocket. As a result, many of these uninsured individuals either end up with poor quality healthcare or have to bear financial hardship. The financial stress that is encountered due to rising medical expenses is believed to affect the lifestyle of all family members for years. India has a huge working population of about 400 million. Nearly 90 percent of this work force is in the unorganized sector. There are numerous occupational groups in economic activities, passed on from generation to generation, scattered all over the country with differing employer-employee relationship. Those in the organized sector of the economy, whether in the public or private sector, have access to some of health service coverage. While the unorganized sector workers have no access. The National Commission for Enterprises in the Unorganized Sector (NCEUS) has recommended a specific scheme of health insurance in case of incidences of illness and hospitalization for workers and their families. The Eleventh Five-Year Plan introduced a new scheme based on cashless transaction with the objectives of improving access to health care and protecting the individual and her family from exorbitant out-of-pocket expenses. Under the scheme, coverage is given to the beneficiary and her family of five members. The health insurance scheme is to achieve good coverage among the below poverty people. With this background this study is taken up to measure women's awareness level and constraints in taking health insurance scheme in rural Coimbatore.

EARLIER RESEARCH

Gumber and Kulkarni (2000) tried to explore the availability of health insurance system for the poor especially women, their needs and expectations of a health insurance system and the likely constraints in extending current health insurance benefits to workers in the informal sector. Ahuja and De (2004) confirmed that the demand for health insurance is limited where supply of health services is weak and explained interstate variation in demand for health insurance by poor in relation to variation in healthcare infrastructure. This apart, the study also found that healthcare infrastructure is positively related to demand for health insurance by poor, whereas the proportion of below poverty line (BPL) population is negatively related. In order to build demand for health insurance, it is necessary to address the demand side and at the same time design the insurance schemes by taking into consideration the paying capacity of the poor. Health care expenditure has also been found to influence the decision to participate in a given health insurance scheme (Kronick and Gilmer, 1999). The relationship between health care expenditure and health insurance purchase decision is premised on the fact that families with higher probability of requiring hospitalization will purchase health insurance.

METHODOLOGY

The womenfolk of the rural Coimbatore who were engaged in agricultural activities, construction work, mill workers, brick-klin work and SHGs, etc. were considered for the study. There were 65 households and they constituted the sample size. For the current study data were collected from the women through a pre-tested interview schedule which was administered to the respondents to elicit information about awareness and constraints in taking health insurance scheme. The preliminary draft of the questionnaire was pretested on the respondents. This helped in improving the questionnaire and also gave an indication as to the kind of responses that would be forthcoming with few additions and deletions. The final questionnaire was developed and used for collection of information from the respondents.

DISCUSSION

Having health insurance does not protect a person against illness, but it can provide a measure of protection against illness, financial risk or reduce their health expenditure at the time of use of health care services. Therefore, an attempt made to examine whether the women workers in this study are aware of health insurance or not. Table 14.1 shows the awareness and sources of health insurance schemes among the respondents. It is revealed that 72 percent of the respondents have awareness about health insurance scheme and 28 percent are not aware about them. This is mainly due to the Tamil Nadu Government health insurance scheme which covered the entire population below poverty line. The continuation of this scheme gave real impetus to all in Tamil Nadu. Although health insurance is not a new concept and people are also getting familiar with it, yet this awareness has not reached the desired level to demand health insurance products. Moreover, there are a number of sources. Mainly the sources which create awareness about health insurance include TV followed by agents, newspapers and friends.

TABLE 14.1

Awareness and Sources about Health Insurance Scheme

Particulars		*Frequency*	*Percentage*
Awareness	Yes	47	72.3
	No	18	27.7
Sources	TV	26	40.0
	Newspaper	14	21.5
	Agents	16	24.6
	Friends	9	13.8
Total		65	100.0

Source : Filed Survey, 2012.

CONSTRAINTS FOR NOT HAVING HEALTH INSURANCE

Factor analysis was used to identify the underlying pattern of relationship between various constraints for not having health insurance and whether these constraints can be grouped in terms of a composite variable. The Cronbach's alpha to test the reliability or internal consistency of the scale gave a value of 0.914 greater than the norm of 0.70 indicating good scale reliability. To determine the appropriateness of applying factor analysis, the KMO and Bartlett's test measures were computed and the results are presented in Table 14.2. KMO statistics is 856 which is signifying higher than acceptable adequacy of sampling. The Bartlett's test of Sphericity was also found to be significant at one percent level providing evidence of the presence of relationship between variables to apply factor analysis. The communalities for each variable were assessed to determine the amount of variance accounted by the variable to be included in the factor rotations. All the variables have value greater than 0.50 signifying substantial portions of the variance accounted by the factors.

TABLE 14.2
KMO and Bartlett's Test Measures

KMO and Bartlett's Test	
Kaiser-Meyer-Olkin Measure of Sampling Adequacy	.856
Bartlett's Test of Sphericity Approx. Chi-Square	444.928
Degrees of freedom	55
Significance level	.000

Source : Estimation based on Field Survey, 2012.

Table 14.3 enlists the eigen values, their relative explanatory powers and factor loadings for 12 linear components identified within the data set. The Kaiser rotated component matrix presented in Table 14.3 reveals that factor one had significant loadings on six

TABLE 14.3
Rotated Component Matrix

Reasons	*Component*	
	1	*2*
Delay in processing claim	.872	
No proper awareness regarding schemes	.886	
Lack of comprehensive coverage		
Lack of reliability and flexibility	.714	
Lack of cooperation from administration		.864
Lack of illness	.699	
Financial constraint	.731	
No commensurate benefits		.762
Lack of family support	.651	
Linked hospitals are not easily accessible		.835
Difficulty in availing services in hospitals		.849
Eigen value	5.977	1.261
Percentage of variance	54.336	11.465
Cumulative percentage	54.336	65.801

Note : *Extraction Method*: Principal component analysis. *Rotation method*: Varimax with Kaiser Normalization, rotation converged in 3 iterations.

Source : Estimation based on Field Survey, 2012.

dimensions namely Delay in processing claim, No proper awareness regarding schemes, Lack of reliability and flexibility, Financial constraint, Lack of family support and lack of illness. Factor one explains 54 percent of the variance. Factor 2 had significant loadings on four dimensions namely Lack of cooperation from administration, No commensurate benefits, Linked hospitals are not easily accessible and Difficulty in availing services in hospitals and explains only 11 percent of the variance. These are the various factors acting as constraints in joining the health insurance scheme among women working in the unorganized sector.

CONCLUSION

The rural women who suffer from illness are mainly utilising costly health care services from the private providers. The Government health care set up is unable to provide quality care to the rural population. However, the demand for health care on introduction of health insurance or risk sharing scheme mainly depends on quality of care provided under the scheme. The government should also improve awareness campaign to raise the level of awareness for the health insurance scheme in the rural areas. This would effectively enlighten the citizens on the health insurance scheme and also positively affect their willingness to pay for the schemes. The existing health facilities should be equipped and well-managed, rather than build new ones in the same or close locations. Increase in medical expenses is a huge burden for everyone and for people in the informal sector. Therefore, it is recommended that some insurance scheme should be introduced to cater to this section of the population. The Government should also educate people about the importance of these schemes consequent upon rise in medical costs. Regulators need to bring about change in the guidelines in order to allow only the right and efficient players to enter the health insurance market.

REFERENCES

Ahuja, R. and I. De (2004), "Health Insurance for the Poor Need to Strengthen Healthcare Provision," *Economic and Political Weekly*, Vol. 39, No. 41, pp. 4491-93.

Bloom, G. (2004), "China in Transition: Challenges to Urban Health Services". In *Health Care Transition in Urban China*. Bloom, G., S.H. Tang (ed.), Ashgate Publishing Limited, England, 127-42.

Charu, C. Garg (2006), "Is Health Insurance Feasible In India?: Issues in Private and Social Health Insurance", cited in Sujata Prasad and C. Sathyanala (eds.), *Securing Health for all: Dimensions and Challenges*, Institute for Human Development Publication, New Delhi, pp. 430-51.

Gumber, A. and V. Kulkarani (2000), "Health Insurance for Informal Sector: Case Study of Gujarat", *Economic and Political Weekly*, Vol. 35, No. 40, pp. 3607-13.

Kronick, R. and T. Gilmer (1999), "Explaining the Decline in Health Insurance Coverage, 1979-95", *Health Affairs*, 18(2): 30.

Sen, A. (1999), "Economic Policy and Equity: an Overview", in V. Tanzi, K. Chu, S. Gupta (eds.), *Economic Policy and Equity*, Washington, D.C: IMF, pp. 28-42.

Strauss, John and Duncan Thomas (1998), "Health Nutrition and Economic Development," *Journal of Economic Literature*, Vol. 36, No. 2, pp. 766-817.

World Health Organization (2001), "Maternal Mortality in 1995: Estimates Developed by WHO, UNICEF, UNFPA", WHO/.RHR01.9.Ge.

15

Gender Disparity in Childhood Immunization in Rural Coimbatore, Tamil Nadu

S. Sampath Kumar and R. Maruthakutti

INTRODUCTION

Gender differences are as old as human culture and arose from the biological differences between males and females. With human evolution, cultures have maintained some differentiation of gender roles. (Ghose and Malik, 2007) But the extensive transformations have taken place with the passage of time. Gender beliefs and practices define roles, opportunities and limitations for women and men, greatly influencing their life in all societies. Aspects of daily life shaped by gender include use of language and means of self expression, dress and appearance, education, work opportunities, family structure and size and each individual's health (Paulson, 2005). The patrilocal joint family is still the common family concept in India. Living together with parents, grandparents, aunts, uncles and cousins improves social understandings; but the joint family system has some negative implications especially concerning gender equality. With few exceptions, joint families adhere to patrilocal residence. Gender discrimination has its roots not only in the seemingly senseless traditions and old-fashioned religious beliefs, but is deeply woven into the socio-economic fabric (Mullatti, 1992).

GENDER AND HEALTH DISPARITY

The child's health and survival depend upon the degree of care with which the child is brought up. Child care starting from birth to the end of childhood is an important consideration in understanding the determinants of child health. Child health in the form of breastfeeding, immunization and timely and appropriate treatment in case of illness can reduce health risk during childhood. The type of care provided to the child may be broadly divided into two types: medical and non-medical. Medical care comprises of immunization, timely and appropriate treatment of illness and medical attention at birth. The non-medical care consists of feeding practices, timing of initiation and duration of breastfeeding and introduction of supplementary feeding.

South Asia is well-known in the world for skewed sex ratio. Further, the worrying fact in India is the continuing decline in sex ratio indicating that morbidity and mortality are higher among females than males. The sex ratio in the age group of 0-6 years has declined significantly in the recent decades. The deteriorating trend may be due to lack of medical and non-medical support to females. A growing number of countries have adopted population and development policies like universal immunization, food security and minimum standard of life to meet health care and education needs of women. Yet, gender inequality persists in most of the countries around the world (Chelala, 2005).

GENDER AND IMMUNIZATION STATUS

An important indicator of child health status in a given country is the proportion of children protected through immunization against potentially life-threatening diseases. Protection level in a population of children not only assesses the prevalence of specific disease protection but also provides an indication of parental awareness, attention and the extent of the preventive health services available and accessible. In India, nearly 20 to 25 percent of child deaths are due to six common immunisable childhood diseases like diphtheria, pertussis, tetanus, polio, measles and tuberculosis. There are marked gender differences in immunization and acute polio statistics. These differences become wide with the age of children and with the intensity of care received. Data from rehabilitation centers and polio camps show gender differences too. These differences are prominent in the villages and are reflected in the marked absence of girls with polio from these villages seeking care. Further these differences may be attributed to lack of health care for girl children, neglect of girls with polio, and high mortality of girls with polio (Wyatt, 2004). A study in Rajasthan reports greater incidence of immunization among males for each vaccine. In Jaipur, about 8 percent female and 17 percent male children were fully immunized. In Tonk district the corresponding ratios were 13 percent and 17 percent, respectively. Lack of knowledge stands first and cultural belief follows next in both the regions for not immunising children. In Jaipur, 57.9 percent female and 54.5 percent male children have not received any vaccine (Saha, 2003). Similar findings are reported by Vani (2004) on the basis of econometric estimates, which are based on unit-record data for over 4000 children between the ages of 1 and 2 years living in rural households drawn from 16 major states in India. Out of 4333 children analyzed, 55 percent of the boys and 50 percent girls had been fully vaccinated. The proportion of children who were fully vaccinated was substantially higher when their mothers were literate (66 percent and 32 percent respectively) as compared to the mothers who were proximate literate (59 percent and 28 percent) or illiterate (42 percent and 18 percent).

An analysis made using the National Family and Health Survey (1998-99) data suggests that the situation in 1992-93 was dismal with 70 percent of children aged 12-60 months in rural areas not fully immunized and close to 40 percent with no immunization at all. When no-immunization and full-immunization picture was analysed it was found that there was significant difference in improvement in gender difference. In no-immunization while the gap between boys and girls remains statistically significant in 1999, it decreased from 5.4 to 1.3 percent points during NFHS-3 in 2005. The fact that results in gender differences in full-immunization are not as good as those in no-immunization indicates that the problem of discrimination is more likely the result of household decisions rather than failures of health-care system (Gaudin and Yazbeck, 2006).

Pande (2003) examines the role of sex composition of surviving older siblings in gender differences in childhood nutrition and immunization using data from the National Family Health Survey, 1992-93. Selective neglect of children with certain sex and birth-order combinations operates differentially for girls and boys.

Disaggregating national averages is important for a better understanding of social disparities in health. National Family Health Survey-2 data have been used to analyze socio-economic, gender, urban-rural and regional inequalities in immunization in India for each of the 17 large states. Results show that on average the southern states have better immunization levels and lower immunization inequalities than many of the northern states. Gender inequalities persist in most states, including the south, and seem unrelated to overall immunization or the levels of other inequalities. This suggests that gender differentials reflect deep-seated societal factors rather than health system issues *per se* (Pande and Yazbeck, 2003). After analysing the NFHS-2 data Yu (2004) also observed that female disadvantages in childhood immunization concentrate among girls with one or more surviving older sisters.

Other evidences suggest that with government efforts universal immunization programme become successful in eradicating diseases in different parts of the country. (Sharma *et al.*, 2008) It is also confirmed that in an urban slum of Chandigarh there has been relatively better utilization of immunization services for females as compared to other services such as proper nutrition, proper treatment during illness, timely admission in hospitals etc. All this happen because immunization is available free of cost and often at door-steps or else at a walking distance from home as compared to other services which require money and time.

Using NFHS-2 data Sharma (2005) found that immunization coverage for girls is slightly more as compared to boys in India. However, with regard to administering of individual vaccines girls are slightly less advantaged. A study carried out in Chandigarh reveals that males were immunized with measles vaccine more than females but sex differences were not statistically significant (Sharma *et al.*, 2008).

The paper has two main objectives: first, to explore the awareness level of rural mothers with regard to immunization, diseases prevented by immunization of children and secondly to assess gender differences in childhood immunization.

AREA OF THE STUDY

Coimbatore known as Kovai is the second largest city in the state of Tamil Nadu. It is the administrative headquarters of Coimbatore District with an average literacy rate of 78 percent with male literacy of 81 percent and female literacy 74 percent. In urbanization Coimbatore stands next to Chennai in Tamil Nadu. Among the districts outside Chennai, Coimbatore is seen as a trend setter in every aspect of development—infrastructure, health sector, hospitality, industrial and educational. It's considered to be the centre for textile, textile machines, pump and other tools development.

METHODS

The survey covered north and south divisions of Coimbatore Taluk in Tamil Nadu; each division consists of two Panchayat Blocks. Coimbatore North includes Periyanaickenpalayam and Sarkarsamakulam Blocks, and Coimbatore South consists of Thondamuthur and Maddukkarai Blocks. Each of these Panchayat Blocks consists of varying number of village panchayats. The sampling process involved selection of one village panchayat using lottery method from each block of Coimbatore. From each village panchayat 20 percent of the mothers having at least one male and one female child under the age of 15 years were selected through a systematic random sampling method.

TOOLS FOR DATA COLLECTION

Based on the existing literature on gender discrimination, especially concerning the upbringing of children, questions were developed to elicit information on gender discrimination. As the study population comprises rural women with varying levels of literacy, it was decided to use the interview method with the schedule rather than using questionnaire.

FINDINGS

Socio-economic Background

The data related to socio-economic status of the mothers give valuable lead to any social science study and further it provides detailed and deeper assessment with the main study variables. In the present study 65 percent of them aged between 26-35 years and in excess of half of them belong to backward community and on an average their family income falls between Rs. 2000 to Rs. 4000. The educational status of the respondents was considerably poor: 60 percent of them have received up to secondary level education and 30 percent were illiterate. Poor economic condition and lack of education forced them to work as agricultural labourers (39 percent) and 38 percent remain as housewife. About 94 percent of them have no savings and 65 percent of them were non-migrants.

The study areas were the typical Indian village, where 53 percent mothers were living in single room houses and 77 percent of them live in tiled houses. Seven out of ten houses (71 percent) have no toilet facility. With respect to availability of electricity, most of the respondents have such facility through free electricity scheme of the Government and 11 percent of them live without such minimum facility.

KNOWLEDGE, SOURCE AND USES OF IMMUNIZATION

The Universal Immunization Programme targeted to cover at least 85 percent children against the vaccine preventable diseases. Children are required to be immunized against some of the childhood diseases, which can turn out to be fatal in the absence of timely vaccination. To reduce the incidence of morbidity and mortality,

TABLE 15.1
Knowledge, Source and Uses of Immunization (N: 335)

Variable	*Categories*	*Frequency*	*Percentage*
Knowledge about Immunization	No knowledge	9	2.7
	Had	326	97.3
Source of Information on Immunization	None	9	2.6
	Doctors	100	29.9
	Television	1	0.3
	Health visitors	5	1.5
	Village Health Nurse	200	59.7
	Teacher	20	6.0
Awareness about Uses of Immunization	Not aware	45	13.4
	Aware	290	86.6
Awareness about Diseases prevented by Immunization	Not aware	45	13.4
	Partially aware	58	17.3
	Fully aware	232	69.2

Government of India has made arrangements for free vaccination services of the required doses of BCG, DPT, polio and measles vaccines to protect children against tuberculosis (BCG); diphtheria, pertussis (whooping cough), tetanus (DPT); polio and measles respectively (Ministry of Health and Family Welfare, 1991).

The awareness programme by any government and non-government organizations on health maintenance efforts and prevention of diseases did not give the desired result due to some unbreakable hurdles of cultural nativity, lesser orientation on literacy and self determination of 'No Vaccination' irrespective of any infections. But the study findings exhibit contrasting picture as 97 percent of the mothers have knowledge about immunization out of which 60 percent of them attribute the village health nurse as their source of information and for 30 percent mothers, doctors are the main source. (Table 15.1) With regard to consciousness about diseases prevented by immunization, 69 percent of them have full awareness and the rest are either partially aware or not aware. (Table 15.1) Similar observation has been reported by Saha (2003) that large proportion of the mothers had knowledge of immunization in urban areas and a high percentage had knowledge of polio eradication.

GENDER INEQUITY IN IMMUNIZATION STATUS

From a study in Chitwan district of central Nepal it is found that son preference was observed in the perception of mothers; however, it was not related to completion of immunization (Funabashi, 2000). Pandey (1995) from his study in Maharashtra argues that the girl children who faced discrimination and inequality were not immunized against BCG, DPT, polio and measles.

The present study demonstrates distinctive view point that the mothers show some consistency in vaccinating male and female children from birth to 9 months in all the age sub-groups. (Table 15.2) The data display that there is a steady decline thereafter in immunizing children in the age group of under 5 years where the number of children not immunized increases from 1 percent both for boys and girls at birth to 21.5 percent (average of Male: 28 percent, Female: 15 percent) at 9 months. As the age of the children progresses, the vaccination status of children declines. Though there is a steady overall decline, the respondents do not show much difference between male and female children in vaccinating them irrespective of their age. Among those who were under-5 years of age some difference is marked between male and female children and who

Table 15.2
Age of the Child and Immunization Status from Birth to Nine Months (N: 758)

Sl. No.	Age and Immunization Status	At Birth (BCG + OPV)				1½ Months (DPT + OPV)				2½ Months (DPT + OPV)			
		M	%	F	%	M	%	F	%	M	%	F	%
(1)	(2)	(3)	(4)	(5)	(6)	(7)	(8)	(9)	(10)	(11)	(12)	(13)	(14)
1.	Under 5 Years Immunized	94	98.9	94	98.9	90	94.7	89	93.7	82	86.3	85	89.5
	Not Immunized	1	1.1	1	1.1	5	5.3	6	6.3	13	13.7	10	10.5
2.	5-9 Years Immunized	135	100	119	99.2	135	100	119	99.2	134	99.3	119	99.2
	Not Immunized	0	0	1	0.8	0	0	1	0.8	1	0.7	1	0.8
3.	10 Years and above Immunized	142	100	171	100	142	100	171	100	140	98.6	170	99.4
	Not Immunized	—	—	—	—	—	—	—	—	2	1.4	1	0.6

(Contd.)

TABLE 15. 2 (Contd.)

Sl. No.	*Age and Immunization Status*	*3½ Months (DPT + OPV)*				*9 Months Measles + OPV*			
		M	*%*	*F*	*%*	*M*	*%*	*F*	*%*
(1)	*(2)*	*(15)*	*(16)*	*(17)*	*(18)*	*(19)*	*(20)*	*(21)*	*(22)*
1.	Under 5 Years Immunized	80	84.2	80	84.2	68	71.6	80	84.2
	Not Immunized	15	15.8	15	15.8	27	28.4	15	15.8
2.	5-9 Years Immunized	134	99.3	119	99.2	133	98.5	113	94.2
	Not Immunized	1	0.7	1	0.8	2	1.5	7	5.8
3.	10 Years and above Immunized	140	98.6	170	99.4	139	97.9	169	98.8
	Not Immunized	2	1.4	1	0.6	3	2.1	2	1.2

TABLE 15.3

Age of the Child and Immunization Status from 1½ Years to 15 Years (N: 758)

Age and Immunization Status	1½ Years- Booster DPT+ OPV				5 Years DT				10 Years TT				15 Years TT			
	Male	%	Female	%	Male	%	Female	%	Male	%	Female	%	Male	%	Female	%
(1)	(2)	(3)	(4)	(5)	(6)	(7)	(8)	(9)	(10)	(11)	(12)	(13)	(14)	(15)	(16)	(17)
Under 5 Years																
Immunized	62	65.3	72	75.8	15	15.8	11	11.6	–	–	–	–	–	–	–	–
Not Immunized	33	34.7	23	24.2	80	84.2	84	88.5	95	100	95	100	95	100	95	100
5-9 Years																
Immunized	131	97	113	94.2	127	94.1	102	85	16	11.9	18	15	–	–	–	–
Not Immunized	4	3	7	5.8	8	5.9	18	15	119	88.1	102	85	135	100	120	100
10 Years and above																
Immunized	139	97.9	167	97.7	136	95.8	163	95.3	104	73.2	116	67.8	11	7.7	7	4.1
Not Immunized	3	2.1	4	2.3	6	4.2	8	4.7	38	26.8	55	32.2	131	92.3	164	95.9

Table 15.4
Age of the Child and Nature of Immunization Status of the Child (N: 758)

Nature of Immunization	*Age Group of the Child*							
	Under 5 years		*5- 9 years*		*10 years and above*		*Total*	
	Male	*Female*	*Male*	*Female*	*Male*	*Female*	*Male*	*Female*
(1)	*(2)*	*(3)*	*(4)*	*(5)*	*(6)*	*(7)*	*(8)*	*(9)*
Not immunized	3 (3.2)	1 (1.1)	—	1 (0.8)	—	—	3 (0.8)	2 (0.5)
Partially immunized	15 (15.8)	8 (8.4)	14 (10.4)	24 (20.0)	38 (26.8)	53 (31.0)	67 (18.0)	85 (22.0)
Fully immunized	77 (81.1)	86 (90.5)	121 (89.6)	95 (79.2)	104 (73.2)	118 (69.0)	302 (81.2)	299 (77.4)
Total	95 (100)	95 (100)	135 (100)	120 (100)	141 (100)	171 (100)	372 (100)	386 (100)

Note : Figures in parentheses denote percentages.

are not immunized in the case of DPT and OPV at 1½ years. (Table 15.3) This is not consistent with findings of the National Family Health Survey-3 and Saha (2003) shows that boys are slightly more likely than girls to be fully vaccinated and boys are more likely to receive each of the individual vaccines than female children.

With respect to nature of immunization status of children it is observed that male children in the age groups of 5-9 years, and 10 years and above were fully immunized than their female counterparts. (Table 15.4) In the age group of less than 5 years, however, more female children were fully immunized than male children. Thus, there is less concern for female children in the age group of above 5 years in vaccinating them.

CONCLUSION

It is concluded that with education and empowerment women do not show any bias in allocating resources irrespective of the sex of the child. The parents treat equally both boys and girls. Resource allocation is not consciously planned and both the boys and girls receive equal attention in the matter of health care. The nature of work, economic position, educational level and fertility behaviour of the mother, availability of resources and the family size are the major determining factors of health care allocation. The mothers have knowledge about eradication of diseases through vaccinations, which is attributable to government efforts for universal immunization and mass awareness campaign followed by service campaigns conducted at various levels such as community health centre and primary health centre levels.

REFERENCES

Census of India (2001), http://censusindia.gov.in/Census_And_You/gender_composition.aspx.

Chelala, Cesar (2005), "A Sad World Wide Gender Gap", Retrieved from http://www.commondreams.org.

Funabashi Amane (2000), "The Gender Difference in Vaccination in Chitwan District, Nepal", *Bulletin of National Institute of Public Health*, 49(3), 301-02, http://sciencelinks.jp/j-east/article/.

Gaudin, Sylvestre and S. Abdo Yazbeck (2006), "Immunization in India 1993-99: Wealth, Gender, and Regional Inequalities Revisited", *Social Science and Medicine,* 62, 694-706.

Ghosh, Sudipta and S.L. Malik (2007), "Auditing Gender Equality among Santhals, www.isical.ac.in/wemp/papers/paper Sudipta Ghose.doc.

Mullatti, Leela (1992), Changing People of the Indian Family, The Changing

Family in Asia, UNESCO Principal Regional Office Asia and the Pacific, Thailand, http://unesdoc.unesco.org/images/0009/000988/098809EB.pdf.

Pande, R.P. (2003), "Selective Gender Differences in Childhood Nutrition and Immunization in Rural India: the Role of Siblings", *Demography,* Aug. 40(3), 395-418.

Pande, R.P. and A.S. Yazbeck (2003), "What's in a Country Average? Wealth, Gender, and Regional Inequalities in Immunization in India", *Social Science & Medicine*, 57(11), 2075-88.

Pandey, D. (1995), "Girl Child and Family in Maharashtra", *Social Change,* 25(2-3), 217-25.

Paulson, Susan (2005), "Opinion-Gender Insights can Improve Services", http://www.reproline.jhu.edu/english/6read/6issues/6network/v18-4/nt1847a.html/.

Saha, Chandana. (2003), *Gender Equity and Equality: Study of Girl Child in Rajasthan*, New Delhi: Rawat Publications.

Sharma, Suresh (2005), "Gender Differences in Child Health: Evidence from NFHS-2" presented at the XXVIIth Annual Conference of Indian Association for the Study of Population (IASP) on 'Poverty, Reproductive and Child Health and Population Stabilization, at Population Research Centre, Punjab University, Chandigarh, http://www.iassh.org/web_ abs/121.pdf.

Sharma, M.K., K. Dinesh Kumar, Naveen Mangat Goel, Chetna (2008), "Measles Immunization Coverage in an Urban Slum of Chandigarh (India)", *The Internet Journal of Epidemiology,* 6(1).

Vani, K. Borooah (2004), "Gender Bias among Children in India in their Diet and Immunization against Disease", *Social Science and Medicine*, 58: 1719-31.

Wyatt, H.V. (2004), Journeys and Voices: A Collection of Excerpts. The Female Client and the Health Provider: Using Poliomyelitis as a Marker, http://www.idrc.ca/en/ev-28402-201-1-DoTopic.html/.

Yu, Shengchao (2004), "Childhood Immunization in India: Roles of Family Structure, Women's Autonomy, and Village Health Service Provision", http://repository.upenn.edu/ dissertations/AAI3152130.

16

Gender Differentials in the Detection of Diabetes in Ahmedabad, Gujarat

RAMAN SHETTY, VINAY RANSIWAL, BIRANCHI JENA, ADIBABU KADITHI AND CLIFFORD D'SOUZA

INTRODUCTION

Worldwide, diabetes has emerged as a major non-communicable disease (NCD) with high rate of prevalence and a steadily increasing demographic burden. Diabetes along with other NCDs such as chronic respiratory diseases, cardio vascular disease (CVD) and cancer affected 36 million deaths globally in the year 2008. The number has increased over the years and diabetes alone caused the death of 46 millions in 2011. While the total deaths caused by communicable diseases, nutritional deficiencies and maternal and perinatal conditions are projected to decline by 3 percent by 2015, the deaths due to chronic diseases are projected to increase by 17 percent. The common risk factors of NCDs like unhealthy diet, excessive use of alcohol, tobacco, high blood pressure, increased blood sugar and cholesterol, insufficient physical activity and obesity are progressively taking root across different population groups, affecting younger and previously "low-risk" groups. The economic impact of these modifiable risk factors as a cause of poverty and as a hindrance to economic development in many countries is underappreciated and has not invited global response commensurate to the challenge.

Diabetes presents a major challenge to patients, health systems and national economies. The World Health Organization (WHO) together with the International Diabetes Federation (IDF) is working to raise awareness on diabetes worldwide along with improving the quality of care. Although research has improved the means of living quality life with the disease, prevention of diabetes has remained elusive. A comprehensive and integrated plan of action based on the existing knowledge of cost-effective and reliable solutions led by government, coupled with vigorous efforts to update our understanding of the disease by the scientific community, is the means to achieve success against diabetes.

Community-based survey reports are not available for Gujarat to estimate the prevalence rates. Prevalence of diabetes and Impaired Fasting Glucose (IFG) are very high and alarming in the city of Ahmedabad in Gujarat. The sex specific prevalence was 16.8 percent and 11.11 percent for males and females respectively.

Despite a host of literature on prevalence, reliable data on the registry of diabetes is lacking in most parts of the world including India. Without such data fight against diabetes is a formidable task. Weak points in the diagnosis, effective treatment and prevention of diabetes have to be identified, prioritised and acted upon for future benefits. Otherwise the losses due to direct costs to treatment and indirect costs to national economies can be massive. The knowledge of extent and effectiveness of current diabetes care has to be completely understood for improving the care process of the growing pandemic. The care seeking behaviour for a chronic condition like diabetes is bit complex and undermined, as the knowledge on the complications of diabetes is very low. When it comes to gender variation in the care seeking behaviour, it is further complex as the decision making for the same is predominantly influenced by the breadwinner in a patriarchal society. There is, therefore, a need to develop good information flow to understand the differentials in the prevalence rate and also in the current situation in exposure to the risk factors. The knowledge of diabetes among women is very critical due to the growing incidence of Gestational Diabetes Mellitus (GDM).

The current national or state initiatives in the collection of data are incongruent and call for a concerted approach to gather information and track progress. Then there is a need for the development of an international accord for measurable and comparable improvements in diagnosis, effective treatment and prevention of diabetes. Delineating the appropriate data required for the public healthcare providers, policy and decision makers will enable sound investment for the future of diabetes care. The affected population would experience an improved quality of life. The savings to the healthcare system through avoidance of diabetes complications could be rechanneled and the whole economy would benefit from a more productive workforce. The continuous flow of information would also help in understanding the social aspects of diabetes including gender variations in seeking care in the community and managing GDM effectively for self and in the community.

METHODOLOGY

The data for the analysis has been obtained from the project 'Changing Diabetes Barometer, Gujarat'. The 'Changing Diabetes Barometer' (CDB) initiative is a public-private partnership community programme running in the state of Gujarat by Novo Nordisk Education Foundation (NNEF) in collabouration with the Government of Gujarat. The programme was initiated in response to the urgent and pressing need for intensive action against diabetes.

It primarily involved for complementing the existing capacity in healthcare resources, spreading awareness about diabetes and concomitant complications, and creating linkages with Gujarat Government to function through public-private partnership (PPP) in order to make Gujarat a model state in India. The 'Changing Diabetes Barometer' initiative aims to improve lives of people with diabetes in Gujarat and reduce costs associated with this progressive chronic disease.

The project collects information on behalf of Government on socio-economic-demographic background of the population along with anthropometric and clinical parameters like Random Blood Sugar (RBS) and Blood Pressure (BP). The programme follows the operational guidelines for National Programme for Prevention and Control of Cancer, Diabetes, Cardiovascular Diseases and Stroke (NPCDCS), Ministry of Health & Family Welfare, Government of India for the measurement of RBS and BP. Random blood sugar test was done through strip method with the help of Glucometer, Test strip and Lancet. A lancet was used to pierce the skin and obtain blood from the tip of a finger. The blood sample was placed on the test strip. The test strip package provides exact instructions, including blood sample size. Usually this is accomplished by placing the blood drop against the edge or top of the strip and then the glucometre screen was observed. It should show a "waiting" or "processing" symbol, and will emit a beep when the sample has been tested. The results will be displayed as a number on the screen. Similarly, blood pressure is measured in a digital blood pressure measurement apparatus in the programme. For the purpose of the study, the following diagnostic criteria are used to classify the diabetes status in the community:

For people with unknown diabetes status:

RBS value less than 140 mg/dl: Non-Diabetes
RBS value between 140 and 200 mg/dl: Impaired Glucose Tolerance (IGT) or pre-diabetes
RBS value more than 200 mg/dl: Diabetes mellitus

For people with known diabetes status (already diagnosed with diabetes):

RBS value less than 180 mg/dl: Controlled diabetes
RBS value more than 180 mg/dl: Un-Controlled diabetes

Again, the World Health Organisation (WHO) classification 2004 was used for the various categories of Body Mass Index (BMI). The following categories of BMI are used in the current study:

BMI of less than 18.5 = Under-weight
BMI between18.5-24.99 = Normal or ideal weight
BMI between 25-29.99 = Pre Obese
BMI 30 or more than 30 = Obese or over weight

Similarly, the following criteria were used for the classification of Waist Hip Ratio (WHR):

WHR of 0.95 or above for male: High WHR
WHR of below 0.95 for male: Normal WHR
WHR of 0.85 or above for female: High WHR
WHR of below 0.85 for female: Normal WHR

As a part of the programme, data collected during June 2012 and August 2012 in the district of Ahmedabad have been analysed. The current analysis provides an observational outline of the people who came to the screening camps. A total of 12140 people screened during this period were included in the analysis. Bi-variate tables and uni-variate odds ratio were used to explain the variation in the explanatory variables.

RESULT

Of the total 12,140 people who had come for the screening, 52 percent (6351) were female and 48 percent (5789) were male. This shows the high acceptance rate for female participants for getting their diabetes status checked in the camps.

TABLE 16.1

Gender-wise Status of Diabetes of the Participants in the Diabetes Screening Camp

(*in percent*)

	Female	*Male*
Diabetes Status at the camp		
Unknown Diabetes	92	87
Known Diabetes	8	13
N	6351	5789
Screening outcome at the camp		
Diabete	7.6	12.
Pre-Diabetes	10.8	11.9
Non-Diabetes	79.1	71.7
Newly Diagnosed Diabetes	2.5	3.5

Of the total, a higher proportion of male participants coming to the camp are already aware about their diabetes status (13 percent) as compared to their female counterparts (8 percent). Again, more male participants were diagnosed with diabetes for the first time (3.5 percent) then the female participants (2.5 percent). The overall diabetes detection rate in the camps revealed that 16.4 percent men are suffering from diabetes as compared to 10.1 percent women. Although there is high margin of difference in the diabetes detection rate in the camp between male and female participants, there is a matter of concern for the pre-diabetes detection rate among females. The rate is almost equal to the pre-diabetes detection rate among male participants (Table 16.1).

It has been observed that the detection rate of diabetes in the screening camp increased significantly with age. A detection rate of 5.2 percent for male participants below 40 years is increased to 20 percent for the age group between 40 and 60 and further increased to 24.6 percent with more than 60 years of age. Similar trend is also observed for female participants, although the detection rate was comparatively lower for the age group (Figure 16.1). Of the total known diabetes, 50 percent of the female patients were found to be controlled diabetes, whereas this proportion was 45 percent for male patients. This indicates female patients either maintain a good treatment regimen or a better diet and exercise, which helps in keeping the blood sugar level within the desired level as compared to the male patients.

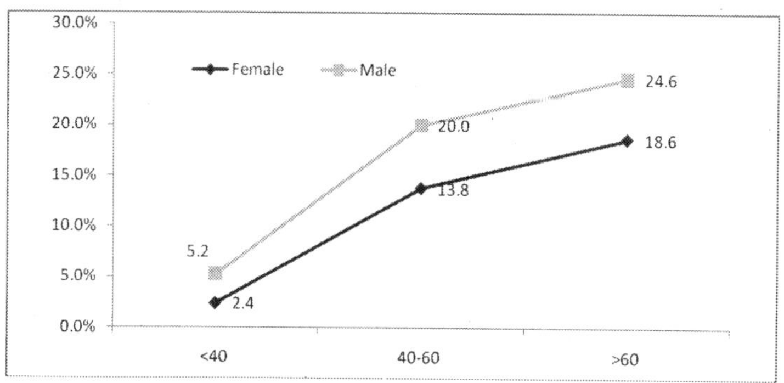

Figure 16.1 : Gender Variation in the Detection of Diabetes by Age Group (in percent)

TABLE 16.2

Age-wise Distribution of Uncontrolled Diabetes among Male and Female

(in percent)

Un-Controlled Diabetes	*Female*	*Male*	*N*
<40 years	7.2	7.3	47
40 years to 60 years	63.3	56.3	381
More than 60 years	29.5	36.3	219
N	237	410	647

As far as age is concerned, there is no variation in women and men in the age group of below 40 years in managing diabetes and keeping the blood sugar at the desired level. Around 7 percent of both male and female patients in the age group of below 40 years were unable to maintain their blood sugar level at 180 mg/dl or less. A higher proportion of females in the age group of 40-60 years and males in the age group of 60 years and above were unable to maintain their average blood sugar level below 180 mg/dl (Table 16.2).

The diabetes screening camp helps in improving the diagnosis rates. Therefore, such camps are of high importance particularly in places where the diagnostic rate is very low. The diagnostic rate for diabetes remains at very low level in India, mainly because of the low awareness level. The success of the screening camps, therefore, depends on the proportion of people detected with diabetes mellitus for the first time. The current analysis revealed that 2.5 percent of female and 3.5 percent male were newly-diagnosed with diabetes mellitus. However, by considering the overall diabetes detection rate, the newly-diagnosed numbers indicated that there is an improvement of 25 percent in the diagnostic rate for females and 21 percent improvement in the diagnostic rate for males.

TABLE 16.3

Age-wise Distribution of Newly-Diagnosed Diabetes among Males and Females

(in percent)

Newly Diagnosed Diabetes	*Female*	*Male*	*N*
<40 years	15.7	15.9	57
40 years to 60 years	54.7	65.7	219
More than 60 years	29.6	18.4	84
N	159	201	360

Once it comes to age for the diagnosis of diabetes for the first time, a major proportion of males and females gets diagnosed in the age-group of 40-60 years. However, comparatively a higher proportion of males get diagnosed in the the age-group of 40-60 years and higher proportion of female get diagnosed in age-group of more than 60 years (Table 16.3). Although variations are observed in the prevalence of diabetes by socio-economic variables like education, income, type of diet, life style pattern etc., some anthropometric variables like height, weight, waist and hip measurement are presented as major factors of variation in the detection (prevalence) of diabetes. Body Mass Index (BMI) and Waist Hip Ratio (WHR) are two estimated variables that are most commonly used to describe the relative risk associated in the detection of diabetes.

More than half of the male participants who visited the screening camp found to have normal weight with the BMI measurement within the range of 18.5 and 24.99. However, comparatively more female participants in the screening camp were found to be obese (Table 16.4). The association between BMI and uncontrolled diabetes was clearly found in the screening data, as the proportion of uncontrolled diabetes increased linearly with increase in BMI. However, more obese men have difficulty in keeping their blood sugar level within the desired level (Table 16.5).

TABLE 16.4

BMI-wise Distribution of All the Participants in the Screening Camps

(in percent)

BMI	*Female*	*Male*	*N*
Under Weight (< 18.5)	25.3	17.8	2639
Normal Weight (18.5 to 24.99)	43.2	52.2	5762
Pre-Obese (25 to 29.99)	21.7	23.8	2758
Obese (> =30)	9.8	6.2	981
N	6351	5789	12140

TABLE 16.5

BMI-wise Distribution of Uncontrolled and Newly Diagnosed Diabetes Detection Rate

(in percent)

BMI categories	*Uncontrolled diabetes detection rate*		*Newly diagnosed diabetes detection rate*	
Underweight (BMI < 18.5)	*Female*	*Male*	*Female*	*Male*
Normal Weight (BMI between 18.5-24.99)	0.7	3.3	0.9	1.8
Pre-Obese (25 to 29.99)	3.0	7.0	2.1	2.9
Obese (> =30)	7.0	9.4	3.7	5.3
N	7.2	10.3	5.9	6.1

The detection rate of diabetes is found to be almost same for the both the sexes at BMI of above 30, although there is a minor variation in the newly-diagnosed diabetes rate at the screening camps for males and females at different levels of BMI (Figure16.3). As far as the uncontrolled diabetes is concerned, there are comparatively more variations in the uncontrolled diabetes for male and female at various levels of BMI. (Figure 16.2)

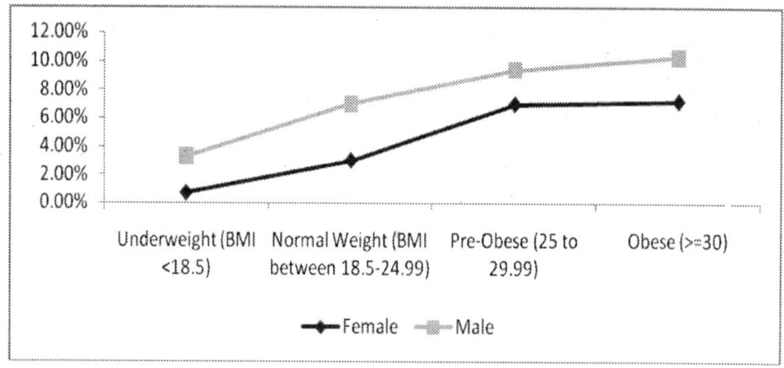

Figure 16.2 : Gender Variation in the Detection of un-Controlled Diabetes by Differential BMI

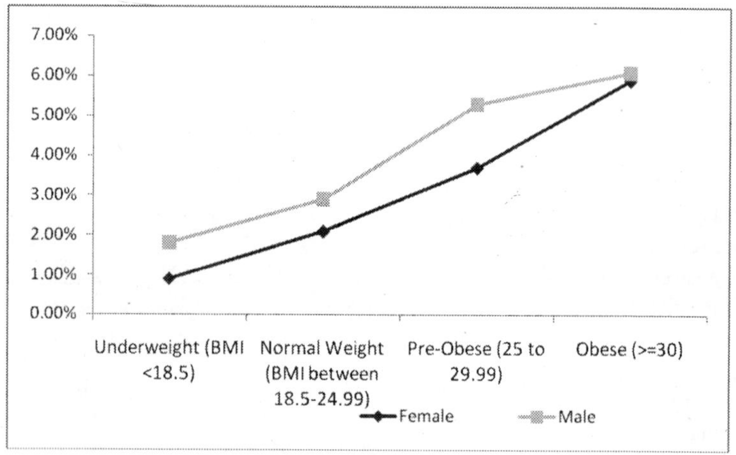

Figure 16.3 : Gender Variation in the Newly -Detected Diabetes by Differential BMI

Like BMI, Waist Hip Ratio (WHR) is also a risk factor for diabetes status. In the present analysis, it was found to have a notable variation between normal WHR and high WHR as well as between males and females for both uncontrolled diabetes and newly-diagnosed diabetes. However, WHR was found to be comparatively higher risk factor in case of uncontrolled diabetes than a person diagnosed for the first time with diabetes (Table 16.6). Of all the participants in the screening camp who had already been diagnosed for diabetes, 11.2 percent of the females and 14.4 percent of the males were without any medication. This implies that treatment rate is better for female patients than male patients. However, the results did not show any significant variation in the treatment rate for controlled and uncontrolled diabetes.

TABLE 16.6

WHR-wise Distribution of Uncontrolled and Newly Diagnosed Diabetes Detection Rate

(in percent)

WHR categories	*Uncontrolled Diabetes detection rate*		*Newly Diagnosed Diabetes detection rate*	
	Female	*Male*	*Female*	*Male*
Normal WHR	0.9	2.7	0.8	1.5
High WHR	2.8	4.4	1.7	2.0

DISCUSSION

Although India is building on the healthcare system with quality healthcare professionals, health care policies and treatments, only a small fraction of the people live well with the disease. This is because most people with diabetes remain undiagnosed or diagnosed at a later stage with a number of diabetes related complications. In line with the 'rule of halves', developed for hypertension, the diminishing effectiveness of existing efforts seek newer approaches for the management of disease. The present data explain that 24 percent of the females were undiagnosed and 21 percent male remain undiagnosed for diabetes, which is negating the rules of half concept. A study in Malwan, Maharashtra indicates that 70 percent diabetes patients remain undiagnosed, basically due to low educational status and lack of health care facilities. Although the screening camps were opportunistic in nature, there was a high probability of bias in the number of known diabetes patients in the camp. Thus, awareness, education and lack of health care centres in the proximity remain the major challenges in improvement in the diagnosis rate of diabetes.

The analysis found a high incidence of diabetes with increased age of the people. In a few studies, high prevalence of diabetes was attributed to ageing and increased BMI.· However, the variation in the detection of diabetes in the screening camp was comparatively less in the age group of less than 40 years than for the older age group. Girls are 1.3 to 1.7 times more likely than boys to develop Type-2 diabetes during childhood. (WHO, 1999; Deo, 2006; Gu, 2003) Although the reason for the increased risk among girls is not clear, it may be related to an increased risk of insulin resistance as seen in adolescent girls with polycystic ovarian syndrome (PCOS).

High prevalence of diabetes in the first degree relatives as well as vertical transmission through more than two generations is commonly seen among Indians. The prevalence of diabetes increases with increasing family history of diabetes. (Pinhas-Hamiel, 1996) The data in the programme indicate that people with family history are 3.68 times more at risk for diabetes as compared to those without having family history. There was no significant variation in such risk for both male and female participants in the screening camp (Odds Ratio for male being 3.6 and for female it is 3.5).

A study reveals that factors associated with diabetes for both men and women were aged 40 years and above, and having a low gross annual household income, obesity and a family history of diabetes and among women high WHR is associated with high risk of diabetes. (Scott, 1997). The current data from Gujarat provide similar results. The WHR is found to be significantly associated with diabetes with an odds ratio of 3.1. However, females with high WHR are at more risk (OR= 3.5) than the males with high WHR (OR= 3.09).

A study in China show prevalence rates of general obesity and overweight classified by BMI were 15.0 percent (15.7 percent for men and 14.3 percent for women, $p<0.01$) and 19.2 percent (20.8 percent for men and 17.7 percent for women, $p<0.01$), respectively, and the overall prevalence rate of abdominal obesity was 37.6 percent (31.1 percent for men and women 43.9 percent for women, $p<0.01$). (Fagot-campagna, 2000) The data for Gujarat indicate similar trend with total prevalence of obesity and overweight (31 percent). General obesity in Gujarat was found to be comparatively less at 8.1 percent (9.8 percent for women and 6.2 percent for men, $P<0.01$) than the overweight proportion which stood at 22.7 percent (21.7 percent for women and 23.8 percent for men, $P<0.01$). However, women were found to be more obese than men unlike the distribution in the study from China and this may pose a potential risk factor for women in Gujarat to be diagnosed with diabetes in near future. Abdominal obesity measured by WHR is found to be 43.4 percent for women and 38.7 percent for men, which corroborates the study of China. Analysis stratified by gender in the China study reveals that men with a higher level education level, a white-collar job, a cadre job, or higher family income were the high risk group, and women with higher level of education or higher family income were the low risk group. (Dabelea, 2007)

As far as medication and management of diabetes is concerned, it was observed that medicine compliance was better for women than men, with higher proportion of women were on medication after the status of the diabetes is known. Women disclosed their diabetes more readily and integrated management into their daily lives, whereas men were more reluctant to disclose to friends and family about their diabetes status and were less observant of self-management practices in social settings.

CONCLUSION

It is found that there is large gender variation in the existing and the newly-diagnosed diabetes cases. The results reveal that the intervention in terms of free diabetes screening services has been quite effective for the age group of 30 years and above for the improvement in the diagnosis of diabetes. The screening camps were also useful to both men and women to practice diet and exercise regimen, especially for those found with impaired glucose tolerance level. In other words, the free screening services are more effective for early adult age groups to make life style changes as a cost effective measure for managing diabetes in a resource poor settings like ours.

There is wide disparity in the utilisation of public health facilities at different levels. While the tertiary hospitals are overloaded, the first referral systems like Primary Health Centres (PHCs) are underutilized. Utilization of the first referral unit was lower for diabetes, as the medication is very limited in PHCs and even the next level referral unit such as Community Health Centres (CHCs). More than 12 percent of the known diabetes patients not seeking health care and treatment are more due to non-availability of treatment at the first referral units than due to the lack of physical access to the health facilities. Therefore, making the first referral units self-sufficient to manage diabetes is the need of the hour to contain the ill effects of diabetes epidemic.

References

Dabelea, D. *et al.* (2007), "Incidence of Diabetes in Youth in the United States," *JAMA*, 297, 2716.

Wang, Hao *et al.* (2012), "Epidemiology of General Obesity, Abdominal Obesity and Related Risk Factors in Urban Adults from 33 Communities of Northeast China: the CHPSNE Study;" *Public Health* , 12:967.

Fagot-Campagna, A. *et al.* (2000), "Type 2 Diabetes among North American Children and Adolescents: An Epidemiologic Review and a Public Health Perspective," *J Pediatr*, 136, 664.

Grant, Grant (2009), "Gender-specific Epidemiology of Diabetes: A Representative Cross-sectional Study," *International Journal for Equity in Health*, 8:6.

Gu, D. *et a*l. (2003), "Prevalence of Diabetes and Impaired fasting Glucose in Chinese Adult Population International Collaborative Study of Cardiovascular Disease in Asia," *Diabetologia*, 46, 1190-8.

http://www.idf.org/sites/default/files/Diabetespercent20Atlaspercent203rd percent20edition.pdf (Accessed on 29-05-2012).

http://www.who.int/gho/ncd/en/index.html (Accessed on 29-05-2012).

Pinhas-Hamiel, O. *et al.* (1996), Increased Incidence of Non-insulin-dependent Diabetes Mellitus among Adolescents. *J Pediatr*, 128, 608.

Scott, C.R, J.M. Smith, M.M. Cradock and C. Pihoker (1997), "Characteristics of Youth-Onset Non-insulin-Dependent Diabetes Mellitus and Insulin-Dependent Diabetes Mellitus at Diagnosis," *Pediatrics*, 100, 84.

Mathew, Rebecca (2012), "Self-management Experiences among Men and Women with type 2 Diabetes Mellitus: A Qualitative Analysis," *BMC Family Practice* , 13:12.

Sudha, S. Deo, *et al.* (2006), "To Identify the Risk Factors for High Prevalence of Diabetes and Impaired Glucose Tolerance in Indian Rural Population", *Int J Diab Dev Ctries*, 26, 19-23.

Sudha, S., Deo, *et al.* (2006), "To Identify the Risk Factors for High Prevalence of Diabetes and Impaired Glucose Tolerance in Indian Rural Population," *Int J Diab Dev Ctries*, 26, 19-23.

17

Gender and Health in Kerala

K. GANGADHARAN AND DIVYA KARIKKAN

The most fundamental aspect of human life is health. It forms an integral part of overall socio-economic development of a nation. In terms of resources for economic development, nothing can be considered of higher importance than health of the people. The progress of society greatly depends on the quality of its people—women and men. Unhealthy people can hardly be expected to make any significant contribution towards developmental programmes. Health is man's greatest possession, for it lays a solid foundation for his happiness. The concept of health keeps changing from time to time and of course varies from person to person. For example, according to some people absence of disease is a healthy condition; some even accept obese is a good state of body in comparison to normal or ideal weight. The most accepted scientific definition put forth by the World Health Organisation states "Health is a state of complete, physical, mental and social well-being and not merely the absence of disease or infirmity". (WHO, 1948). This definition of health projects four different dimensions—physical, mental, social and spiritual. A person who enjoys health in these four aspects is said to be in a state of good health.

Health is an important factor in the achievement of social status, particularly for women, whose health is conditioned to a great extent by social attitudes. The health status of women includes their mental and social condition as affected by prevailing norms and attitudes of society in addition to their biological and psychological problems. Society delineates women's roles partly according to their biological functions and partly from prevailing attitudes regarding their physical and mental capacity. These social attitudes also influence the provision and use of preventive and curative health care, including maternal care. The health care facilities provided to women by a community particularly in the form of materiality services are a significant index of the emphasis that community places on the health of its women.

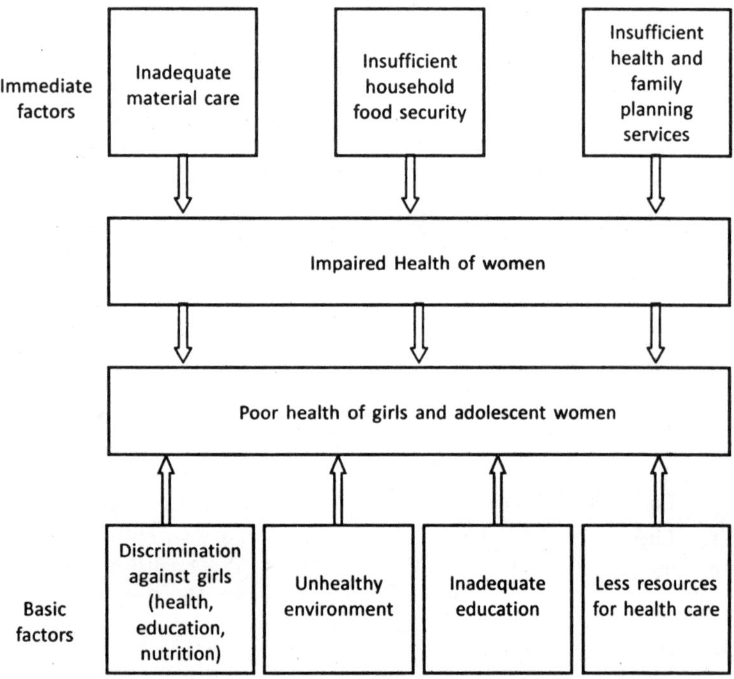

Factors Affecting Poor Health Among Women and Girls

THE STATUS OF WOMEN IN KERALA

It is widely acknowledged that women in Kerala are better off than their counterparts elsewhere in India. Development scholars attribute to past and present levels of female literacy rate and education, late age at marriage, declining fertility and greater life expectancy to establish this fact. Of late, these conventional indicators are under scanner as various other indicators like decreasing sex ratio in the 0-6 age group, lower work participation rate than the national level, increasing violence against women and low political participation are becoming issues of concern.

Table 17.1 presents the socio-economic indicators of Kerala. When the female population as a percentage of the total population in Kerala is about 52 percent, it is only about 48 percent at the all-India level. According to the 2011 Census, the urban population in

TABLE 17.1

Basic Socio-economic Development Indicators of Kerala-2012

Sl. No.	*Item*	*Unit*	*Kerala*	*India*
1.	Total population (2011 Census)	'000s	33,387	12,10,193
2.	Males as a % of total population (2011 Census)		48	51.54
3.	Females as a % of total population (2011 Census)		52	48.46
4.	Rural population as a % of total population (2011 Census)		52.28	68.84
5.	Urban population as a % of total population (2011 Census)		47.72	31.16
6.	Sex ratio (2011 Census)		1084	940
7.	2001-11 Decadal Growth of Population	Per cent	4.86	17.64
8.	Literacy rate (2011 Census)	Per cent	93.91	74.04
9.	Total SC population (2001 Census)	'000s	3124	166635
10.	Total ST Population (2001 Census)	'000s	364	84326
11.	SC population as a % of total population (2001 Census)		9.8	16.2
12.	ST population as a % of total population (2001 Census)		1.1	8.2
13.	Total workers (2001 Census)	'000s	10283.89	402234.72
14.	Net area sown (2008-09)	'000 ha	2088.95	141360 (P)
15.	Area sown more than once (2008-09)	'000 ha	605.98	53740 (P)

Source : Government of Kerala, 2012.

Kerala constitutes nearly 48 percent while it stands at about 31 percent at the all-India level. The sex ratio in Kerala is also skewed in favour of women with a sex ratio of 1084 when there is an adverse sex at the national level. The state has low percentage of SC (9.8) and ST (1.1) population. (Table 17.1) From the brief socio-economic profile presented in Table 17.1 it is observed that Kerala stands at a better footing with regard to the socio-economic indicators. More particularly, women in the state enjoy higher status as compared to their counterparts in other states of the country.

DEMOGRAPHIC AND HEALTH STATUS OF WOMEN

The role of women's literacy in achieving health transition in Kerala has been well documented. Health achievements are reflected in life expectancy and infant and maternal mortality figures (Table 17.2). Life expectancy of women in Kerala is clearly higher than that of India as a whole but it is also about 5 years more than that of men in Kerala. Infant and maternal mortality figures in Kerala are much lower than those of all India. Underlying these achievements is the significantly higher age at marriage, particularly the percentage of girls marrying after 21 years of age. While these factors have contributed greatly to the demographic and development scenario in Kerala, sole emphasis on them tends to mask the fall out of health transition in the state and particularly its adverse implications on women. These implications are particularly strong where reproductive health of women is concerned. Low and declining levels of fertility have brought women in the reproductive age under tremendous pressure in terms of decisions on child birth and pre-natal care. It is not unlikely that this pressure is reflected in the rising level of caesarean-section deliveries in Kerala and its possible association with private sector institutions. It is common knowledge that contraception is almost entirely women's terrain, reflected in the high levels of sterilization of women. Health and demographic transitions have been achieved at the cost of intervention into women's bodies and lives in ways that require serious critical reflection and inquiry. In Kerala women have higher life expectancy. Kerala has a sex ratio of 1084 females per 1000 males as compared to all India average of 940 females per 1000 males according to the 2011 census. There is a difference between the life expectancy of females and males in Kerala. In Kerala, women have higher life expectancy and they are more prone to obesity and experience higher stress level than men. In case of infant mortality and maternal mortality rates they are lowest in Kerala compared to other states and also far below the national average.

TABLE 17.2

Basic Health Indicators in Kerala and India during 2007 and 2012

Sl.No.	*Health Indicators*	*Kerala*		*India*	
		2007	*2012*	*2007*	*2012*
1.	Birth rate' ('000 population)	15	14.8	23.8	22.1
2.	Death rate ('000 population)	6.4	7	7.6	7.2
3.	Infant mortality rate ('000 population)	14	13	58	47
4.	Child mortality rate 0-4 years ('000 population)	3	2	17	15
5.	Maternal mortality rate (per lakh live birth)	110	81	300	212
6.	Total fertility rate (children per woman)	1.7	1.7	2.9	2.6
7.	Couple protection rate (in percent)	72.1	62.3	52	52
8.	Life at birth—Male	70.9	71.4	61.8	62.6
	Female	76	76.3	63.5	64.2
	Total	73.45	74	62.7	63

Source : Government of Kerala, 2012.

HUMAN DEVELOPMENT AMONG WOMEN IN KERALA

In Kerala, the state has performed well in various development indicators. The birth and death rate, have lowered and life expectancy has increased in Kerala. The literacy rates of women are high. The use of family planning methods is widespread and fertility rate has declined. According to NFHS data, universal marriages of women existed in Kerala. In Kerala, the elderly population, especially women who had been widowed, divorced and separated have a number of economic, social and health problems. These issues continue to remain unaddressed at the policy level. The mean age of marriage of women was 21 years. According to NFHS data, women aged 20-24 years married by 18 years are only 15.4 percent. The total fertility rate (children per women) is 1.9 percent. The NFHS-III data show that 29 percent of women had caesarean deliveries. Many of them were conducted in private clinics. In addition, women from Kerala have also been found to be suffering from a number of non-communicable diseases. Breast cancer and thyroid cancer was found to be high in Kerala. They also suffer from obesity and hyper tension. Diabetes is also on the rise among women. Mental illness among women in the state is found to be much higher than the national average. Violence against women was high within homes and harassment in public was higher compared to other states. A number of reproductive health problems not related to pregnancy and child birth also continue to be common among women which need urgent attention.

IMMUNIZATION COVERAGE

Immunization is one of the most successful and cost-effective health interventions and prevents debilitating illness, disability and death from vaccine-preventable diseases such as diphtheria, hepatitis A and B, measles, mumps, pneumococcal disease, polio, rotavirus diarrhoea, tetanus and yellow fever. Table 17.3 presents the target and achievement in immunisation in Kerala in 2011. It is observed that Kerala has achieved 98 per cent target in immunization during the year while it is 33.78 percent in Andhra Pradesh, 73.71 percent in Karnataka and 65.93 percent in Tamil Nadu. It means that Kerala is ahead of other states in immunisation in the country.

TABLE 17.3

Target and Achievement of Immunization during 2011

State	*Target*	*Achievement*	*Per cent*
Andhra Pradesh	1480000	500003	33.78
Karnataka	1149000	84904	73.71
Tamil Nadu	1147000	756171	65.93
Kerala	486000	458860	98.05

Source : India Stat.com and Directorate of Health Services.

MAJOR HEALTH PROBLEMS IN KERALA—COMMUNICABLE DISEASES

Communicable diseases such as Dengue, AIDs, Malaria, Leptospirosis, Hepatitis, Chikungunya, HINI fever, etc. are increasing over the years. Thiruvananthapuram district in Kerala is almost endemic to Dengue and it reports about two-third of the total cases in the state. Presence of co-morbidity is a major problem which leads to mortality in case of communicable diseases.

Dengue Fever: Dengue was reported for the first time in Kerala in 1997. Subsequently, it spread far and wide and now it has become endemic in certain areas especially in Thruvananthapuram district. India has recorded over 37,000 dengue cases, including 227 dengue deaths in 2012 (Government of Kerala, 2012). Among the southern states of India, the highest percent of dengue deaths were reported in Kerala during 2011 (10 out of 1281) and Karnataka reported the least percentage of dengue deaths (5 out of 405). During 2012 Kerala reported the maximum of over 3033 dengue cases and about 12 deaths occurred up to September 2012. The details of Dengue cases and the deaths reported in Kerala from 2007 onwards have been shown in Table 17.4. During the last five years, it is observed that leprosy, tuberculosis, diarrhoeal diseases, pneumonia, enteric fever, respiratory infection, and chicken pox have worsened (Table 17.5). A state actually in the forefront of health care advancement has suffered a lot due to the spread of communicable diseases and this sort of health care deprivation occurred mainly due to environmental

TABLE 17.4

Details of Dengue Fever Reported in Kerala

(Per cent)

Year	*Cases*	*Deaths*	*Mortality*
2007	677	11	1.62
2008	733	3	0.41
2009	1425	6	0.42
2010	2597	17	0.65
2011	1304	10	0.77
2012	3033	12	0.39

Source : Directorate of Health Services.

degradation and lack of proper solid waste management system in the urban and rural areas of the state.

TABLE 17.5
Prevalence Rate of Public Health Diseases during 2007 and 2012

Diseases	*Prevalence rate per 10000 population*	
	2007	*2012*
Malaria	0.06	0.19*
Leprosy	0.21	0.26
Tuberculosis	0.40	0.52
Diarrhoeal diseases	14.14	19.76
Pneumonia	0.76	1.51
Enteric fever	0.19	0.25
Measles	0.08	0.06
Respiratory infection	233.88	305.12
Chicken pox	0.41	0.76

Source : Government of Kerala, Directorate of Health Services.

GENDER DEVELOPMENT

The Eleventh Plan placed considerable emphasis on gender auditing and gender budgeting of major development policies and programmes. Gender auditing is concerned with the assessment of the gender impact of policies and programmes not just in technical terms but also in terms of overcoming the personal and institutional biases in the culture of the relevant organizations which hinder the achievement of gender equality objectives. The Twelfth Five-Year Plan emphasis is to increase women's employability in the formal sector as well as their asset base. It will improve the condition of self-employed women. Focus will be on women's workforce participation particularly in secondary and tertiary sectors, ensuring decent work for them, reaching out to women in agriculture and manufacturing, financial inclusion, and extending land and property rights to women. The paradox of the status of women in Kerala lies in the confusion between 'gender equality' and 'gender equity'. The notion of gender equality assumes that the needs and interest of women and men are identical, whereas the notion of gender equity presumes they are different. Policies and plans should take this into consideration and the differential needs be addressed to achieve gender justice.

CONCLUSION

Development effectiveness through gender mainstreaming signifies performance in bringing about change in increased productivity, improved social development and enhanced gender equality in rights, resources and political voice that generally disadvantage women. Most of the gender-related and health-related demographic researchers agree over 'women's pivotal role in health'. By empowering women through education, especially health education, the health and the mortality condition of the people as a whole could be improved. Some important radical steps are required for empowering the health sector in Kerala and specially the gender aspect of health care. They mainly include integrating MDGs in planning process, policy formulation, and programme implementation with equity focus. Improved service delivery—convergence, capacity development, and quality, newer technology to reach poor also has to be undertaken. Strengthening of public health system with primary care network in rural and urban areas should be another focus area. Increase in public spending on health with more than 2 percent GDP should also be considered. The National Urban Health Mission programme should be implemented with maximum focus on environmental cleanliness and measures to augment health care affordability and accessibility of the poor sections.

REFERENCES

Dash, Dhanlaxmi (2005), *Women, Environment and Health*, Jaipur: Mangal Deep Publications.

Elango, K., A. Ayyam Perumal and J. Mohan Raj (2008), *Emerging Issues on Gender and Women Development*, Delhi: Abhijeet Publications.

Goel, S.L. and Aruna Goel (2008), *Women, Health, Education*, New Delhi: Deep and Deep Publications.

Government of India (2008), *Kerala Development Report*, New Delhi: Government of India, Planning Commission.

Government of India (2011), *Census of India, 2011*, Thiruvanathapuram: Directorate of Census Operations.

Government of Kerala (2012), *Economic Review*, Thiruvananthapuram : State Planning Board.

http://sakhikerala.org

www.kerala.gov.ac.in

Index